THE NOTION OF FETTER IN EARLY BUDDHISM

The Notion of Fetter in Early Buddhism

DIPEN BARUA

ADITYA PRAKASHAN
New Delhi

First published in India, 2018

ISBN 978-81-934621-0-2

Price : ₹ 795/-

Published by Aditya Prakashan, 2/18, Ansari Road,
New Delhi – 110 002.

email: contact@adityaprakashan.com
website: www.adityaprakashan.com

Printed at Thomson Press (India) Ltd.

To
My Late Mother Juti Bala Barua
and
Father Joysen Barua

Contents

Acknowledgements

This work is a revised version of my MPhil research entitled "Developments of the Concept "Fetter" (*Saṃyojana*) in the Pāli Canon" which I submitted to The University of Hong Kong (HKU) for my Master of Philosophy Degree in 2017. Professor Venerable K.L. Dhammajoti admitted me as a research student in 2014 and supervised my studies until his retirement in 2015. I feel so blessed to have had the chance to learn from him. I am since most indebted to Professor G.A. Somaratne for his earnest supervision, and Professor Toshiichi Endo for his tireless support as co-supervisor. I am grateful towards Professor Oliver Abeynayake (Sri Lanka), and Professor Georgios T. Halkias (HKU), examiners of my MPhil thesis, for their guidance.

I am forever indebted to the Centre of Buddhist Studies of HKU for supporting my MPhil studies through the Glorious Sun Group Postgraduate Scholarship. Special thanks to Mrs. Sun-Man Janis Chan for careful proofreading of my entire work. Appreciation also goes to other friends (too numerous to name individually) whose comments and suggestions were extremely fruitful.

I am grateful to Professor Guang Xing of HKU for his ongoing support. My special thanks to Professor M.A. Deokar of Savitribai Phule Pune University (formerly University of Pune), and Professor Ujjwal Kumar of Calcutta University, India. They have encouraged me to come to study at HKU. Their constant support was central to my higher studies at HKU.

I also wish to express my deep appreciation to my masters Venerable Paññānanda and Venerable Shilananda for their support throughout my studies. Sadly, close to the end of my MPhil studies, my beloved mother Juti Bala Barua passed away. My dream of higher studies was nurtured by her careful instructions. I express my deep gratitude to her, and my father Joysen Barua who is always concerned about me. Finally, the Aditya Prakashan in New Delhi, India, has very kindly accepted to publish this present work. I hope my efforts would contribute in a humble way towards more elucidating works on the subject of Fetter in the future. My heartfelt gratitude to the publisher.

Preface

The discourses of the Buddha in the Pāli Canon contain, taken to be the standard, of ten psychological factors called 'fetters' (*saṃjoyana*). The individual factors in this list appear in various other contexts playing the roles of mental defilements of varying degrees as obstacles and hindrances to achieving progress in the soteriological path leading to *Nibbāna*. This list of fetters appears in the discourses as either a continuous single list (AN V 17: *dasayimāni saṃyojanāni*) or divided into two groups: the five downward fetters (*orambhāgiya-saṃyojana*) and the five upward fetters (*uddhambhāgiya-saṃyojana*) implying that these psychological factors are responsible for the worldly person's 'self'-existence (*bhava*) and in turn birth or appearance in the experiential worlds of varying pains and pleasures within, metaphorically defined, the vertical universe (AN V 17; see also DN III 234; SN V 60–61). The first five fetters in this list are: (1) 'person' view (*sakkāya-diṭṭhi*), (2) doubts (*vicikicchā*), (3) attachment to precepts and vows (*sīlabbata-parāmāsa*), (4) sensual desire (*kāmacchanda*), and (5) ill-will (*vyāpāda*). As the Commentary explains, these are the fetters that produce births in the lower, that is, the sensual sphere (Mp II 130: *oraṃ vuccati kāma-dhātu, tattha uppatti-nipphādanato taṃ oraṃ bhajantī ti orambhāgiyāni*). The next five fetters in the list are: (6) lust for the fine-matrial (*rūpa-rāga*), (7) lust for the immaterial (*arūpa-rāga*), (8) conceit (*māna*), (9) restlessness (*uddhacca*), and (10) ignorance (*avijjā*). Again, the same Commentary states that these fetters produce births in the higher, that is, both the fine-material and the immaterial spheres (Mp II 130: *uddhaṃ vuccati rūpārūpa-dhātu, tatth'uppatti-nipphādanato taṃ uddhaṃ bhajantī ti uddhambhāgiyāni*). Thus, these ten factors are called fetters because they chain the worldly person to the sensual, the fine-material, and the immaterial spheres of 'self'-existence (*bhava*). As the twelve-factored formulation of the Dependent Co-arising theory shows, 'self'-existence is conditioned by clinging and craving of a contacting and feeling worldly person who is conscious of a dyad of name-and-matter both internally and externally with his every sensory experience and holds into them with varying intentions as 'I' and 'my self' due to his ignorance into the not-self teaching of the Buddha. It is this clinging, and also what comes before, that chain the worldly person to 'self'-existence and in turn to birth in this metaphorically vertical world of suffering. If this is the case, what is referred to as fetters should be different ways of talking about the same factors of craving and clinging determined by varying intentions conditioned by ignorance. Craving is represented by craving for sensuality (*kāma-taṇhā*), craving for 'self'-existence (*bhava-taṇhā*) and craving for 'self'-discontinuity (*vibhava-taṇhā*). Clinging is the differing ways of holding into sensuality, views, vows, and self. Thus, it could be concluded that the fetters represent an extended version of this clinging and its conditioning factors such as ignorance, intentions and craving, because it is the psychological factor of clinging or attachment that really chains the worldly individual to a 'self'-existence in either a lower or a higher manifestation as birth (*jāti*), the source of varying sufferings such as ageing-and-death (*jarā-maraṇa*).

One who intends to be free from 'self-existence follows the insight scheme to destroy both the downward and the upward fetters that produce birth in the three spheres. The sensual sphere is the hardest to be freed from. Therefore, the practitioner of the insight scheme does it in three stages:

first, he destroys the first three downward fetters, comes to the noble stage of stream-entry and becomes free from being born in hells, the lowest of the sensual realm; second, he who has already destroyed the first three downward fetters now weakens lust (*rāga*), hatred (*dosa*) and delusion (*moha*) and comes to the noble stage of once-return while carrying the potential to return only once to the sensual sphere; third, he destroys all of the five downward fetters and comes to the noble stage of non-return, and becomes free from the sensual sphere irrevocably. After this, the practitioner in the insight scheme, destroys the five upward fetters and comes to the noble stage of *arahat* and becomes free from both the fine-material and the immaterial spheres irreversibly.

This scheme is comparable to the *jhāna* scheme that is often practiced by the Buddhist practitioner by combining it with the insight scheme. In this scheme, the practitioner attains the first *jhāna*, becomes free from the sensual sphere temporarily and dwells in the fine-material sphere. Then, he attains the first immaterial *jhāna*, becomes free from the fine-material sphere temporarily and dwells in the immaterial sphere. Finally, he attains the cessation of perception and feeling, becomes free from even the immaterial sphere. However, in this last case the person is always a noble one who is either a non-returner or an *arahat*, meaning he is also a practitioner of the insight scheme. If the person is a non-returner, when he comes out of the cessation he automatically turns into an *arahat* irrevocably.

The popular canonical quote (e.g., AN II 238) on the Four Noble Persons defines the first three—stream-enterer, once-returner, and non-returner—in relation to their giving up of fetters (*saṃyojana*) but the *arahat* in relation to his destruction of mental taints (*āsava*). This mixing of the categories of both fetters and mental taints for the gradual presentation of the Four Noble Persons compels us to understand that either there is a close connection between fetters and taints or, as I have argued elsewhere, there is a problem in classifying the Four Noble Persons in relation to their destruction of fetters. As mentioned above, the goal of the Buddhist path and practice is to attain the cessation of suffering by way of ending birth by ceasing 'self'-existence (*bhava-nirodha*) in the three spheres: the sensual, the fine-material, and the immaterial (SN V 56). There is no doubt that the Buddha uses varying metaphorical categories to represent the psychological defilements that maintain the worldly person's 'self'-existence and in turn birth in the three spheres. This could be seen from the category of taints (*āsava*) that is defined in the discourses to be three (DN II 81; AN I 165; SN V 56): (1) sensuality (*kāmāsava*), (2) 'self'existence (*bhavāsava*), (3) ignorance (*avijjāsava*). These taints tell us that they are subtler ways of identifying the same mental defilements that are presented as fetters or chains. If one becomes an *arahat* with the destruction of ten fetters. This means that with the vanishing of the taint of sensual desire, the practitioner becomes free from the sensual sphere, and with the vanishing of the taints of 'self'-existence (and ignorance), he becomes free from both the fine-material and the immaterial spheres. This is clearly analogous to the soteriological function of the fetters. Hence, it takes us to a general conclusion that taints and fetters are more or less the same and that difference between them lies mostly in the categories chosen to define the noble persons.

Even though with a doctrinal study into such category variations one would be able to make sense out of such varying category presentations of the early discourses attributed to the Buddha, one would also always find one's interpretations and conclusions to be doubtful when seen the varying possibilities and approaches that are available to study the doctrinal materials of these early discourses and their subsequent interpretations and adaptations in the different Buddhist traditions. In this regard, Dipen Barua's admirable study of the fetter concept through historical and soteriological lines takes us a big step forward into understanding not only the subject matter itself for he brings many new insights into it but also the need for exploring the doctrinal concepts to discern their functional changes in the soteriology presentations during and after the formulation periods of the Pāli Canon and its Commentaries of the Theravāda Buddhist tradition. Dipen Barua explores more specifically the function of labeling the soteriological progresses achievable along the noble path to *Nibbāna* and concludes that this function of fetter is a result of a doctrinal development that took place within the Pāli Canon, with the transition from the *Sutta*-s to the *Abhidhamma*. He observes that it is initially the *Dhammasaṅgaṇi*, a Canonical *Abhidhamma* text, that systematizes the description of the four progressive soteriological stages with reference to fetters for it is in it that once-return is first defined with reference to the attenuation of sensual lust and ill-will—not with reference to the attenuation of lust, hatred, and delusion as in the *Sutta*-s—, the fourth and the fifth fetters in the list, and the *arahat*-ness with reference to the destruction of the last five fetters, not with reference to the destruction of cankers as in the *Sutta*-s. Dipen Barua examines this soteriological and some other functions of fetters in great detail by systematically applying both the doctrinal and historical approaches to a vast body of both the Canonical and the Commentarial Pāli texts of the Theravāda Buddhist tradition. For those who wish to pursue studies into doctrinal development in Buddhist traditions, Dipen Barua's this masterpiece remains exemplary!

G.A. Somaratne, PhD (Northwestern)
Assistant Professor
Centre of Buddhist Studies
The University of Hong Kong
04.11.2017

Abbreviations

Note 1: In this work, the Pāli quotations of the first four *Nikāya*-s, the *Sutta Nipāta*, and the *Itivuttaka* are from the Pāli Text Society (PTS) editions. The Pāli quotations of the *Abhidhamma Piṭaka*, the *Niddesa*, and the *Paṭisambhidāmagga* are from the Vipassana Research Institute (VRI) editions. And, the Pāli quotations of the *Sutta* and the *Abhidhamma-aṭṭhakathā*-s are also from the VRI editions.

Note 2: All translations from primary sources (the Pāli Canon and Its Commentaries) are mine unless otherwise stated. When I translate Pāli passages into English from the first four *Nikāya*-s, I often consult the English translations by Bhikkhu Bodhi, Bhikkhu Ñāṇamoli, and Maurice Walshe (for details please see the Bibliography).

AN	*Aṅguttara Nikāya*
Abhidh-s	*Abhidhammattha Saṅgaha*
As	*Atthasālinī* (*Dhammasaṅgaṇi–aṭṭāhakathā*)
DN	*Dīgha Nikāya*
Dhp	*Dhammapada*
Dhs	*Dhammasaṅgaṇi*
Iti	*Itivuttaka*
Iti-a	*Itivuttaka-aṭṭhakathā*
Kv	*Kathāvatthu*
Kv-a	*Kathāvatthu-aṭṭhakathā*
MN	*Majjhima Nikāya*
Mp	*Manorathapūraṇi* (*Aṅguttara Nikāya-aṭṭhakathā*)
MpṬ	*Majjhima Nikāya-aṭṭhakathā-ṭīkā*
Nidd I	*Mahāniddesa*
Nidd I-a	*Mahāniddesa-aṭṭhakathā* (*Saddhammapajjotikā*)

Nidd II	*Cullaniddesa*
Nidd II-a	*Cullaniddesa-aṭṭhakathā* (*Saddhammapajjotikā*)
Paṭis	*Paṭisambhidāmagga*
Paṭis-a	*Paṭisambhidāmagga-aṭṭhakathā* (*Saddhammappakāsinī*)
Pp	*Puggalapaññatti*
Pp-a	*Puggalapaññatti-aṭṭhakathā*
Ps	*Papañcasūdanī* (*Majjhima Nikāya-aṭṭhakathā*)
PTS	Pali Text Society
SN	*Saṃyutta Nikāya*
Skt	Sanskrit
Sn	*Sutta Nipāta*
Spk	*Sāratthappakāsinī* (*Saṃyutta Nikāya-aṭṭhakathā*)
Sv	*Sumaṅgalavilāsinī* (*Dīgha Nikāya-aṭṭhakathā*)
Th	*Theragāthā*
Thī	*Therīgāthā*
Vibh	*Vibhaṅga*
Vibh-a	*Vibhaṅga-aṭṭhakathā* (*Sammohavinodanī*)
Vism	*Visuddhimagga*
VRI	Vipassana Research Institute
vol.	volume

Chapter 1 – **Introduction**

1.1 Introduction

This chapter introduces the textual sources of the concept "fetter" (*saṃyojana*) within the Pāli tradition. The Pāli tradition comprises of a vast body of Pāli literature both Canonical and Commentarial. In the Pāli Canon, the concept "fetter" denotes the notion of binding which has different functions and scopes of operation. One of the functions is to mark progress of the four stages of enlightenment. But, we consider this function is a doctrinal development in the Pāli Canon. Evidence is available to show that the concept "fetter" develops from the *Sutta*-s to the *Abhidhamma*. Therefore, the concept "fetter" is worth studying both from a soteriological point of view and from a historical point of view. This introductory chapter formulates the research scope by considering various lists of fetter and also three types of functions: as householder binding, as intra-psychic binding, and as existential binding. Taking these into consideration, we will show why the present study is important in Buddhist studies.

1.2 Introduction to the Study

The concept "fetter" (Pāli: *saṃyojana* or *saññojana)* plays an important role in the Pāli Canon and its Commentaries. Many scholars in Buddhist studies, especially those following the Pāli tradition, like Bhikkhu Bodhi (1980, 54), H.G.A. van. Zeyst (1990, 234), T.W. Rhys Davids and William Stede (1993, 656) link the concept "fetter" with a list of ten defilements which bind sentient beings into the cycle of existence (*saṃsāra*). In the *Sutta*-s (AN V 17; SN V 61–62; DN III 216), the ten defilements are named: personality-belief (*sakkāya-diṭṭhi*), doubt (*vicikicchā*), clinging to rules and vows (*sīlabbata-parāmāsa)*, sensual desire (*kāma-chanda*), ill-will (*vyāpāda*), desire for form (*rūpa-rāga*), desire for formlessness (*arūpa-rāga*), conceit (*māna*), restlessness (*uddhacca*) and ignorance (*avijjā*). The *Saṃyojana Sutta* of the *Dasaka Nipāta* in AN divides these ten fetters into two kinds, as follows:

> The five lower fetters [*pañc'orambhāgiyāni saṃyojanāni*]: personality-belief, doubt, clinging to rules and vows, sensual desire, ill-will; the five higher fetters [*pañc'uddhambhāgiyāni saṃyojanāni*]: desire for form, desire for formlessness, conceit, restlessness, and ignorance (AN V 17).[1]

With these two lists of ten fetters, the Theravāda tradition commonly defines the four supra-mundane paths known as the stream-entry (*sotāpatti*), the once-returning (*sakadāgāmi*), the non-returning (*anāgāmi*), and the arahatship (*arahatta*).[2] Maurice Walshe (1995, 27) in summarizing the tradition says that one becomes a stream-enterer by discarding the first three of the five lower fetters, a once-returner by greatly weakening the fourth and fifth lower fetters, a non-returner by completely destroying the fourth and fifth lower fetters, and an arahat by destroying the five higher fetters. This study is undertaken to show that this classification does not fully describe the four stages in the first four *Nikāya*-s, but it was developed during the compilation of the *Dhammasaṅgaṇi*, the first treatise of the Pāli *Abhidhamma Piṭaka*. By doing so, this study will show the enumeration of the four stages with the list of ten fetters together with the lower and higher fetters was mainly defined in the *Kathāvatthu* of the *Abhidhamma Piṭaka*.

---

[1] *sakkāyadiṭṭhiṃ, vicikicchā sīlabbataparāmāso, kāmacchando, byāpādoti, imāni pañcorambhāgiyāni saṃyojanāni; rūparāgo, arūparāgo, māno, uddhaccaṃ, avijjā, imāni kho pañcuddhambhāgiyāni saṃyojanāni.*

[2] These hierarchical spiritual stages are referred in the *Sāmañña Sutta*, the *Brahmañña Sutta* of the *Mahā Vagga* (SN V 25) and elsewhere.

Apart from the existential binding, this study will also show the concept "fetter" applies to two different functions "intra-psychic" and "householder" bindings which are reflected in the first four *Nikāya*-s. These bindings represent various interpretations of fetter from context to context in the Pāli Canon itself. Meanwhile, this study intends to investigate why the description of the four stages with the method of fetter is prevalent throughout the Pāli Canon, while different methods are available in the first four *Nikāya*-s. Many scholars such as Govinda Chandra Pande (1999), A.K. Warder (2000) and Richard F. Gombrich (2006) have pointed out that the Pāli Canon underwent a long period of doctrinal development and interpretation. Same for the concept "fetter". Therefore, this study intends to trace the concept "fetter" from its earlier application to its later development. This study will also examine the earlier and later *Sutta*-s, and some of the texts in which the doctrine of fetter is expounded.

Buddhist teachings, according to the Theravāda tradition, are contained in the Pāli Canon that exists today. Among them, many are considered to be the early Buddhist teachings. According to Paul J. Griffiths (1983, 59), the early Buddhist teachings are to be identified as "pre-Aśokan Indian Buddhism". Steven Collins (1990, 89) defines early Buddhism from the time of the Buddha to the time of King Aśoka who reigned around 270–30 BCE. T.W. Rhys Davids (1911, 188) offers a chronological order of the Pāli Canon from the time of the Buddha to the time of King Aśoka. Maurice Winternitz (1977, 17–18) examines the Bhārhut and Sāñchī inscriptions which illustrate a collection of Buddhist texts called "*Piṭaka*-s," divided into the five *Nikāya*-s and established some time before the 2nd century BCE. Pande (1999, 16 & 43) summarizes the tradition as saying that the entire Pāli *Tipiṭaka* was written down in Sri Lanka in the 1st century BCE, and the *Nikāya*-s would go back to the 3rd Century BCE. He asserts that the growth of the *Nikāya*-s fell between the 5th and the 3rd centuries BCE. Pande also mentions many

Sutta-s in the *Nikāya*-s reveal patchwork in which the application of *anusaya, āsava, ogha, kilesa, saṃyojana* changed from early to late period. In a similar approach, Gombrich (2006, xii) mentions that a vast body of materials in the Canon was produced over many years, therefore "it is not surprising that misunderstanding or diverse interpretations arose in the process". Drawing from the above mentioned sources, we can safely say that the doctrinal development took place within the Pāli Canon itself throughout the period of its compilation which finally fossilized into a standard collection in the texts that exist today. In this Canon, we will show that the concept of fetter has developed from the *Sutta*-s to the *Abhidhamma*.

The focus of this study is on the doctrine of fetter from a perspective of doctrinal development in the *Sutta* and the *Abhidhamma Piṭaka*-s. Some scholars have shown various references to fetter and its development within both *Piṭaka*-s. Bhikkhu Anālayo (2006, 219) says there are considerable variations in the use of the term "fetter" in the discourses. He shows the variations in several *Sutta*-s, such as MN I 361 and MN I 483 which mention "the eight 'fetters' in relation to killing, stealing, false speech, malicious speech, rapacious greed, spiteful scolding, angry despair, and arrogance,' and 'the fetter of householder'". Pande says (1999, 43), "*saṃyojana* originally has a general meaning in which the metaphor is clear. Later it was elaborated into diverse lists". Soonil Hwang (2006, 27) is exceptional as he argues that the four stages with the method of fetters were entirely developed in the *Abhidhamma*. The present study also aims to prove that the concept "fetter" was a developed notion which was subsequently interpreted in various ways in the *Sutta* and the *Abhidhamma Piṭaka*-s.

1.3 The Scope of the Research

Etymologically, *saṃyojana,* a neuter noun in Pāli, derives from *saṃyuñjati* (*saṃ* + *yuñjati*) meaning "binding firmly" or "binding together." The prefix *saṃ* means "together," and the word *yojana* derives from the root √*yuj* meaning "to yoke," "to join," or "to bind." In the *Nikāya*-s, it is used to mean "fetter" or "bond". In Canonical (DN II 302; MN I 61) passages an alternative form *saññojana*[3] is also used in the same sense. In the *Pāli-English Dictionary*, Davids and Stede (1993, 743) state *saññ* is a frequent spelling of *saṃy*, and *saññojana* and *saṃyojana* offer the same meaning: *saṃyojana=saññojana*. Additionally, Monier Williams (2003, 1112) in the *Sanskrit-English Dictionary* gives another implication of *saṃyojana*, for example, copulation or sexual union.

In the *Mahā-satipaṭṭhāna Sutta* in DN and the *Satipaṭṭhāna Sutta* in MN, fetter appears as an intra-psychic phenomenon, a conditioning factor that occurs depending on the sense bases and sense objects (MN I 61; DN II 302–03). In this context, the concept "fetter" refers to the psychic force of binding. This is one interpretation of fetter in the *Sutta*-s, which is different from the existential binding. Several *Sutta*-s, for example the *Saṃyojana Sutta* of the *Saḷāyatana Vagga* in SN, record that the meaning of fetter was not clear for many monks, and they questioned each other saying: "friends! 'the fetter' and 'the things to be fettered', are these things different in meaning and different in phrasing; or are they one in meaning and just different in phrasing?" (SN IV 282).[4] In response to this question, the concept of fetter with the example of two oxen who are joined together by a yoke was introduced in the same *Sutta*. The *Sutta* explains that their bondage is not caused by either of the oxen, but by the yoke itself.

The term *saṃyojana* also appears in the *Sutta*-s to denote the suffering of life in *saṃsāra*. The *Devatā-saṁyutta* of the *Sagāthā Vagga* (SN I 39), for example, analyzes the role of fetter as the binding force that traps sentient beings in the world (*loka*), and the complete eradication of the fetter of craving

---

[3] *yañca tadubhayaṃ paṭicca uppajjati saññojanaṃ tañca pajānāti.*

[4] *saññojananti vā āvuso saññojaniyā dhammāti vā ime dhammā nānatthā nānāvyañjanā, udāhu ekatthā vyañjanameva nānanti.*

leads one to final liberation, *Nibbāna*. The *Itivuttaka* narrates that the Buddha speaks about the notion of fetter as being employed to account for the suffering of life within *saṃsāra*. In his word, "because of the fetter of craving [*taṇhā-saṃyojana*] all sentient beings, being conjoined, go wandering and transmigrating on for a long, long time" (Iti 8).[5]

Different *Sutta*-s enumerate fetters into different categories: the fetter of delight (*nandi-saṃyojana*) is found in SN I 39, the fetter of craving (*taṇhā-saṃyojana*) is found in AN I 223 & 224, and the fetter of existence (*bhava-saṃyojana*) is found in SN I 71, SN V 145; AN I 231. The eradication of each of these fetters is identified as liberation which refers to the "advanced doctrine" on account of differing spiritual attainments of the practitioner.

In addition, the list of fetter is varies in different *Sutta*-s. For example, a list of "three fetters" (*tīni-saṃyojanāni*) often occurs in the *Nikāya*-s, as follows:

1. The fetters of personality-belief (*sakkāya-diṭṭhi)*, doubt (*vicikicchā)*, and clinging to rules and vows (*sīlabbata-parāmāsa*) (DN III 216).

The *Sutta*-s describe that through the eradication of these three fetters one can become a stream-enterer (DN II 92).

The *Satta-saññojana Sutta* (AN IV 7) records a list of seven fetters as follows:

2. The fetters of compliance (*anunaya)*, hatred *(paṭigha)*, views *(diṭṭhi)*, doubt (*vicikicchā*), conceit *(māna)*, desire for existence (*bhava-rāga)*, and ignorance (*avijjā*).

The *Macchariya-saṃyojana Sutta* (AN IV 8) records another list of seven fetters with a slight variation as follows:

3. The fetters of compliance, hatred, views, doubt, conceit, envy (*issā*), and selfishness (*macchariya*).[6]

---

[5] *taṇhāsaññojanena hi bhikkhave saṃyuttā sattā dīgharattaṃ sandhāvanti saṃsarantī'ti.*

[6] *issā* and *machariya* fetters are also referenced by passing in the *Sakkapañha Sutta* (DN II 277).

The functions of the above two lists of fetters are not the same. According to the *Nikāya*-s, through the eradication of the first list of seven fetters, final liberation can be attained, but the second list does not appear to serve such a purpose. The *Saññojana-pahāna Sutta* of the *Sattaka Nipāta* in AN, for instance, develops the theory that when one has abandoned the first list of seven fetters, "cut it off at the root, made it like a palm stump, then there is no future becoming, the person has completely made an end of suffering" (AN IV 08).[7]

A list of ten fetters, which further divided into two classes, is found in the *Sutta*-s (DN III 216; SN V 61–62, 136–37, 241–42, 251; AN V 17), as follows:

4. The five lower fetters: personality-belief, doubt, clinging to rules and vows, sensual desire and ill-will; and
5. The five higher fetters: desire for form, desire for formlessness, conceit, restlessness and ignorance.

It is interesting to note that the *Abhidhamma* texts such as the *Dhammasaṅgaṇi* record a separate list of ten fetters, and in a different order with sensuality (*kāma-rāga*) as the first in the sequence. The list is:

6. The fetters of sensual desire (*kāma-rāga*), hatred (*paṭigha*), conceit (*māna*), view (*diṭṭhi*), doubt (*vicikicchā*), clinging to rules and vows (*sīlabbata-parāmāsa*), desire for becoming (*bhava-rāga*), envy (*issā*), selfishness (*macchariya*), and ignorance (*avijjā*) (Dhs VRI 166).

The *Sunakkhatta Sutta* (MN II 254–55) gives another delineation of the use of fetter, as follows:

7. The fetter of the lure of the world (*lokāmisa-saññojana*), the fetter of imperturbability (*āneñja-saññojana*), the fetter of the base of nothingness (*ākiñcaññāyatana-saññojana*), and the fetter of the base of neither-perception-nor-non-perception (*nevasaññānāsaññāyatana-saññojana*).

Apart from the above mentioned lists, different kinds of usages of the concept "fetter" are also found in the *Nikāya*-s, which

---

[7] *ucchinnamūlaṃ tālāvatthukataṃ anabhāvakataṃ āyatiṃ anuppādadhammaṃ ... sammā mānābhi samayā antamakāsi dukkhassāti.*

delineate additional demarcations of fetter. For example, while the *Tevijjavacchagotta Sutta* (MN I 483) records "the fetter of householder" (*gihi-saññojana)* as a bondage of a householder, the *Potāliya Sutta* (MN I 360) describes it as unwholesome psychological state of a householder.

The *Dukanipāta* (AN I 63) contains two distinctive interpretations of fetter which are named "internal fetter" (*ajjhatta-saññojana*) and "external fetter" (*bahiddhā-saññojana*). The internal fetter describes the person who returns to this world, and the external fetter describes the person who does not return to this world. The *Abhidhamma* treatises, i.e., the *Vibhaṅga* (VRI 215) interprets these two categories of fetters into two kinds showing the internal fetter with the five lower fetters, and the external fetter with the five higher fetters.

In the *Sutta* and the *Abhidhamma Piṭaka*-s, moreover, the definition of the attainment of once-returning and arahatship through the destruction of fetter is found in diverse ways. Firstly, in DN, MN, SN & AN, the once-returning is defined through the destruction of the first three fetters of personality-belief, doubt, and clinging to rules and vows, and through the attenuation of desire (*rāga*), hatred (*dosa*), and delusion (*moha*) (AN IV 12).[8] Secondly, the *Abhidhamma* texts such as the *Kathāvatthu* (VRI 49–51) contain another alternative definition of once-returning. It is documented with reference to the destruction of the first three fetters and greatly weakening of fetters of sensual desire (*kāma-chanda*) and ill-will (*vyāpāda*). Although both definitions are accepted in Buddhist tradition, the second one is not recorded in the first four *Nikāya*-s at all. But this interpretation is found in the *Abhidhamma*, and together with elimination of respective *anusaya*-s in the *Paṭisambhidāmagga* (VRI 11) and the *Niddesa* (Nidd II VRI 148)[9] of the *Khuddaka Nikāya*. This study is undertaken to

---

[8] *tiṇṇaṃ saṃyojanānaṃ parikkhayā rāgdosamohānaṃ tanuttā sakadāgāmi hoti.*

[9] In both texts the four stages are always defined through the destruction of ten fetters and seven latent tendencies (*anusaya*) together.

show these diversities of this doctrinal exposition in the *Sutta* and the *Abhidhamma Piṭaka*-s.

A traditional interpretation of the arahatship is defined through the abandonment of ten fetters and interprets an arahat as one who has eradicated the five higher fetters. Ven. Nyanatiloka (1952, 50), Zeyst (1990, 234) and Walshe (1995, 27) refer to the traditional interpretation and state the five higher fetters are: desire for form (*rūpa-rāga*), desire for formlessness (*arūpa-rāga*), conceit (*māna*), restlessness (*uddhacca*), and ignorance (*avijjā*). However, this exposition is not recorded in any *Sutta*-s of DN, MN, SN & AN. Rather, in these *Nikāya*-s (SN III 193; AN I 144; MN I 141; DN III 133) the stage of arahatship is defined as one who has destroyed the cankers (*khīṇa-āsava*), and completely eradicated the fetter of existence (*parikkhīṇa-bhava-saññojana*). Therefore, it is an important aspect of this study to investigate when the elucidation of arahatship in connection to the higher fetters was developed.

Another key question is that the spiritual breakthrough of the four stages is not always associated with fetters. For example, the *Kāyagatāsati Vagga* of the *Ekaka Nipāta* (AN I 45) states one can realize the fruits of stream-entry, once-returning, non-returning, and arahatship through the development and cultivation of mindfulness (*sati*). The *Macchariya Sutta* of the *Pañcaka Nipāta* (AN III 840) presents the four stages in terms of abandoning the five things of selfishness (*macchariya*) with regard to dwellings (*āvāsa*), families (*kula*), gains (*lābha*), praise (*vaṇṇa*), and the Dhamma (*dhamma*). The *Anicca, Dukkha, Anatta Sutta*-s and the *Nibbāna Sutta* of the *Chakka Nipāta* (AN III 442–43) define the four stages in terms of insight into impermanence, suffering and non-self. Yet in the *Indriyasaṃyutta* of the *Mahā Vagga* (SN V 200), the four stages are elucidated with five faculties: faith (*saddhā*), energy (*viriya*), mindfulness (*sati*), concentration (*samādhi*) and wisdom (*paññā*). Showing the above evidence, it is a further curiosity to discern the affiliation between the fetters as well as the other possible interpretations for gradual spiritual paths. Though in the *Nikāya*-s these methods are available to describe the four stages, the method with fetters is prevalent throughout the *Sutta* and the *Abhidhamma Piṭaka*-s. This study will investigate why the description of the four stages with the method of fetters is prevalent, while other methods are available.

The investigation into the fetter and its various functions in the *Sutta* and the *Abhidhamma Piṭaka*-s would potentially inform us about the tendencies of doctrinal growth and interpretation. Looking at the account of compilation of DN, MN, SN, AN, the *Paṭisambhidāmagga,* the *Niddesa*, and the *Abhidhamma* texts, there is also a possible hint that the concept "fetter" developed from context to context in the Pāli Canon itself. Later, only after a period of final development, the scheme of "ten fetters" to describe the four supra-mundane stages is established in the Theravāda tradition. Highlighting the scheme of fetters and their expansion, this study puts forward the proposition that the ten and other listed fetters are not a conclusive, closed compilation. All these different conceptual and systematized functions are undertaken for examination in this study.

1.4 Background to the Issue

A few scholars have worked on the importance of spiritual hierarchy with regard to the traditional list of ten fetters, although the work on the concept "fetter" is not a well-developed study in Buddhist studies. Importance is given to the following works in this work:

1.4.1 Studies on the Fetters in Relation to the Four Stages

Gary Ow (2000) has analyzed Ānanda's spiritual progress towards arahatship through the eradication of ten fetters. He identifies the four supra-mundane stages in relation to the ten fetters as listed in Narada Maha Thera's (1956) translated text *A Manual of Abhidhamma*, and U. Kyaw Min's (1980) *Buddhist Abhidhamma Meditation and Concentration.* Ow has not paid attention to the *Nikāya* materials on the path to enlightenment. His dissertation's Chapter 4 "The Ten Fetters" and Chapter 7 "How He Overcame the Ten Fetters to Attain the Four Stages of Enlightenment," are relevant for the current study but these are mostly based on secondary resources due to insufficient canonical references.

Among studies on fetter, the works of Anālayo (2006) are of importance. Anālayo argues that fetters are used in the discourses in diverse contexts but all are in the sense of binding process. Anālayo says:

> In the discourses there is considerable variation in the usage of the term "fetter," which suggests that to speak of "fetter" does not always necessarily refer to a fixed set, but may sometimes include whatever falls under the same principle, in the sense of fettering and causing bondage (Anālayo 2006, 219).

Elaborating on this, Anālayo (2006, 219–21) points out that the list of ten fetters is not necessarily relevant in the context of actual *satipaṭṭhāna* practice, but the fetter brings out the direction to the context of sense bases and their objects. Though his comment regarding the scheme of ten fetters in the context of *satipaṭṭhāna* practice is thoughtful, it would be simplistic to sum up various disparate definitions of fetter into the one single scheme. Bhikkhu Sujato (2012, 79) has carried out a similar work on mindfulness and its history based on the *Nikāya*-s. In the study while he discusses fetter in the context of sense bases and their objects, the different variations of the concept "fetter" are excluded in his discussion.

Another outstanding contribution of Anālayo is a comparative study of the Pāli *Majjhima Nikāya* and the Chinese *Madhyama Āgama*. In this study Anālayo (2011, 95) refers to all of the Pāli *Majjhima Nikāya*'s recording of fetters paralleling those of the *Āgama*. Comparing both texts, he argues that the *Madhyama Āgama's* interpretation of fetter does not relate to direct mindfulness to the senses and their respective forms, but merely as conditions for the arising of a fetter. He further opines, the *Āgama's* interpretation of fetter is "not to be mindful of senses or their objects as such, but of the fetter that may arise at any sense-door" (Anālayo, 2011, 95). Finally, Anālayo suggests the function of fetter in the *Āgama*-s is similar to that of the two (Mahā)-*Satipaṭṭhāna Sutta*-s in the *Nikāya*-s. In his study, though the list of five lower fetters is discussed, the list of five higher fetters has entirely been omitted. Therefore, for what reason the lists of lower and higher fetter have been used in the *Nīkaya*-s is unclear, and this study is undertaken to illuminate them. Two more books of Anālayo (2009 & 2010), based on the Pāli discourses, also focus on the study of fetters. They clarify various types of craving and grasping. Some sections of both books are relevant to this study in terms of some individual fetters.

Tzungkuen Wen's (2009) study on the *Sukkhavipassaka* contains a comprehensive documentation of the position of "dry-insight practitioner". This study, in its chapter one, proposes an initial chronological sequence to the path of awakening and the four stages of spirituality, taking various evidence from the Pāli Canon. Although the study describes the stream-entry and the once-returning in relation to the eradication of fetters, the elaboration of once-returning is somehow different from the *Nikāya* definition. Referring to SN V 61 Wen says, "the five lower fetters (*orambhāgiya-saṃyojana*) for the description of the once-returner are the first three fetters plus sensual desire (*kāmarāga*) and ill will (*vyāpāda*)" (Wen, 2009, 31–32). Here his reference to SN is not well-cited, because in the *Sutta*-s the once-returner is defined with reference to the eradication of the first three fetters and with the attenuation of *rāga, dosa,* and *moha*. The present study will show that Wen's interpretation is a later development in the *Abhidhamma*. In addition to this, the "introduction" to Bhikkhu Ñāṇamoli and Bhikkhu Bodhi's (1995, 42–43) translated volume of the *Majjhima Nikāya* is important. Here the non-returner is defined with reference to fetters as Wen describes. As sources, it was referred to MN I 6.11–13, 19, and MN I 22.42–45. In the same context, the arahat is defined with reference to the complete removal of the five higher fetters. But this definition is not found in the same text. Their reference to the *Sutta*-s does not list the five higher fetters as it was described, rather the arahat or final stage of spirituality is defined in the following order:

> 'May I, by realizing for myself with direct knowledge, here and now enter upon and abide in the deliverance of mind and deliverance by wisdom that are taintless with the destruction of the taints let him fulfil the precepts, be devoted to internal serenity of mind, not neglect meditation, be possessed of insight, and dwell in empty huts (Ñāṇamoli and Bodhi, 1995, 117).
>
> [B]hikkhus who are arahants with taints destroyed, who have lived the holy life, done what had to be done, laid down the burden, reached the true goal, destroyed the fetters of being, and are completely liberated through final knowledge (Ñāṇamoli and Bodhi, 1995, 235).

Similarly, in "introduction" to the Walshe's (1995, 26–27) translation of the *Dīgha Nikāya* contains the four stages with reference to fetters as Bodhi and Ñāṇamoli observe. From the above discussion it is clear that the standard description of the four stages with the method of ten fetters is not recorded in the *Sutta*-s, but found in the *Abhidhamma*.

G.A. Somaratne (1999) following a critical approach presents the concept of fetter to identify several types of non-returner with reference to the five higher fetters. He cites several passages from the *Nikāya*-s in support of his proposition. While clarifying the Four Noble Persons in relation to the traditional list of ten fetters, he points out its weakness. He gives the example of various types of non-returner. Somaratne (1999, 124) is the first in Buddhist studies, who sees the weakness of the scheme of five higher fetters in regard to the definition of non-returners. He (*ibid.*, 144) says the term *uddhacca* (restlessness) in the list of five higher fetters is later replaced by redactors or copiers. Using the example of liberation with the eradication of cankers (*āsava*), he (*ibid.*, 129) concludes that "cankers" (*āsava*) and "fetters" are more or less the same and they differ mostly in the terms used rather than in meaning. There is no doubt that fetters and cankers are the same in terms of their functions, but further investigation is essential to illustrate why the word *saṃyojana* is more suitable to categorize the

Four Noble Persons, instead of *āsava*. Also, throughout the Pāli canon it is evident that the function of fetter has been enlarged from context to context, instead of *āsava*. Even the texts that contain *āsava* have also undergone development, from three to four in the *Abhidhamma*.

Another point Somaratne (*ibid.*, 129) clarifies in terms of "lower" and "higher" fetters is that the Buddha did not intend to create a fixed list of fetters, rather he tried to convey the nature of one's spiritual attainment by using the concept. Further, Somaratne (*ibid.*, 130) suggests that the standardization of Noble Persons in relation to the fetters took place in early Buddhist history. His thoughtful assumption is evidently valid in the historical development of the concept of fetter. However, we will show that the list of ten fetters with the Four Noble Persons took place entirely in the *Abhidhamma*. Because, in the *Sutta* and the *Abhidhamma Piṭaka*-s the methods to define the Four Noble Persons with fetters are different.

Somaratne also shows two similar lists of fetters from the *Aṅguttara Nikāya*—seven "latencies" (*anusaya*) and seven "fetters" (*saṃyojana*). Clarifying these two lists, he (*ibid.*, 144–45) says, these seven latencies exist at a latent level for a child, and for the mature people, they exist as engrossed levels. They are not only obsessed by these fetters but they do not understand how to eradicate them. This study will show that these two lists directly influence the composers of the *Dhammasaṅgaṇi* when they set up another list of fetters in the *Abhidhamma*. Somaratne's work on fetters is of particular relevance to the current area of interest, especially his suggestion that fetters function differently from context to context. In this connection, a critical-historical approach is indeed needed to scrutinize the development of the concept of fetter.

1.4.2 Discussion on between Saṃyojana and Āsava

You-Mee Lee's (2009) research work on the *Āsava* and *Kilesa* contains the function of both *āsava* and *saṃyojana*. Lee (2009, 44–45) says that fetter is proximately related to *āsava* and that all fetters originate from it. Taking the lower and higher fetters for granted she proposes eradicating fetters means eliminating *āsava*. In regard to the meaning of *āsava*, her opinion is also close to that of Somaratne who says "cankers" and "fetters" are more or less the same and they differ mostly in the terms used rather than in meaning. However, it is necessary to examine why *saṃyojana* and *āsava* are named as defilements, but only *saṃyojana* is frequently applied to explain the four stages. Apparently the *Nikāya*-s show that in Buddhist history *saṃyojana* plays a more crucial role in describing the four stages than *āsava*.

1.4.3 Discussions on the First Three Fetters (tīni-saṃyojanāni)

After the discussion on fetters and their functions, a review is delivered on the list of three fetters—personality-belief, clinging to rules and vows, and doubt-on which a few scholars have given their critical observations. For example, Norman C. McClelland (2010) says the framework of the first three fetters in relation to the stage of stream-entry has Brāhmanic religious influence. He explains each of the three fetters originated from Vedic religious practice. McClelland contends:

> Each of these fetters is actually a belief, practice, or mainstay of Brāhmanic or Vedic religion, a major competitor of Early Buddhism. In the case of the first fetter the belief in a real self was the belief in ātman and Brahman. In the second case, one was expected to have at least an initial respect for, if not absolute confidence in, the Buddha and his teachings as being in no way inferior to those of the Brahmanic priests. As for the third fetter, attachment to rites and rituals, this meant abandoning any trust in the blood sacrificial rites and rituals of the Brahmanic priests (McClelland, 2010, 51).

Regarding the fetter of clinging to rules and vows, Gombrich also concurs with McClelland. But, Gombrich (2009, 14) observes that the Buddha used a lot of old words and gave them new meanings following his custom. For example, *silabbata* (Skt: *śīlavrata*) is a brāhmin word for 'ritual' which was used to refer to ethical intention in Buddhism. The study on the fetter *sīlabbata-parāmāsa* has also been documented in Damien V. Keown's (1985) PhD dissertation "Ethical Perfection in Buddhist Soteriology," Richard K. Payne's (2004, 723–26) encyclopedia entry "Ritual," and Davids' (1907) *Buddhism: Its History and Literature* respectively. Keown (1985, 68–99) discusses this fetter with reference to the *Visuddhimagga* as a ground of one of the five false views listed in the *Abhidharmakośa*. He defines *sīlabbata-parāmāsa* as the lifelong practice of *agnihotra* sacrifice which is ritual baths and other such observances in the hope of liberation. Up to this point, only secondary source studies are available on *sīlabbata-parāmāsa*. The Pāli Canon explains *sīlabbata-parāmāsa* in a broader sense. For example, the verse 271 of the *Dhammapada* indicates that Buddhist monks are encouraged to go beyond the clinging to rules and observances. On the other hand, the *Aṅguttara Nikāya* (AN I 225) says that rules and ceremonies in themselves can be either skilful or unskilful. In this regard, it is clear that the problems are not just certain rules and ceremonies as such, but rather the act of clinging to them that has unskilful effects.

1.4.4 Study Remarks on Nandi-saṃyojana

Several scholars have discussed some particular fetters which are given importance in this study. This section focusses on a particular fetter *nandi-saṃyojana* (fetter of delight). Alexander Wynne (2007, 89) says that the word *nandi-saṃyojana* is consistent with the principle of craving which is the cause of suffering—the Second Noble Truth. The Commentary to the *Khaggavisāna Sutta* of Sn, the *Niddesa* (*Nidd* II VRI 42, 79 & 84) defines delight as craving (*nandi vuccati taṇhā*). Though the *Niddesa* identifies *nandi* as *taṇhā,* the functions of them have slight difference which will be discussed by consulting the *Sutta*-s. In this regard, we will show the function of *nandi* is not as same as *taṇhā*, rather the function of *nandi-rāga* is as *taṇhā*.

1.4.5 Other Studies Related to the Development of the Concept of Fetter

The present study views the concept "fetter" as something that has developed within the Pāli Canon. A few scholars have occasionally observed this development in their studies. For example, Pande (1999, 43) says that in the early period of Buddhist teachings the term *saṃyojana* signifies a general meaning which was clearly encapsulated by a metaphor, but later it was expanded into diverse lists. He (*ibid.*, 38) also remarks on *āsava* that in the earliest texts there were three kinds of *āsava*, and later they were increased to four. In his study, he does not further analyze on fetter. However, this study will cite sources to support its opinion that the concept of fetter is a developed doctrine. To support this opinion, it further scrutinizes the study conducted by Hirakawa Akira (1990) who says the two lists of ten fetters that we find in the *Abhidhammattha Saṅgaha,* with slight differences, were standardized during the compilation of the *Abhidhamma* texts. He says, in the *Sutta* list of ten fetters two additional fetters-envy (*issā*) and selfishness (*macchariya*) were included and was made another list of ten fetters in the *Abhidhamma*. According to Hirakawa (1990, 198), "the ten fetters from the *abhidhamma* texts... developed during the period when the Pāli *abhidhamma* texts were being compiled". Although Hirakawa's assumption is insightful, this study will show that the *Abhidhamma* list is older than the traditional *Sutta* list. The traditional list of fetter was later developed for which the *Dhammasaṅgaṇi* plays a crucial role. In a third opinion, Hwang (2006) says the traditional list of ten fetters to describe the spiritual stages was entirely developed within the *Abhidhamma*. According to Hwang:

> [E]xplaining the four noble persons entirely in terms of their giving up of the traditional ten fetters is a later development, within the *abhidhamma*. It is in the *Dhammasaṅgiṇi* that a once-

> returner was first explained in this sense. It says that one attains the second path, a once-returner, while diminishing sensual desire and ill-will (*kāmarāgavyāpādānaṃ patanubhāvāya*); whereas one attains the third path, a non-returner, while giving up sensual desire and ill-will without any remainder *(kāmarāgavyāpādānaṃ anavasesappahānāya).* This new interpretation was later applied in the *Puggalapaññatti* and also appeared in the *Dharmaskandha* in the Chinese *abhidharma* (Hwang, 2006, 27).

From the above analyses, there is strong evidence for the development of the concept of fetter. Hwang's understanding of the developed nature of the concept of ten fetters in relation to the four stages of enlightenment is to be *Abhidhammic*. But, it fails to mention the central role of fetter in the *Sutta*-s. Consulting the *Sutta*-s and the *Abhidhamma* evidence, this study will further illuminate how and why the concept of fetter has been developed. In this order, Davids and Stede's (1993, 39) assumption is thoughtful, they argue that the stage of non-returning does not mean the abandoning defilements, but the cultivation of certain good mental habits, such as understanding the non-self (*anatta*) and the five *indriya*-s. They say the stage of non-returning is defined through cutting off bonds in the *Abhidhamma*. Though this study agrees with them relatively, evidence is available to show that the stage of non-returning is explained through the destruction of the three fetters and attenuation of greed, hatred and delusion in the *Sutta*-s.

Furthermore, the *Niddesa* (Nidd II VRI 11) and the *Paṭisambhidāmagga* (VRI 151) discuss the four stages together with the method of fetter and latent tendencies (*anusaya*), the description of which was not found in the *Sutta*-s and the *Abhidhamma*. Several scholars, such as Hirakawa (1990, 128), G.P. Malalasekera (1998, Vol.II, 116) and Paul Fuller (2005, 86), say both texts pre-date of the *Abhidhamma* literature, but some scholars such as Hajime Nakamura (1999, 48) and Osker von Hinüber (1996, 60) say both texts were compiled after the *Abhidhamma* literature. This study, however, intends to show that both texts as a whole could have not been complied at a time before the *Abhidhammic* texts, rather subsequently or later

Abhidhamma. Hirakawa (1990, 155 & 202–03) further classifies a list of underlying tendencies (*anusaya*) from which the list of nine fetters was developed. Though the list of nine fetters is not mentioned in his book, it probably belongs to the *Sarvāstivāda* tradition as the list is recorded in the Sanskrit *Abhidharma* texts. While Hirakawa identifies competing lists of fetters to show the developed nature of the concept, again it may not be that fetters are further developed from the list of *anusaya*, because his claim shows a far gap from the historical development of the fetters and underlying tendencies.

Reviewing the above secondary sources and presenting the research scope, the present study pays tribute to scholars who have made useful contributions to the investigation of the development of the concept "fetter". This is the approach of the present study. In conducting this research, the concept "fetter" is to be studied mainly focusing on various lists of fetter and their functions which have not been examined systematically. This study ultimately hopes to advance one step towards the study of the concept "fetter" in the Buddhist scholarship.

1.5 Methodology and Sources

The approach of this study is from a perspective of doctrinal development. It elucidates the concept "fetter" from its earlier appearance to later development, trying to uncover different usages of fetter in the Pāli Canon. However, one may claim that the Buddha himself standardized some of his doctrines at a later stage of his life time. One may argue that because the Buddha's teachings have been memorized by different disciples, and during the process of compilation of the Pāli Canon, different arrangements have taken place in the texts, therefore there is less of a possibility that the doctrine within the Pāli Canon could have been developed. It is true that even the Buddha's own teachings during his lifetime have gone through changes, depending on the needs of his disciples and followers; it is very difficult to differentiate between earlier and later stratification of the discourses from the period of the Buddha to the compilation of the texts. This proposition is similarly observed by Tse-fu Kuan (2008, 6) in his work on the textual analysis of mindfulness in early Buddhism. Several scholars have also given their observations on this matter. For example, Pande says:

> To explain this 'identity-in-difference' we must resort to the hypothesis that the *Nikāya*-s are frequently 'edited' texts embodying doctrines deriving from a common source (Pande, 1999, 24).

Meanwhile, L. Schmithausen says:

> [D]ivergences are caused not only by the different needs of the particular situation, e.g. the time at disposal, but also by the intentions of the instructor. There must have been, certainly, not only chanters simply choosing and combining elements from a given stock of tradition, but also preachers personally engaged in practice and theory, and it is hardly conceivable that such persons did not develop new ideas—even though they themselves need not have taken these ideas to be new in substance—and that they did not try to incorporate them into tradition by means of modification, supplementation, etc., of the already existing material, a part of which to have acquired a rather fixed literary form quite early. Such a process, especially when carried out on received material, is likely to have entailed certain discrepancies and incoherences (Schmithausen, 1981, 201).

Following their opinions, this study also attempts to show the concept "fetter" was interpreted from context to context, and it was developed from earlier to later texts of the Pāli Canon. Though this argument may not be accepted by some scholars, this study hopes to clarify some doctrinal issues relating to the concept of fetter.

One thread of research in Buddhist studies runs through the Pāli Canonical and its Commentarial literature. The Pāli Canon is known as the *Tipiṭaka*: the *Vinaya*, the *Sutta* and the *Abhidhamma Piṭaka*-s. Erich Frauwallner (cited by Kuan, 2008, 5) says the *Abhidhamma Piṭaka* represents a later development and was composed between 200 BC and 200 AD. This study will consider this aspect into account and identify the divergent interpretations of the concept "fetter" between the *Sutta*-s and the *Abhidhamma*. Warder (2000, 11) states that the *Tipiṭaka* is recognized by Buddhists to be not earlier than a hundred and thirty-seven years after the Buddha's *parinibbāna*, and the doctrine had undergone some development during the period. This study also involves identifying the components in the texts and the contexts in which certain doctrinal development occurs.

The limit of this study is especially within the *Sutta* and the *Abhidhamma Piṭaka*-s of the Pāli Canon. The *Vinaya Piṭaka* is not included because it does not contain much about fetter. It takes into account the Commentaries on the respective *Piṭaka*-s, to explain certain points of the doctrine "fetter".

The current study takes the *Sutta* and the *Abhidhamma Piṭaka*-s into account as the "primary sources". The development of the concept "fetter" will be discussed in three sections. The first section discusses the various usages of fetter, including the intra-psychic, existential and householder binds; the second section shows the description of the four stages with the fetters and without fetters in the first four *Nikāya*-s. The third section explains the concept of fetter with the traditional list of ten fetters and their usages. This section demonstrates that the traditional list of ten fetters became closely associated with the four supra-mundane paths, stream-entry, once-returning, non-returning, the arahatship, during the compilation of the *Abhidhamma* materials. This section also shows the *Abhidhamma* list of ten fetters is actually older than the traditional list (*Sutta* list).

For the first and the second sections, the *Sutta Piṭaka*'s five divisions: the *Dīgha Nikāya*, the *Majjhima Nikāya*, the *Saṃyutta Nikāya*, the *Aṅguttara Nikāya*, and the *Khuddhaka Nikāya* are consulted. The first four and some books of the *Khuddhaka Nikāya*, i.e., the *Itivuttaka* and the *Sutta Nipāta* are of immense value for the first two sections. For the third section the *Abhidhamma Piṭaka* together with the *Niddesa* and the *Paṭisambhidāmagga* are consulted. The four volumes of the *Abhidhamma Piṭaka,* the *Dhammasaṅgaṇi*, the *Vibhaṅga*, the *Puggalapaññatti* and the *Kathāvatthu* are given high value.

To strengthen the argument, this study will also consult the *Abhidhammattha Saṅgaha*, a manual of the *Abhidhamma Piṭaka*.

This study also takes into account previous scholars' works as "secondary sources" and draw from their insights at the appropriate contexts. For the English translation of the Pāli version of the *Sutta Piṭaka*, we have consulted the excellent translations by Venerable Bhikkhu Bodhi, Venerable Ñāṇamoli, Maurice Walshe, etc. We consult the Pāli Text Society (PTS) version of the *Sutta Piṭaka* literature for the first two sections of the discussion. The third section which is based on the *Abhidhamma Piṭaka*, the *Niddesa*, and the *Paṭisambhidāmagga* will be from the Vipassana Research Institute (VRI) version of Pāli literature. The entire Pāli Commentarial literature will also be consulted from the VRI publications.

1.6 Chapter Outline

This study will define the three fundamental contexts in which the different functions and development of the concept "fetter" are positioned. Besides the introduction and conclusion, this work is divided into main three chapters.

Chapter 1: This chapter introduces the textual sources of the concept "fetter" in the Pāli Canon. It discusses the research scope, different lists of fetters and their functions, literature review and methodology. It shows why the study is important in Buddhist studies.

Chapter 2: This chapter discusses the earlier usages of the concept of fetter by consulting the *Saḷāyatana Vagga* of SN and the two *Satipaṭṭāna Sutta*-s of DN and MN respectively. Chronologically, then spans the concept by consulting various *Sutta*-s from the first four *Nikāya*-s, the *Itivuttaka*, and the *Sutta Nipāta* in the fifth *Nikāya*. At this point, the chapter demonstrates that the different individual fetters such as fetter of *taṇhā, nandi*, *bhava, gihi*, *lokāmisa*, *āneñja*, *ākiñcaññāyatana*, and *nevasaññānāsaññāyatana* have their respective functions. This chapter also shows an analysis of a Vedic term *pāśa* (fetter), which has similar functions as the terms *saṃyojana* and *bandhana* in early discourses of the Pāli Canon.

Chapter 3: This chapter includes a classification of the usages of fetter on the basis of discussion in Chapter 1. It discusses how a person attains enlightenment. Different methods are found in the first four *Nikāya*-s for attaining enlightenment. It discusses why the Pāli tradition emphasizes the method with fetters, when other different methods were available. It argues that the method of fetters is prevalent in the Pāli Canon to emphasize the existential binding of the concept of rebirth in the Buddhist teachings.

Chapter 4: This chapter shows the description of the four stages with the method of fetters was developed within the *Abhidhamma*, initially in the *Dhammasaṅgaṇi*. A large portion of this chapter is devoted to showing the development of the concept "fetter". It discusses the *Niddesa* and the *Paṭisambhidāmagga* were composed not before *Abhidhamma* but either subsequently or in later *Abhidhamma* texts. A large portion of the chapter is composed by consulting the *Abhidhammattha Saṅgaha* which systematically describes the four stages with the traditional list of ten fetters. It argues the term *saṃyojana* best suits to describe the four stages than other terms denoting the defilements. It also discusses the function of ignorance *(avijjā)* being a root of not knowing the Four Noble Truths and why it is placed as the last of the two lists of ten fetters.

Chapter 5: Taking into account all of the above chapters, this chapter furthers the arguments in chapter 4 which intends as the final phase of composition of fetter in relation to the four stages of spiritualty, the definition of which became stable in the Theravāda tradition. Through an analysis of various lists of fetters, it suggests that the Theravāda tradition only accepted the traditional list of ten fetters with reference to the Four Noble Persons, and ignored other different lists of fetters in relation to spiritual stages found in the Pāli Canon itself. Also, the tradition discounts the other methods to describe the four stages which are recorded in the first four *Nikāya*-s.

1.7 Conclusion

Based on the discipline and the methodological issues espoused above, in conclusion, it is believed the functions of fetter have great importance in the Pāli Canon. So far as the developmental notion of the concept of fetter is concerned, at least, a few scholars like Hirakawa, Hwang and Pande have remarked that the list of ten fetters is not strictly the earliest scheme, rather it was subsequently enlarged and developed to describe the four stages of liberation in the Pāli Canon. Taking other scholars' previous research into consideration, the current study, together with the Pāli Canonical sources demonstrates the concept of fetter has undergone developmental changes in contrast to traditional contextualization. In addition, it was shown that the scholars who chose to maintain the concept "fetter" in relation to the four stages limited themselves by not presenting a step beyond its traditional repetition.

Chapter 2 – *Saṃyojana* and Its Conceptual Variations in the *Sutta Piṭaka*

2.1 Introduction

This chapter presents various concepts of fetter as evident in the *Sutta Piṭaka*. It is divided into four parts. Part one starts with several questions on the function of *saṃyojana*. By addressing them, it aims to investigate *chanda-rāga* as the initial phase of fetter in the *Sutta*-s which plays a major role as an "intra-psychic bond". It will show the eradication of this fetter defines final liberation. Part two aims to discuss the concept of fetter with both "intra-psychic bond," and "existential bond". This section gives a comprehensive picture of fetters—*nandi, taṇhā* and *bhava*—which is understood as the earlier phases of fetter in the existential setting, and the eradication of one of them defines liberation. Part three explores *gihi-saṃyojana*, delineation of which closely resembles the five precepts, which is different from the previous two. Other fetters such as *rūpa-saṃyojana* and fetters in relation to the *jhāna* states will also be addressed in this part. It will be clearly seen that the concept of fetter has various conceptual definitions from context to context in the *Sutta*-s. Finally, part four concludes this chapter with a comparison between *bandhana* and the Vedic terminology *pāśa* (fetter) found in the *Sutta*-s, both of which are similar to the concept *saṃyojana*.

Part One

2.2 The Doctrinal Meaning of *Saṃyojana*

The term *saṃyojana* occurs in the Pāli Canon in a variety of forms and associations. Before dealing with this topic, one should consider what *saṃyojana* refers to. In the *Aṅguttara Nikāya*, the Buddha mentions that the fetter is mental infatuation things which are basis for desire and lust (*chanda-rāga*) (AN III 264). In the Commentaries, Buddhaghosa (Sv VRI 104) equates the term *saṃyojana* with *bandhana* (*saṃyojanānīti bandhanāni*), meaning that "fetter" and "bondage" are parallel. Bhikkhu KL Dhammajoti (2015) says, according to the *Abhidharma-mahā-vibhāṣā*, fetter has three meanings: 'binding', 'union with *duḥkha*' and 'mixing with poison'. Dhammajoti elaborates:

> The first meaning is said to be derived from the *sūtra*. The second, because the fetters of the sphere of sensuality unite beings with *duḥkha* in that sphere; likewise for those of the fine-material and immaterial spheres. The third, because the *ārya*-s are disgusted with even the best state of birth and with the with-outflow *dhyānas*, as with excellent food mixed with poison (Dhammajoti, 2015, 367).

Bodhi (2000, 21–22) and Griffiths (1986, 28) assert that *saṃyojana* is a technical term used to denote various kinds of attachment to things of the world. Griffiths states:

> [Fetter is] a technical term in Buddhist psychology, denoting various kinds of exhaustively analyzed attachment to the things to the world, things which do not, given the Buddhist analysis, warrant any such attachment (Griffiths, 1986, 28).

Bodhi (1980, 54) identifies the ten kinds of attachment that bind sentient beings to *saṃsāra*. Bodhi's comprehension is to consider that the use of *saṃyojana* is in the sense of a binding force which binds beings to *saṃsāra*, the cycle of existence. This study would be presenting this as a relatively late interpretation of the doctrine. Through a careful examination, one can show that *saṃyojana* appears in the Pāli Canon to convey different meanings at its earlier phase of occurrence, thereby, proving that the concept of fetter has undergone several variations in its soteriological purpose.

2.3 Questions Leading to the Earlier Appearance of Fetter

Passages in many *Sutta*-s show that many monks were not clear about the role of *saṃyojana*. They seem to be confused about the role of fetter and that led them to ask questions amongst themselves. A passage from the *Saṃyojana Sutta* of the *Saḷāyatana Vagga* in SN demonstrates their question, as:

> Friends! "the fetter" and "the things to be fettered" [*saññojaniyā dhammā*], are these things different in meaning and different in phrasing; or are they one in meaning and just different in phrasing (SN IV 282)?[1]

In the foregoing passage, the term *saññojaniyā dhammā* can be translated literally as "the things to be fettered" preserving the passive sense of the future participle, in contrast with Bodhi's (2000, 1186, 1314–15, 1587–88) treatment in his *Saṃyutta* translation as "the things that fetter". Sujato (2012, 79) also prefers the term "things that fetter". Competing translation include Davids and Stede's (1993, 656) translation of the term *saññojaniyā* is "connected with the *saṃyojanas*" or "favorable to the *saṃyojanas*". The present author notes the coherence of Davids and Stede's translation with the simile of the oxen given subsequently in this section, which treats the black and the white oxen as objects to be joined rather than the active agents of joining.

Returning to the above-referred question, we would like to claim that the term *saññojana* (*saṃyojana*) signifies a psychological affiliation with sense bases and sense objects, because this question is important in understanding of the activities of the six faculties. On the role of *saṃyojana*, a passage of the *Koṭṭhita Sutta* of the *Saḷāyatana Vagga* states:

---

[1] *saññojananti vā āvuso saññojaniyā dhammāti vā ime dhammā nānatthā nānāvyañjanā, udāhu ekatthā vyañjanameva nānanti.*

> Is the eye the fetter of forms or are forms [visual objects] the fetter of the eye? Is the ear the fetter of sounds or are sounds the fetter of the ear? Is the nose the fetter of scents or are scents the fetter of the nose? Is the tongue the fetter of tastes or are tastes the fetter of the tongue? Is the body the fetter of contacts or are contacts the fetter of the body? Is the mind the fetter of phenomena or are phenomena the fetter of the mind (SN IV 162–63; SN IV 165–66)?[2]

Here an additional point should be pointed out. While *saṃyojana* is associated with sense bases and sense objects, the above questions show the "intra-psychic bind" rather than "existential bind". That is to say, it would have led to the misconceptions among monks about the function of *saṃyojana* in a confusing way. The following section shows how the *Sutta*-s interpret their question.

The question is: 'the fetter' and 'the things to be fettered', are these things different in meaning and different in phrasing; or are they one in meaning and just different in phrasing? Several *Sutta*-s deal with this question using an agricultural simile of two bulls bound together by a yoke. The *Sutta*-s (SN IV 163, 166, 282–83), for example, say that when a black ox and a white ox are joined with a single harness or yoke, the black ox is not the fetter of the white ox, and the white ox is not the fetter of the black ox, rather the single harness or yoke by which they are joined—that is the fetter there.

It is noteworthy in this example that the *Sutta*-s present two bulls whose bondage is caused by a yoke. In the same manner the fetter in regard to the sense bases and their objects should be understood as not attributable to either its inner or its outer conditions but to the binding force of

---

[2] *cakkhu rūpānaṃ saññojanaṃ rūpā cakkhussa saññojanaṃ, sotaṃ saddānaṃ saññojanaṃ saddā sotassa saññojanaṃ, ghānaṃ gandhānaṃ saññojanaṃ gandhā ghānassa saññojanaṃ, jivhā rasānaṃ saññojanaṃ rasā jivhāya saññojanaṃ, kāyo phoṭṭhabbānaṃ saññojanaṃ phoṭṭhabbā kāyassa saññojanaṃ, mano dhammānaṃ saññojanaṃ, dhammā manassa saññojananti.*

unwholesome thoughts. These thoughts can be defined as desire and lust (*chanda-rāga*) which together possess defilements (*kilesa*).[3] This study aims to show that the concept of *chanda-rāga* is the earlier occurrence of the concept of fetter in the *Sutta*-s. Taking examples from the *Sutta*-s, now it undertakes to explore why *chanda-rāga* is the earlier state of the doctrine "fetter".

2.4 *Chanda-rāga* as Fetter

Answer to the questions can be found in passage from the *Koṭṭhita Sutta* of the *Saḷāyatana Vagga*:

> No my friend [Koṭṭhita], the eye is not the fetter of forms [visible objects], nor are forms the fetter of the eye, rather whatever desire and lust [*chanda-rāga*] that arise in dependence on both—that is the fetter there. The ear is not the fetter of sounds, nor are sounds the fetter of the ear, rather whatever desire and lust that arise dependent on both—that is the fetter there. The nose is not the fetter of odors, nor odors the fetter of the nose, rather whatever desire and lust that arise dependent on both—that is the fetter there.
>
> The tongue is not the fetter of tastes, nor tastes the fetter of the nose, rather whatever desire and lust that arise dependent on both—that is the fetter there. The body is not the fetter of tangible feelings, nor tangible feelings the fetter of the body, rather whatever desire and lust arise dependent on both—that is the fetter there. The mind is not the fetter of mental phenomena, nor are mental phenomena the fetter of the mind, rather whatever desire

[3] According to Dhammajoti (2015), the term *kilesa* is understood in the sense of 'defilement' or 'impurity'. About the usage of the term Dhammajoti elaborates:

> The occurrence of this term is rare in the *sūtra-piṭaka*. Its use was historically preceded by that of *upakleśa*, although subsequently the latter generally came to be understood as 'secondary defilements'—those which proceed from *kleśa*. At this later stage, it is explained that *upakleśa*-s are also the *kleśa*, but they additionally include other defilements which are not called *kleśa*. Examples of these secondary defilements are moral immodesty, avarice and restlessness which are said to be emanations (*niṣyanda*) from greed (*rāga*). (Dhammajoti, 2015, 365)

and lust that arise dependent on both—that is the fetter there (SN IV163–64; SN IV 165, 166, 283).[4]

From the above-passage, it is noted through the example of two bulls that fetter should be understood as a binding notion, "the single yoke by which they are yoked or joined together (*yena ca kho te ekena dāmena vā yottena vā saṃyuttā*), and "desire and lust that arise there in dependence on both" (*yañca tattha tadubhayaṃ paṭicca uppajjati chandarāgo*). Here, while the latter definition of desire and lust connotes conditionality and a degree of causal relation between sense bases and sense objects, and the aforementioned desire and lust, such connotation is absent in the first definition of *saṃyojana*, which emphasizes the linkage of two bulls. The absence of the idea of conditionality would separate *saṃyojana* from causal co-relations that form the basis of *paṭicca-samuppāda.*

Included in the above-discussion (see 2.2), the response to the questions "'the fetter' and 'the things to be fettered'," *chanda-rāga* is applied to mean the fetter in the *Sutta*-s. The response to the subject "the things to be fettered" is

---

[4] *evameva kho āvuso* [*Koṭṭhita*] *na cakkhu rūpānaṃ saññojanaṃ, na rūpā cakkhussa saññojanaṃ. Yañca tattha tadubhayaṃ paṭicca uppajjati chandarāgo taṃ tattha saññojanaṃ. Na sotaṃ saddānaṃ saññojanaṃ, na saddā sotassa saññojanaṃ. Yañca tattha tadubhayaṃ paṭicca uppajjati chandarāgo taṃ tattha saññojanaṃ. Na ghānaṃ gandhānaṃ saññojanaṃ, na gandhā ghānassa saññojanaṃ. Yañca tattha tadubhayaṃ paṭicca uppajjati chandarāgo taṃ tattha saññojanaṃ.*

Na jivhā rasānaṃ saññojanaṃ, na rasā jivhāya saññojanaṃ. Yañca tattha tadubhayaṃ paṭicca uppajjati chandarāgo taṃ tattha saññojanaṃ. Na kāyo phoṭṭhabbānaṃ saññojanaṃ, na phomṭhabbā kāyassa saññojanaṃ. Yañca tattha tadubhayaṃ paṭicca uppajjati chandarāgo taṃ tattha saññojanaṃ. Na mano dhammānaṃ saññojanaṃ, na dhammā manassa saññojanaṃ. Yañca tattha tadubhayaṃ paṭicca uppajjati chandarāgo taṃ tattha saññojanaṃ.

[Both sentences are omitted in the PTS and VRI Pāli versions of the *Saḷāyatana Vagga* in SN (SN VRI 85–86)]: the following sentences are omitted in the PTS (SN IV 163) and VRI (SN 86–87) Pāli versions of the *Koṭṭhita Sutta* in the *Saḷāyatana Vagga: Na kāyo phoṭṭhabbānaṃ saññojanaṃ, na phoṭṭhabbā kāyassa saññojanaṃ, yañca tattha tadubhayaṃ paṭicca uppajjati chandarāgo taṃ tattha saññojanaṃ.*

elucidated with only sense bases, excluding sense objects, for which *chanda-rāga* is the fetter. For example, the *Saññojana Sutta* of the *Saḷāyatana Vagga* states:

> The eye, monks, is a thing that to be fettered; the desire and lust for it is the fetter there. The ear is a thing that to be fettered; the desire and lust for it is the fetter there. The nose is a thing that to be fettered; the desire and lust for it is the fetter there. The tongue is a thing that to be fettered; the desire and lust for it is the fetter there. The body is a thing that to be fettered; the desire and lust for it is the fetter there. The mind is a thing that to be fettered; the desire and lust for it is the fetter there (SN IV 89 & 108; SN V 89).[5]

Here it seems that the *Sutta*-s do not give a clear explanation of *saññojanīyo dhamma*, because the *Saññojana Sutta* demonstrates that the *saññojanīyo dhamma* is only the sense bases, at the exclusion of sense objects. It would pose a contradiction as the simile of the oxen makes clear the dependence on both sense objects and sense bases as the things to be linked, while the definition here excludes the sense objects. This could be a reason that the sense bases are media through which the sense bases interact with the objects and it is through them that the objects enter the range of the sense bases. Besides, *saññojanīyo dhamma* is also applied with the five aggregates in the *Khandha Vagga* of SN, as follows:

> Form is a thing that to be fettered; and the desire and lust for it is the fetter there. Feeling...perception...volitional formations... consciousness is a thing that to be fettered; and the desire and lust for it is the fetter there (SN III 166–67).[6]

[5] *cakkhuṃ bhikkhave saññojanīyo dhammo, yo tattha chandarāgo taṃ tattha saññojanaṃ. Sotaṃ saññojanīyo dhammo, yo tattha chandarāgo taṃ tattha saññojanaṃ. Ghānaṃ saññojanīyo dhammo, yo tattha chandarāgo taṃ tattha saññojanaṃ. Jivhā saññojanīyo dhammo, yo tattha chandarāgo taṃ tattha saññojanaṃ. Kāyo saññojanīyo dhammo, yo tattha chandarāgo taṃ tattha saññojanaṃ. Mano saññojanīyo dhammo, yo tattha chandarāgo taṃ tattha saññojanaṃ.*

[6] *rūpaṃ saññojaniyo dhammo yo tattha chandarāgo, taṃ tattha saññojanaṃ. Vedanaṃ... saññā... saṃkhārā... viññāṇaṃ saññojaniyo dhammo, yo tattha chandarāgo, taṃ tattha saññojanaṃ.*

The above discussion suggests that the notion of *saṃyojana* is used to illustrate "intra-psychic bind" in a proper way. Because the fetter *chanda-rāga* implies the six sense bases and their objects in the *Sutta*-s which leads to the subsequent function in the intra-psychic bond. Another point is that on being questioned by monks who were perplexed regarding the function of *saṃyojana*, the *Koṭṭhita Sutta* and other *Sutta*-s present a detailed commentary to the specific term and its applications. Hence, as a concluding remark of the role of *saṃyojana*, it would be appropriate to comment that it serves to illustrate how *chanda-rāga* functions as fetter for the six sense bases and their objects, and this could be the earlier usages of fetter in the *Sutta*-s.

2.4.1 How Abandoning Chanda-rāga Leads to Final Liberation

This section proposes that one attains final liberation through relinquishing *chanda-rāga*. Before dealing with this topic, it is necessary to examine why *chanda-rāga* plays a major role in relation to the notion of *saṃyojana* and its application. Some contents of the two *Sutta*-s of the *Saḷāyatana Vagga* are cited to answer this question.

Firstly, the *Antevāsika Sutta* (SN IV 136–38) illustrates that when a monk, having seen a form, heard a sound, ...cognized a mental phenomenon, with the eye, ear, ...mind respectively, evil unwholesome things, memories and intentions which are connected with the fetters (*pāpakā akusalā dhammā sarasaṅkappā saññojaniyā*) arise in him and he dwells within them, then the monk resides in suffering. And, having seen a form, heard a sound...etc., connected with the fetter do not arise in him, he does not dwell within them, then the monk resides happily.

Secondly, the *Parihānadhamma Sutta* (SN IV 76–77) refers to similar contents as when evil unwholesome things, memories and intentions which are connected with the fetters, arise in him, he endures them, does not destroy them, then he declines away from wholesome states. In reverse order, when evil unwholesome things do not arise in him and he does not tolerate them, abandon them, then he never falls from wholesome states.

The most significant point from the above illustrations is that the concept of fetter denotes the unwholesome states which arise dependent on the intra-psychic affiliation. Though not explicitly stated in these *Sutta*-s, the reference to unwholesome states connected with the fetters infer *chanda-rāga*. In AN III 264, the Buddha is also said to have mentioned that unwholesome states are mental infatuations which are called *chanda-rāga*. The Buddha says:

> Monks! One wanders about the mental infatuation things in the past that are the basis for desire and lust [*chanda-rāga*]. As one had the mental infatuation things in the past that are the basis for desire and lust, desire arises. The desire when springs up, one is fettered by those mental infatuation things. That mental infatuation is what I call the fetter (AN III 264).[7]

Here, this would be a reason why *chanda-rāga* as unwholesome things initially appeared as fetter. At this point, a important question to be addressed is whether *chanda-rāga* initially denoted fetter in the *Sutta*-s, or it had a different meaning? In order to answer this question, the function of *chanda-rāga* is elaborated in a broader context recorded in the *Sutta*-s. The following section explores how one attains final liberation through relinquishing *chanda-rāga*.

Largely the important implications of *chanda-rāga* intensify in various *Sutta*-s of the *Sutta Piṭaka*. Among them, the *Khandha Vagga* of SN III, the *Mahāpuṇṇa Sutta* (MN III 15–20) and the *Mahākaccāna-bhaddekaratta Sutta* (MN III 192–202) broadly discuss the notion of *chanda-rāga*. In the

[7] *atīte bhikkhave chandarāgaṭṭhānīye dhamme ārabbha cetasā anuvitakketi anuvicāreti. Tassa atīte chandarāgaṭṭhānīye dhamme ārabbha cetasā anuvitakkayato anuvicārayato chando jāyati. Chandajāto tehi dhammehi saññutto hoti. Etamahaṃ bhikkhave saññojanaṃ vadāmi.*

Khandha Vagga (SN III 7) the Buddha is often said to have advised his disciples to abandon *chanda-rāga* from the five aggregates—form, feeling, perception, volitional formations and consciousness. He says, if one is not devoid of *chanda-rāga* in the five aggregates, then with the alteration and change of consciousness there arise the whole mass of suffering. The *Chanda-rāga Sutta* of the *Khandha Vagga* teaches that through abandoning *chanda-rāga* one can break the future arising. The Buddha says:

> Monks! abandon desire and lust [*chanda-rāga*] in form, thus that form will be abandoned, uprooted, made like a palm stump, demolished, so that there is no more subject to future arising. Abandon desire and lust in feeling, thus that feeling will be abandoned, uprooted, made like a palm stump, demolished, so that there is no more subject to future arising. Abandon desire and lust in perception, thus that perception will be abandoned, uprooted, made like a palm stump, demolished, so that there is no more subject to future arising.
>
> Abandon desire and lust in volitional formations, thus that volitional formations will be abandoned, uprooted, made like a 40 palm stump, demolished, so that there is no more subject to future arising. Abandon desire and lust in consciousness, thus that consciousness will be abandoned, uprooted, made like a palm stump, demolished, so that it is no more subject to future arising (SN III 27).[8]

In the above passages, the notion of *chanda-rāga* is interrelated with *taṇhā,* the cause of suffering. Bodhi (2000,

---

[8] *yo bhikkhave rūpasmiṃ chandarāgo taṃ pajahatha, evaṃ taṃ rūpaṃ pahīnaṃ bhavissati ucchinnamūlā tālāvatthukatā anabhāvakatā āyatiṃ anuppādadhammaṃ. Yo vedanāya chandarāgo taṃ pajābhatha [pajahatha], evaṃ sā vedanā pahīnā bhavissati ucchinnamūlā tālāvatthukatā anabhāvakatā āyatiṃ anuppādadhammā. So saññāya chandarāgo taṃ pajahatha evaṃ taṃ saññāya pahīnā bhavissati ucchinnamūlā tālāvatthukatā anabhāvakatā āyatiṃ anuppādadhammā.*

Saṃkhāresu chandarāgo taṃ pajahatha, evaṃ te saṃkhārā pahīnā bhavissanti ucchinnamūlā tālavatthukatā anabhāvakatā āyatiṃ anuppādadhammā. Yo viññāṇasmiṃ chandarāgo taṃ pajābhatha [pajahatha], evaṃ sā viññāṇaṃ pahīnaṃ bhavissati ucchinnamūlā tālāvatthukatā anabhāvakatā āyatiṃ anuppāda-dhammanti.

38) also affirms *chanda-rāga* equally functions as *taṇhā*. Followings are some examples in the *Sutta*-s where *chanda-rāga* functions as *taṇhā*.

The core function of *taṇhā* is the second truth in the Four Noble Truths. The cessation of this is known as *Nibbāna* (SN V 421–23). In the *Sambodhi Sutta* of the *Saḷāyatana Vagga* (SN IV 6–8), the Buddha himself describes his enlightenment experience through the abandonment of *chanda-rāga*. The Buddha says, he could not claim perfect enlightenment in this world among devas, Māras, brahmās, ascetics and brahmins, and humans, until he had directly understood *chanda-rāga*. He further says when he understood *chanda-rāga* as the gratification and danger, then he removed it from the mind. Finally, knowledge and vision arose in him and he experienced he is no more liable to future becoming in the world.

The *Kilesa Saṃyutta* of the *Khandha Vagga* (SN III 232) elucidates *chanda-rāga* as a defilement of the mind (*cittasse'so upakkileso*) with regard to the six sense bases, six sense objects, six sense base-consciousnesses (*viññāṇa*), contact at six sense bases (*samphassa*), feeling born of contact at six sense bases (*samphassajāya vedanā*), perception of six sense objects (*saññā*), intentions involving six sense objects (*sañcetanā*), craving for six sense objects (*taṇhā*), earth, water, heat, air, space, and consciousness element (*dhātu*), and the five aggregates (*khandha*). The *Saṃyutta* further says when the defilement of mind, etc. is abandoned, the mind is stimulated by abandonment in regard to those things that are to be realized by direct knowledge (*abhiññā sacchikaraṇīyesu dhammesūti*). The *Saṭṭhipeyyāla* section of the *Saḷāyatana Vagga* (SN IV 148–57) discusses how *chanda-rāga* can be abandoned internally and externally whatever is impermanent (*anicca*), suffering (*dukkha*) and non-self (*anatta*) in regard to the sense spheres and the five aggregates.

However, it is noteworthy that the terms *chanda* and *rāga* individually and in combination with other terms have several meanings as they are used in the Pāli Canon. For example, *kāma-chanda*—one of the five hindrances (*nīvaraṇa*); *kāma-rāga*, *rūpa-rāga,* and *arūpa-rāga* are within the traditional list of ten fetters. An alternative enumeration of this gives *bhava-rāga-saṃyojana* in the *Abhidhamma* list of ten fetters. These will be discussed in greater length in Chapter 4.

The term *chanda* alone has both negative and positive connotations in the *Sutta*-s themselves. On one hand, the *Bhadraka Sutta* of the *Saḷayātana Vagga* (SN IV 328–29) says *chanda* is the root of suffering, which has a similar function of *taṇhā*. The *Brāhmaṇa Sutta* of the *Mahā Vagga* (SN V 271) recounts that once Venerable Ānanda was asked by Brahmin Uṇṇābha on how *chanda* is to be abandoned. In his reply, Ānanda says that it is effected through the development of spiritual power that possesses concentration due to desire/will (*chanda*), energy (*viriya*), thought (*citta*), and investigation (*vīmaṃsā*). When the Brahmin asked how it was possible that *chanda* could be abandoned by *chanda*. Venerable Ānanda gives an example of going to a park which suggests the necessity of desire, energy, thought, and investigation for the realization of the goal. The *Kīṭāgiri Sutta* (MN I 480) and the *Canki Sutta* (MN II 173) teach that *chanda* possesses a positive aspect which leads to final liberation.

Following up on the explanation of *chanda* in the above *Sutta*-s, Nyanatiloka (1952, 84–85) distinguishes *chanda* into three categories of its usages. They are: (1) as neutral sense of intention, generally mental factors (*cetasika*) clarified in the *Abhidhamma*, (2) as an unwholesome quality that commonly takes place with other terms for denoting desire and greed, and (3) as a positive sense, i.e., righteous will (*dhamma-chanda*).

A similar point is made by Rhys Davis:

> Now we cannot afford to impoverish our ethical (and aesthetical) concepts by squandering this term (*chanda*) out right on (gross) *taṇhā*, and thereby, so to speak, make the devil a present of all desire—even of that *dhamma-chanda* that drove Prometheus to fight Zeus, that drove the Buddha from home to Bo-tree... (Davis, 1910, 244).

While *chanda* would have both positive and negative aspects, in this study we focus on one aspect of *chanda* that always takes place with the term *rāga*.

At this point, it could be argued that *chanda-rāga* was used in the *Sutta*-s as defilement of mind. Our main focus of analysis is how *chanda-rāga* turns out to mean "fetter" in the *Sutta*-s. Following this object, it was observed that *chanda-rāga* connects with fetter in the *Saṃyojana Sutta* of the *Khandha Vagga* (SN III 166), the *Saṃyojana Sutta*, the *Koṭṭhita Sutta*, the *Kāmabhū Sutta*, and the *Saṃyojana Sutta* of the *Citta-saṃyutta* of the *Saḷāyatana Vagga* (SN IV 89, 163–67, 283) respectively. It was also observed that the *Sutta*-s in the *Saṭṭhipeyyāla* section of the *Saḷāyatana Vagga* are repeated with supplementary explanation in the *Mahāpunna Sutta,* and the *Mahākaccāna-bhaddekaratta Sutta* of MN. This suggests doctrinal proximity of the *Saḷāyatana Vagga* and some *Sutta*-s of the *Majjhima Nikāya* setting. It is worth to note the compilation of collection of *Sutta*-s in the *Khandha Vagga* and the *Saḷāyatana Vagga* which would require further research beyond the scope of the present study.

The materials on the compilation of the Pāli Canon and its *Sutta*-s were extensively introduced by several scholars such as Pande (1999), Sujato and Brahmali (2014). In our study it is observed that, though organized differently than DN and MN, the notion of fetter in SN is closely connected with many *Sutta*-s. For example, the *Saḷāyatana-saṃyutta* bears resemblance to the *Satipaṭṭhāna Sutta*-s of DN and MN respectively. It sometimes illuminates that SN has preserved smaller *Sutta*-s but given detailed elaboration in DN and MN.

An extensive research on SN has been conducted by Sujato (2012, 37, 41–42) arriving at the conclusion that SN is the first among the four *Nikāya*-s. He says "the *Dhammacakkappavattana Sutta* was originally the first discourse in the *Saṃyutta*," but currently it is the "number eleven in the Theravāda *Sacca-saṃyutta*; but in the Chinese it is the first in this chapter." He further says after the *Dhammacakkappavattana Sutta*, the *Anattalakkhaṇa Sutta* and the *Ādittapariyāya Sutta* are the earliest discourses among others. With a supplementary note Sujato and Brahmali (2014, 97) further cite Yin Shun, who also suggests SN is the earliest book, and consistently states the order of SĀ in which the *Khandha Vagga* is placed first followed by the *Saḷāyatana*, and at last the *Sagāthā Vagga,* a sequence more consistent with the Four Noble Truths. Following this line, Sujato and Brahmali also see the SĀ's *Vagga* arrangement as more consistent than SN, which is also observed by Bodhi (2000, 27).

Regarding the content of SN, scholars such as Hinüber (1996, 38) mention the first part of SN, the *Sagāthā Vagga*, as completely different from the other *Vagga*-s, and part of this *Vagga* is very old which is close to Vedic texts. Similarly, Nakamura (1999, 38) observes the *Sagāthā Vagga* is undoubtedly very early. Pande (1999, 181) says the *Sagāthā Vagga* is significantly different from other *Vagga*-s in SN. He says though a number of *Sutta*-s are later strata in the *Vagga*-s, as a whole "it has a greater proportion of early *Suttas* than the other *Vaggas*." About the *Vagga*, he refers to Mrs. Rhys Davids' (*The Book of the Kindred Sayings* Vol.I) remarks, who also authoritatively says the *Sagāthā Vagga* contains the oldest doctrine. Davids says, "the matter of them is of the stamp of the oldest doctrine known to us, and from them a fairly complete synopsis of the ancient Dhamma might be compiled" (Davids, Preface, Vol.I, vii). Though many scholars assert the *Sagāthā Vagga* is the oldest and it contains the oldest doctrines of all other *Vagga*-s, however, in examining the doctrine "fetter" one could argue that the other *Vagga*-s such as the *Khandha Vagga* and the *Saḷāyatana Vagga* consist of various doctrines which are earlier than the doctrines in the *Sagāthā Vagga*. In that aspect, the entire *Sagāthā Vagga*'s materials would not have been the oldest, rather these doctrines are heterogeneous and compiled under the similar set.

2.5 Understanding the Concept of Fetter in the *Satipaṭṭhāna* Practice

The previous section on *chanda-rāga* showed the earlier usages of fetter. This section now examines the fetter with reference to the sense bases and sense objects in the *satipaṭṭhāna* practice.

To begin this section, first it is necessary to give a brief survey of *satipaṭṭhāna* practice in both (*Mahā*)-*Satipaṭṭhāna Sutta*-s (DN II 290–358 & MN I 55–63). Though the *Sutta* in DN is significantly longer than the *Sutta* in MN, both contain singular approach in regard to *satipaṭṭhāna* practice. Both *Satipaṭṭhāna Sutta*-s have close connection to the *Saḷāyatana Vagga* of SN in which the fetter is being examined. Now the concept "fetter" is scrutinized with the connection to *satipaṭṭhāna* practice. This practice refers to the arising and abandoning of fetter through the awareness of sense-spheres which is direct contemplation to the six "internal" and "external" sense-spheres (*ajjhattika-bāhira āyatana*). The instruction of this practice is fourfold, as follows:

> Monks! Here a monk understands the eye, and he understands forms [visual objects], and he understands the fetter that arises dependent on both; and he also understands how the fetter that has not yet arisen comes to arise, and he understands how arisen fetter can be abandoned, and he understands how future non-arising fetter that has been abandoned.
>
> He understands the ear, and he understands sounds, and he understands the fetter that arises dependent on both; and.... He understands the nose, and he understands odors, and he understands the fetter that arises dependent on both; and.... He understands the tongue, and he understands tastes, and he understands the fetter that arises dependent on both; and.... He understands the body, and he understands tangibles, and he

> understands the fetter that arises dependent on both; and.... He understands the mind, and he understands mental phenomena, and he understands the fetter that has not yet arisen comes to arise, and he understands how arisen fetter can be abandoned, and he understands how future non-arising fetter that has been abandoned (DN II 302–04; MN I 61).[9]

The above passage from both *Satipaṭṭhāna Sutta*-s of DN and MN indicates how fetter is understood in terms of its arising and abandoning dependent on the sense bases and sense objects. Anālayo's (2011) comparative study on the *Majjhima Nikāya* and the *Madhyama Āgama* examines in depth the fetter in the *satipaṭṭhāna* practice. His study shows the Pāli version of *satipaṭṭhāna* practice leads a practitioner to reflect on the fetter that arises dependent on sense bases and sense objects. But the Chinese version reveals both sense bases and sense objects are merely conditions for the arising of fetter. Anālayo elaborates:

> According to the *Madhyama-Āgama* presentation, the task in this case is thus not to be mindful of the senses or their objects as such, but of the fetter that may arise at any sense-door. This suggests awareness of the fettering force of perceptual experience and its relation to the arising of unwholesome mental reactions and associations to be the central aspect of contemplation of the sense-spheres (Anālayo, 2011, 95).

---

[9] *idha bhikkhave bhikkhu cakkhuñca pajānāti, rūpe ca pajānāti, yañca tadubhayaṃ paṭicca uppajjati saññojanaṃ tañca pajānāti. Yathā ca anuppannassa saññojanassa uppādo hoti tañca pajānāti. Yathā ca uppannassa saññojanassa pahānaṃ hoti tañca pajānāti. Yathā ca pahīnassa saññojanassa āyatiṃ anuppādo hoti tañca pajānāti.*

Sotañca pajānāti, sadde ca pajānāti, yañca tadubhayaṃ paṭicca uppajjati saññojanaṃ tañca pajānāti....Ghānañca pajānāti, gandhe ca pajānāti, yañca tadubhayaṃ paṭicca uppajjati saññojanaṃ tañca pajānāti....Jivhañca pajānāti, rase ca pajānāti, yañca tadubhayaṃ paṭicca uppajjati saññojanaṃ tañca pajānāti....Kāyañca pajānāti, phoṭṭhabbo ca pajānāti, yañca tadubhayaṃ paṭicca uppajjati saññojanaṃ tañca pajānāti....Manañca pajānāti, dhamme ca pajānāti, yañca tadubhayaṃ paṭicca uppajjati saññojanaṃ tañca pajānāti. Yathā ca anuppannassa saññojanassa uppādo hoti tañca pajānāti. Yathā ca uppannassa saññojanassa pahānaṃ hoti tañca pajānāti. Yathā ca pahīnassa saññojanassa āyatiṃ anuppādo hoti tañca pajānāti.

Anālayo then says that understanding of fetter in the *satipaṭṭhāna* practice of the *Madhyama Āgama* version is relatively similar to the two (*Mahā*)-*Satipaṭṭhāna Sutta*-s of DN and MN. He compares:

> DN 22 at DN II 302, 20 and MN 10 at MN I 61, 16 speak of the monk knowing: 1) the fetter, 2) how the unarisen fetter arises, 3) how the arisen fetter is abandoned, 4) how the abandoned fetter will not arise again in the future. MA 98 at T I 584a15 presents the same exercise in terms of the meditator knowing: 1) if a fetter is present, 2) if no fetter is present, 3) if an unarisen fetter arises, 4) if an arisen fetter ceases and does not arise again (Anālayo, 2011, 350, see footnote).

Although the fourfold *Satipaṭṭhāna* practice elaborated in DN and MN was not implemented in the *Saḷāyatana-saṃyutta,* there is still a close connection between them. Because the *Saṃyutta* discusses several fetters such as *chanda-rāga* that arise dependent on sense bases and their objects. The *Satipaṭṭhāna Vagga* of the *Navaka Nipāta* (AN IV 457) also contains a short version of the fourfold training. A crucial point here is that the establishment of *satipaṭṭhāna* is the only context in the formulation of the path which is a gradual training for final liberation. About the fourfold practice of *satipaṭṭhāna* and the *Saḷāyatana-saṃyutta,* Sujato also gives a similar observation. Sajato says:

> Even though the four *satipaṭṭhānas* as such are not mentioned in the *Saḷāyatana-saṁyutta*, yet there is a closer connection between mindfulness and the six sense media than between mindfulness and the five aggregates (Sajato, 2012, 248).

Although no particular reference of fetter is mentioned in the *satipaṭṭhāna* practice in both (*Mahā*)-*Satipaṭṭhāna Sutta*-s, one could examine scholars' observations as to the number and the exact reference of the fetters in order to understand what kinds of fetters are to be abandoned and what they are.

Ñāṇamoli and Bodhi (1995, 42–43 & 1194, see footnote 160), in their translated *Satipaṭṭhāna Sutta* within the *Majjhima Nikāya*, enumerate the traditional list of ten fetters. Walshe (1995, 594, see footnote 687) in his translated *Mahāsatipaṭṭhāna Sutta* within the *Dīgha Nikāya*, refers not only to the traditional list but also to the *Abhidhamma* list of ten fetters. Tan (2009), however, confidently says that the fetter referred to the *satipaṭṭhāna* practice is merely the *Abhidhamma* list and this is the oldest and a more systematized set than the traditional list.[10] Regarding fetters in the *satipaṭṭhāna* practice Anālayo (2006, 219–22), although not specifically referring to the *satipaṭṭhāna*, implies the traditional set of ten fetters. But Sujato (2012, 260–61) remains silent on this point in his study. Examining their assumptions, we observe that Tan heavily relies on the Commentarial explanation, because the Commentaries to both *Satipaṭṭhāna Sutta*-s equate the fetter in the *satipaṭṭhāna* practice with the *Abhidhamma* list. For example:

> In dependence on both [sense bases and sense objects] the fetters arise.... There are ten kinds of fetter which arise as the fetters of sensual desire, repulsion, conceit, view, doubt, clinging to rules and vows, desire for becoming, envy, selfishness, and ignorance (Sv VRI 181; Ps VRI 134).[11]

It is noteworthy that the Commentaries categorize the Four Noble Persons in accordance with these ten fetters, as follows:

> The five kinds of fetter of view, doubt, clinging to rules and vows, envy, selfishness are eradicated through the path of stream-entry; the two [more] fetters of sensual desire, repulsion are greatly

[10] Piya Tan (2009), trans. *Saññojana Sutta* (S41.1/4:281–83), Online source: dharmafarer.org

[11] *yañca tadubhyaṃ paṭicca uppajjati saṃyojananti.... Kāmarāga-saṃyojanaṃ, paṭigha, māna, diṭṭhi, vicikicchā, sīlabbataparāmāsa, bhavarāga, issā, macchariya, avijjāsaṃyojananti dasavidhaṃ saṃyojanaṃ uppajjati.*

weakened through the path of once-returning; [the two more fetters of sensual desire, repulsion are] completely destroyed through the path of non-returning; the fetters of conceit, desire for becoming, and ignorance are eradicated through the path of arahatship (Sv VRI 181).[12]

According to the foregoing passage, it is evident that the Four Noble Persons can be classified without applying the traditional list of ten fetters, and this point will be discussed at length in Chapter 4.

Regarding fetters in the *satipaṭṭhāna* practice, Ñāṇamoli and Bodhi, and Anālayo reserve their area of work within *Sutta*-s. On the other hand, Walshe examines within the *Sutta, Abhidhamma*, and Commentarial explanations. Tan, however, without explicitly citing the Commentarial literature in his own interpretation, sides with the Commentaries. He says the *Abhidhamma* list of ten fetters is the oldest set than the traditional list of ten fetters. More about this topic will be discussed in Chapter 4.

One may, however, ask the question whether it is only through the *satipaṭṭhāna* practice that the traditional and *Abhidhamma* lists of ten fetters could be removed. This study believes that in the *satipaṭṭhāna* practice not only a few lists of fetter, but also other separate fetters such as *chanda-rāga* can be removed. Hence, we contend that the Commentarial explanation and other scholars' opinions in regard to fourfold mindfulness practice with the traditional and *Abhidhamma* lists of fetter are not conclusive, rather they are just a compilation.

One may ask why Commentators did not adopt the traditional list of ten fetters to explain the *Satipaṭṭhāna*

---

[12] *diṭṭhi-vicikicchā-sīlabbataparāmāsa-issā-macchariya-bhedassa tāva pañcavidhassa saṃyojanassa sotāpattimaggena āyatiṃ anuppādo hoti. Kāmarāga-paṭigha-saṃyojanadvayassa oḷārikassa sakadāgāmimaggena, aṇusahagatassa anāgāmimaggena, māna-bhavarāga-āvijjā-saṃyojanattayassa arahattamaggena āyatiṃ anuppādo hoti.*

Sutta-s. This study believes that the traditional list of ten fetters is mostly introduced to explain the existential binding; on the other hand, the *Abhidhamma* list of ten fetters is perceived through contemplation of the current moment. That could be a reason why the commentators accept the *Abhidhamma* list as the whole picture of fetters in the practice of mindfulness. This could also be another reason why there is a different set of fetters in the *Abhidhamma* texts; it is to show the psychological affiliation. This subject will be explained in detail in Chapter 4.

Part Two

2.6 The Existential Conception of Fetter

Until this point, we have explained the concept of fetter as "intra-psychic bind". In order to show the other notions of fetter, this section now turns to the numerous *Sutta*-s in the *Sutta Piṭaka* which show both "intra-psychic" and "existential" bindings of fetter. This section will discuss how the concept "fetter" was gradually employed to account for the suffering of all forms of life as epitomized by the cycle of existence—*saṃsāra*. In the previous section, we have discussed the fetter *chanda-rāga* and its functions in the *Sutta*-s. In this order, now we promptly discuss *nandi-saṃyojana* (fetter of delight), *taṇhā- saṃyojana* (fetter of craving), and *bhava-saṃyojana* (fetter of becoming). All of them play various dynamic roles from context to context in the *Sutta Piṭaka*. Having taken the sequential order, we first discuss *nandi-saṃyojana* and its functions in the *Sutta*-s.

2.6.1 Nandi-saṃyojana and Its Functions

The term *nandi* (delight) has various meanings in the *Sutta*-s, but in combination with *saṃyojana*, i.e., *nandi-saṃyojana*, it appears only in a few *Sutta*-s.[13] Davids and Stede (1999, 388) translate *nandi* (f. *nandī*) usually as joy, enjoyment, pleasure, delight, etc. But, when associated with *saṃyojana* it is always used to denote coarser defilement. *Nandi-saṃyojana* is an important doctrine in the concept of fetter as discussed by Wynne (2007). He quotes several verses from the *Sutta Nipāta* to discuss *nandi-saṃyojana* and its functions. He says that the function of *nandi-saṃyojana* and that of *taṇhā* is the same. According to Wynne:

> [That] the world is fettered by delight [*nandi*] is consistent with the principle that craving is the cause of suffering, i.e. the second Noble Truth. This suggests that the way to liberation is facilitated by comprehending the fact that delight or craving is the cause of one's suffering (Wynne, 2007, 89).

Sujato (2012, 84), though not equating *nandi-saṃyojana* directly with *taṇhā*, concurs with Wynne's assertion. He says, *taṇhā-saṃyojana* fits under the Second Noble Truth. Here it should be pointed out that Wynne takes the concept on *nandi* as *taṇhā* from the *Cūllaniddesa*, the Commentary to the *Pārāyana Vagga* and the *Khaggavisāna Sutta* of Sn. In this Commentary the term *nandi* is identical with *taṇhā*. For example, "delight is called craving" (*nandi vuccati taṇhā*) (Nidd II VRI 42, 79 & 84). At this point, we wish to add the definition is a later development because this phrase has a deeper meaning in the *Sutta*-s. Several *Sutta*-s suggest that the role of *nandi* has various connotations. Before discussing this in detail, it is important to explore the fundamental significance of *nandi-saṃyojana* in the following section.

---

[13] *Nandi-saṃyojana* is found in the *Migajāla Sutta* of the *Saḷāyatana Vagga*, the *Saṃyojana Sutta* of the *Sagāthā Vagga* in SN, and three verses of the *Pārāyana Vagga* of Sn and further annotated in the *Cūllaniddesa* of the *Khuddaka Nikāya*. Out of three stanzas of the *Pārāyana Vagga*, two are repeated in the *Sagāthā Vagga* of SN I 39.

Based on various *Sutta*-s, *nandi-saṃyojana* is presented in two categories: (a) *nandi* as fetter refers to intra-psychic bind, and (b) existential bind. Firstly, in the *Migajāla Sutta* of the *Saḷāyatana Vagga* in SN it is used to explain the intra-psychic bind. This *Sutta* points out that *nandi* is effectively connected to the chain of conditionality giving rise to bondage dependent on sense bases and sense objects. A passage of the *Migajāla Sutta* states:

> There are forms cognizable by the eye [which are] agreeable, enjoyable, attracting, sensually nurturing, tantalizing—and a monk delights in them, cheers them, and remains holding to them. As he delights in them, cheers them, and remains holding to them, delight arises. There being delight, there is passion. Being passion, there is bondage. Bound by the fetter of delight, a monk dwells with a companion (SN IV 36).[14]

In similar ways, when there are sounds, odors, tastes, tactile objects, and mental phenomena cognizable by the ear, nose, tongue, body and mind respectively, and one delights, welcomes, and remains holding to the desirable, pleasing, etc., delight (*nandi*) arises. As there is delight, there is passion. Being passion, there is bondage, and bound by the fetter of delight, he dwells in companion with craving. On the contrary, a monk who does not seek delight in them is a lone dweller. The *Sutta* states dwelling with a companion means dwelling with "craving". On the other hand, lone dweller means dwelling "without craving".

Secondly, two verses from the *Pārāyana Vagga* of Sn explain *nandi-saṃyojana*. Both verses occurred in a dialogue between the Buddha and Udaya. In the section of the *Pārāyana Vagga*, out of seven verses, two verses contain the metaphor of *nandi-saṃyojana*. For example:

---

[14] *santi kho...cakkhuviññeyyā rūpā iṭṭhā kantā manāpā piyarūpā kāmūpāsaṃhitā rajanīyā, tañce bhikkhu abhinandati abhivadati ajjhosāya tiṭṭhati, tassa taṃ abhinandato abhivadato ajjhosāya tiṭṭhato uppajjati nandi, nandiyā sati sārāgo hoti sārāge sati saññogo hoti, nandisaññojanasaññutto kho bhikkhu sadutiyavihārītī.*

> What does the world have as [its] fetter, what does its mean of driving force; through the abandoning of what, that which is called *Nibbāna*?
>
> The world has delight as its fetter, thought is its means of driving force; through the abandoning of craving, that which is called *Nibbāna* (SN 214–15).[15]

It seems that grammatically the above-stanzas have conceptual variations. Although the term *saṃyojana* is in neuter gender in Pāli, here it seems it is qualifying *loko* (n.) which is synonym of *loka*. Scholars, however, have translated the stanzas differently. For example, N.A. Jayawickrama translates as:

> What, indeed, does the world have as fetter; what, indeed, is its driving force; by the rejection of what is it designated as serenity?
>
> The world has delight as its fetter; reflection its driving force; by the rejection of craving it is designated as serenity (Jayawickrama, 2001, 420–10).

Bodhi translates as:

> By what is the world tightly fettered, what is its means of travelling around? With is that one must forsake, in order to say, 'Nibbāna'.
>
> The world is tightly fettered by delight; Thought is its means of travelling about. Craving is what one must forsake, in order to say, 'Nibbāna' (Bodhi, 2000, 131).

Comparing both translations, it seems that Jayawickrama's translation is grammatically correct. Bodhi takes the term *nandī* as instrumental case. Similarly, Wynne (2007, 88)

---

[15] Udaya–*Kiṃsu saṃyojano loko, kiṃsu tassa vicāraṇaṃ/ Kissassa vippahānena, Nibbānaṃ iti vuccati.* Bhagavā- *Nandīsaṃyojano loko, vitakkassa vicāraṇaṃ/ Taṇhāya vippahānena, nibbānaṃ iti vuccati.* Both verses are repeated in the *Devatā-saṃyutta* of the *Sagāthā Vagga* (SN I 39). In the order of the *Sutta*-s in SN, next two verses are also quite similar as Devatā-*Kiṃsu sambandhano loko kiṃsu tassa vicāraṇaṃ/ Kissassa vippahāṇena sabbaṃ chindati bandhananti.* Bhagavā-*Nandi sambandhano loko vitakkassa vicāraṇaṃ / Taṇhāya vippahāṇena sabbaṃ chindati bandhananti.*

translates as "fettered by delight (*nandī*)" by using instrumental case. If it is instrumental, it should be *nandiyā*, but here the term *nandī* is in feminine noun. It seems that Jayawickrama takes the term *nandī-saṃyojana* [*nandi-saṃyojana*] as compound, means "delight as fetter".

Scholars also translate the phrase *vitakkassa vicāraṇaṃ* differently. For example, K.R. Norman (2001, 141) translates it as "speculation is its investigation". Wynne (2007, 88) translates it as "investigation is its doubt". Bhikkhu Thanissaro (accesstoinsight.org) translates it as "with directed thought it's examined". Bodhi (2000, 131) translates it as "thought is its means of travelling about". This study prefers the Bodhi and Jayawickrama's translations to establish the current connotation of fetter with *nandi-saṃyojana*. Scrutinizing their translations, it is noted that Wynne has relied on the Norman's translation and tries to give its meaning following *nandi-saṃyojana* as recorded in the Verse 1115 of the *Posālamāṇava Pucchā* in Sn. The verse is: *ākiñcaññā sambhavaṃ ñatvā nandi saṃyojanaṃ iti/ etaṃ ñāṇaṃ tathaṃ tassa brāhmaṇassa vusīmatoti*. The *Cūllaniddesa* (Nidd II VRI 91) equates the fetter of delight with the desire for formless existence (*nandi-saṃyojanaṃ vuccati arūparāgo*). It is worth noting that "fetter of delight" as *arūpa-rāga* is another classification of *nandi-saṃyojana*. It is a later interpretation of *nandi-saṃyojana* which is applied to define the base of nothingness (*ākiñcaññāyatana*), a meditative achievement. On the base of nothingness, referring to the *Sunakkhatta Sutta* (MN II 252–62), a discussion is given in this chapter under the section "The Concept of Fetter in the Context of the *Jhāna* States". The *Sutta* says various meditative states such as the base of nothingness (*ākiñcaññāyatana*), and neither-perception-nor-non-perception (*nevasaññānāsaññāyatana*), etc., are fetters.

Returning to the above-mentioned verses, it is important to state that here the term *nandi* represents a grosser conceptual aspect since it appears with *saṃyojana*. In this context, *nandi-saṃyojana* can be defined by its two functions: intra-psychic and existential. For intra-psychic, it argues that the "the world has delight as its fetter" is not with outside world but with the five aggregates and six sense bases in which someone seeks delight (*nandi*), and travelling around the physical world. When there is delight, there is passion, being passion, there is bondage, bound by the fetter of delight. Reversely, with the cessation of bondage comes the cession of suffering which is called *Nibbāna*. Here "bondage" is similar to the notion of "craving".

For the existential bind, on the other hand, it argues that the term *nandi* has a similar flavor with *taṇhā* which binds beings into *saṃsāra*. Both terms denote the root of suffering, and conditions on which there is birth, ageing and death (MN I 6).[16] Through investigation into the *Sutta*-s, however, one can trace that the term *nandi* has various functions in addition to its association with *saṃyojana* in the *Nikāya*-s. Therefore, we suggest that the terms *nandi* and *taṇhā* have slight differences in terms of their functions. Now it is necessary to look at how the *Sutta*-s interpret it.

The *Dhammacakkappavattana Sutta,* which according to Sujato is the first among others in the Buddha's teachings,[17] says the term *nandi* is always mentioned with *rāga* as *nandi-rāga* (desire and lust).[18] *Nandi-rāga* accompanied by *taṇhā*

---

[16] *nandi dukkhassa mūlanti iti viditvā bhavā jāti bhūtassa jarāmaraṇanti.*

[17] In the study of *A History of Mindfulness*, Sujato (2012, 37) declares the *Dhammacakkappavattana Sutta* is the first discourse in Buddhist teachings. Though he claims it as the first, Schmithausen (1981) in his article "Liberating Insight and Enlightenment," says, the *Sutta* underwent changes over the years. Schmithausen says:

> The Pāli version of this text, as is well known, has been transmitted in the *Mahāvagga* portion of the *Vinaya* (I 10 ff.) as well as in the *Saṃyuttanikāya* (56.11); the latter seems to have taken over the text from the *Vinaya*, for it includes, apart from the *Sūtra* proper, also a portion of the narrative framework in which it is embedded in the *Vinaya*. In this form, the *Sūtra* probably belongs to a period at least more than one hundred years later than the Buddha's Nirvāṇa. (Schmithausen 1981, 202)

[18] Citing the *Dhammacakkapattana Sutta* Anālayo (2009, 29) in his study *From Craving to Liberation* says, *rāga* features prominently in the Second Noble Truth, along the same line as Wynne who says *nandi* suits under the same principle of *taṇhā*.

(*taṇhā ponobhavikā nandirāgasahagatā*) leads to renewed existence—known as the Second Noble Truth. The term *taṇhā* is divided into three divisions: craving for sensuality (*kāma-taṇhā*), craving for becoming (*bhava-taṇhā*) and craving for extermination or non-becoming (*vibhava-taṇhā*) (DN II 308; MN III 250; SN III 26, 32, 158, 159; SN V 425, 426; SN V 421).[19] Here, the activity of *taṇhā* is always accompanied by *nandi-rāga*. It means wherever *taṇhā* is, there is *nandi-rāga*. It puts forward the example in the *Dutiya Migajāla Sutta* to show that *nandi* does not always occur with the term *rāga*. It also occurs with other terms, e.g., *saṃyojana,* but it gives a similar connotation as *taṇhā*. For example, the *Dutiya Migajāla Sutta* of the *Saḷāyatana Vagga* in SN correlates the arising of *nandi* with the arising of suffering. For example:

> There are forms cognizable by the eye [which are] agreeable, enjoyable, attracting, sensually nurturing, tantalizing—and a monk delights in them, cheers them, and remains holding to them. As he delights in them, cheers them, and remains holding to them, delight arises. With the arising of delight [*nandi*], there is the arising of suffering (SN IV 36; SN IV 60; MN III 267–68).[20]

In a similar way, when there are sounds, odors, tastes, tactile objects, and mental phenomena cognizable by the ear, nose, tongue, body and mind respectively, one delights in, cheers, and remains holding to desirable, pleasing, attracting, etc., delight arises. With the arising of delight, there is the arising of suffering. Reversely, with the cessation of delight, comes the cessation of suffering (SN IV 36). Here it posits that the above passages represent a formula of the Four Noble Truths

---

[19] *yāyaṃ taṇhā ponobhavikā nandirāgasahagatā tatra tatrābhinandinī, seyyathīdaṃ: kāmataṇhā, bhavataṇhā, vibhavataṇhā.*

[20] *santi kho...cakkhuviññeyyā rūpā iṭṭhā kantā manāpā piyarūpā kāmūpāsaṃhitā rajanīyā, tañce bhikkhu abhinandati abhivadati ajjhosāya tiṭṭāhati, tassa taṃ abhinandato abhivadato ajjhosāya tiṭṭhato uppajjati nandi, nandisamudayā dukkhasamudayo.*

based on the sense bases and their objects. For example, the first two truths—suffering and its origin correlated with the six sense bases, and the remaining two truths—cessation and the path tie in with the abandoning of delight in the six sense bases and their objects.

The above analysis indicates a concise statement of the method of dependent co-arising (*paṭicca-samuppāda*) which is usually explained in twelve factors in the *Mahā-taṇhāsaṅkhaya Sutta* (MN I 256–70). In this setting, *nandi* is applied to the understanding of what arises and ceases in relation to the five aggregates. The *Samādhi Bhāvanā Sutta* and the *Paṭisallāna Sutta* of the *Khandha Vagga* (SN III 13–15) explains the dependent co-arising and cessation with reference to the five aggregates—form, feeling, perception, formations and consciousness. Both *Sutta*-s say that when one seeks delight (*nandi*) in the five aggregates, cheers, and remains holding to them, there delight arises. Delight in the five aggregates is clinging, and with their clinging as condition becoming comes to be; with becoming as condition comes birth; with birth as condition, then aging and death, sorrow, lamentation, pain, distress, and despair come to be, such is the origin of this whole mass of suffering. Following the reverse order when one does not seek delight (*nandi*) in the five aggregates, does not cheer it, and does not remains holding to them, as a consequence of this, delight in the five aggregates ceases, and with the cessation of delight comes cessation of clinging; with the cessation of clinging, cessation of existence; with the cessation of becoming, such is the becoming of this whole mass of suffering.

Similarly, regarding the terms *nandi* and *rāga*, several *Sutta*-s of the *Saḷāyatana Vagga* (SN IV 142–43), for example the *Ajjhattanandikkyaya-anicca Sutta*, the *Bahiddhānandikkhaya-anicca Sutta* state when one experiences repulsion by seeing the six sense bases and their objects as impermanent internally and externally, then with the destruction of delight comes destruction of lust (*rāga*), the mind is said to be well enlightened. The *Atthirāga Sutta* of the *Nidāna Vagga* (SN II 99–104), similarly emphasizes that when there are lust (*rāga*), delight (*nandi*), and craving (*taṇhā*) for the four kinds of nutriment,[21] consciousness becomes established and comes to growth. Where consciousness is established and grown, name-and-form appears. Where there is occurrence of name-and-form, there is progress of volitional formations. Where there is progress of volitional formations, there is a future arising of becoming. Where there is a future arising of becoming, there is future birth, aging, and death. Following the reverse approach, there is no future arising of renewed becoming, no future birth, aging, and death. The above interpretations of the term *nandi* and its function would mean that there is an arising condition with something which leads to arising of suffering, and a passing away of it, denotes the cessation of suffering.

The *Mūlapariyāya Sutta* (MN I 6) represents *nandi* as the root of suffering, and with condition there is birth, ageing and death. But in converse order, the *Sutta* indicates the Buddha has understood that delight is the root of suffering, and through the complete destruction, diminishing completely, cessation, letting go, abandoning of craving (*taṇhā*), he has awakened to the unexcelled full enlightenment.[22]

The preceding example may be puzzling because the Buddha says *nandi* is the root cause of suffering. But, while delivering his full enlightenment the Buddha uses the term *taṇhā*, instead of *nandi*, which has to be eradicated to attain final liberation. In order to clarify the function of *nandi*, it is

---

[21] 1. Edible food (*kabalīṅkāra*), 2. Contact (*phassa*), 3. Mental Volition (*manosañcetanā*), and 4. Consciousness (*viññāṇa*).

[22] *nandi dukkhassa mūlanti iti viditvā bhavā jāti bhūtassa jarāmaraṇanti. Tasmātiha bhikkhave tathāgato sabbaso taṇhānaṃ khayā virāgā nirodhā cāgā paṭinissaggā anuttaraṃ sammāsambodhiṃ abhisambuddho'ti vadāmi.*

useful to examine the example of the *Saññojana Sutta* of the *Nidāna Vagga* in SN. This *Sutta* teaches that when one dwells contemplating gratification in things which fetter, craving increases *(saññojanīyesu dhammesu assādānupassino viharato taṇhā pavaḍḍhati)*; with craving as condition, clinging comes to be...such is the origin of this whole mass of suffering (SN II 86; SN II 87, 89–91). In this setting, fetter refers to *chanda-rāga* that arises dependent on sense bases and objects. Here, it is observed that *chanda-rāga* and *nandi-rāga* have the same flavor as *taṇhā*. But *nandi* alone does not have the same essence as *taṇhā*, rather the activity of *nandi* gives rise to increased *taṇhā* which is a cause for grasping. To clarify this point, materials from the first and second *Migajāla Sutta*-s of the *Saḷāyatana Vagga* will be referred to. Both *Sutta*-s (SN IV 36) define the activity of *nandi* as seeking delight, welcome, and remain holding. These activities give rise to craving (*taṇhā*). When this craving intensifies, there is clinging (*upādāna*), from which remaining links of the dependent arising drive on. Revealing these occurrences, the *Dhammacakkappavattana Sutta* shows craving, accompanied by desire and lust, leads to renewed becoming. Therefore, it would be more fitting to say that the activity of *nandi* gives rise to *taṇhā* rather than equating *nandi* as *taṇhā*.

To summarize this section, we assert that according to the *Mūlapariyāya Sutta* of MN, *nandi* functions as the root cause of suffering, as a similar function of *taṇhā*. But the function of *nandi* should be understood as a subtle form of *taṇhā*. The *Dutiya Migajāla Sutta* of the *Saḷāyatana Vagga* in SN gives a different flavor of dependent co-arising saying that the activity of *nandi* gives rise to *taṇhā*. Though *nandi* has a similar function as *taṇhā*, specifically the function of *nandi* is rejoicing in unwholesome things which is the activity for grosser level of *taṇhā* which stems from *nandi* that gives rise to clinging (*upādāna*). Finally, we conclude that the activity of *nandi* gives rise to *taṇhā* in a grosser level. We also suggest that not *nandi* but *nandi-rāga*, functioning as *chanda-rāga*, is equivalent to the role of *taṇhā*. Therefore, this chapter concludes that the Commentarial explanation and Wynne's opinion that *nandi* functions as *taṇhā* need to be revised.

2.6.2 Taṇhā-saṃyojana and Its Functions

The above section on *nandi* has delineated the role of *taṇhā* and its functions. Through investigation into the *Sutta*-s this section now refers to *taṇhā-saṃyojana* and its usages. It will propose that the function of *taṇhā-saṃyojana* more fruitfully depicts the existential bondage of fetter, because it plays a central role in the perpetuation of the cycle of existence, *saṃsāra*.

The previous section (see 2.5.2) has referred to Sujato who advocates that *taṇhā-saṃyojana* comes under the scheme of the Second Noble Truth—the cause of suffering. Numerous studies are available on the term *taṇhā* and its functions. Among them, the clarification by Davids and Stede (1993) is noteworthy. According to them, *taṇhā* appears as one of the central figures in Buddhist teachings which is rarely used in psychology. Davids and Stede say:

> The figure is a strong one, and the word *Taṇhā* is found mainly in poetry, or in prose passages charged with religious emotion. It is rarely used in the philosophy or the psychology. Thus in the long Enumeration of Qualities (Dhs), *Taṇhā* occurs in one only out of the 1,366 sections (Dhs 1059), & then only as one of many subordinate phases of *lobha. Taṇhā* binds a man to the chain of *Saṁsāra*, of being reborn & dying again & again until Arahantship or Nibbāna is attained.... (Davids and Stede, 1993, 330)

Furthermore, Bruce Matthews (1983) research focus is on the *Craving and Salvation*. He specifically examines many parallel terms of craving, including its functions and abandonment. But, in his study he has largely ignored the term *taṇhā-saṃyojana* and its functions. On the other hand, in the study *From Craving to Liberation Excursions into the Thought-world of the Pāli Discourses*, Anālayo (2009, 7) makes the passing remarks that "from the perspective of faring on in *saṃsāra*, craving is the fetter par excellence." While Anālayo's comment on *taṇhā* is insightful into the nature of craving, we would argue that *taṇhā-saṃyojana* plays a major role in the Buddha's teachings.

The juxtaposition of *taṇhā* with *saṃyojana* is fundamental to the role of craving as expressed in the *Taṇhā-saṃyojana Sutta* of the *Itivuttaka.* The *Sutta* draws a clear narration of *taṇhā-saṃyojana* with its existential inference. According to the *Taṇhā-saṃyojana Sutta*:

> Monks! I do not perceive even one other fetter—like the fetter of craving, conjoined by which [fetter] sentient beings transmigrating and wandering on for a long time (Iti 8).[23]

This passage is worth noting here as the term is not coined in this way in any other four *Nikāya*-s—DN, MN, SN, AN. In the *Anamatagga-saṃyojana* of the *Nidāna Vagga* in SN, the Buddha cautions about *taṇhā-saṃyojana*. He says:

> Monks! this cycle of existence is without discoverable beginning. A beginning point is not evident though sentient beings transmigrating and roaming on bound by ignorance and fettered by craving (SN II 178–79).[24]

Comparing both passages, it is seen though the sentence in the *Itivuttaka* best illustrates the role of the fetter of craving, there is a possibility that it was restructured during the compilation of the text. Several scholars have also commented on this text, which consists of the four *Nipāta*-s, with earlier and later substratum. For example, K. Watanabe

---

[23] *nāhaṃ bhikkhave aññaṃ ekasaññojanampi samanupassāmi yena saññojanena saṃyuttā sattā dīgha-rattaṃ sandhāvanti saṃsaranti yathayidaṃ bhikkhave taṇhāsaññojanaṃ.*

[24] *anamataggoyaṃ bhikkhave, saṃsāro, pubbā koṭi na paññāyati avijjānīvaraṇānaṃ sattānaṃ taṇhā-saṃyojanānaṃ sandhāvataṃ saṃsarataṃ.*

(1906, 44–49) says the *Catukka Vagga* of this text is not found in its Chinese translation, because of which he has concluded that the first three *Nipāta*-s are very old. Following a similar track Pande (1999, 66–71) also says the fourth *Nipāta* is likely to be a later interpretation. On the other hand, Winternitz (1977, 68) asserts the second and the third sections of this text are later additions.

The passage from the *Itivuttaka* indicates the existential connotation of fetter which is a notable implication in the *Sutta Piṭaka*. Because *taṇhā* with *saṃyojana* is only applied to define the cycle of existence (*saṃsāra*) in which sentient beings wander and transmigrate for a long, long time. Besides, the *Anamatagga-saṃyutta* of the *Nidāna Vagga* in SN explains that *saṃsāra* is without a discoverable beginning which is the most evident teaching in the Pāli Canon. The *Sutta* (SN II 178–93) says that the Buddha himself, when questioned by others, has expounded *saṃsāra* as having undiscoverable beginning, which is full of suffering, sorrow, and stress. To escape from this existential (*saṃsāric*) bond, it is necessary to experience repugnance towards all formations, necessary to become detached towards them, and necessary to be freed from them. The *Sutta*-s (SN V 226, 440; SN III 149–51) further state that the Buddha straightforwardly says that beings transmigrate and wander on bound by ignorance and fettered by craving (*avijjānīvaraṇānaṃ sattānaṃ taṇhāsaṃyojanānaṃ sandhāvataṃ saṃsārataṃ*). One must try to escape from this through the abandonment away of residue, the cessation of ignorance and the destruction of fetter of craving.

At this point, the above discussion links to the *Bhava Sutta* of the *Tika Nipāta* in AN. The *Sutta* consists of existential connotations which are deceptively simple, yet are profound teachings of the Buddha. According to the *Sutta*, once Venerable Ānanda approached the Buddha and asked him:

> 'Becoming, becoming,' to what extent, Bhante! is there becoming (AN I 224)?[25]

The Buddha replies:

> Kamma is the field, consciousness the seed, and craving the moisture. For beings bound by ignorance and fettered by craving [*taṇhā-saññojana*] their consciousness is to be established in an inferior realm. Kamma is the field, consciousness the seed, and craving the moisture. For beings bound by ignorance and fettered by craving their consciousness is to be established in a middle realm. Kamma is the field, consciousness the seed, and craving the moisture. For beings bound by ignorance and fettered by craving their consciousness is to be established in a superior realm. Thus, there is the production of renewed becoming in the future (AN I 223).[26]

In the passage the inferior, middle, and superior realms correspond to the existence in sensual realm, existence in form-realm, and existence in formless-realm respectively. Though the passage signifies the exhortation of becoming or future arising of beings based on their degree of ignorance and craving, one needs to differentiate between the terms *saṃsāra* and *bhava*. The importance of *bhava* features particularly in the Second Noble Truth, the cause of suffering

[25] *bhavo bhavoti bhante vuccati. Kittāvatā nu kho bhante bhavo hotīti. The Princeton Dictionary of Buddhism* states:

> In the Pāli sources, *bhava* is of three types depending on the strata of the universe in which it occurs: namely, sensuous becoming (*kāmabhava*) in the sensuous realm (*kāmadhātu*), subtle-material becoming (*rūpabhava*) in the subtle-materiality realm (*rūpadhātu*), and immaterial becoming (*arūpabhava*) in the immaterial realm(*ārūpyadhātu*) (Buswell & Donald, 2014, 111).

[26] *Kammaṃ khettaṃ, viññāṇaṃ bījaṃ, taṇhā sineho. Avijjānīvaraṇānaṃ sattānaṃ taṇhā-saññojanānaṃ hīnāya dhātuyā viññāṇaṃ patiṭṭhitā, patthanā patiṭṭhitā. Kammaṃ khettaṃ, viññāṇaṃ bījaṃ, taṇhā sineho. Avijjānīvaraṇānaṃ sattānaṃ taṇhāsaṃyojanānaṃ majjhimāya dhātuyā viññāṇaṃ patiṭṭhitā, patthanā patiṭṭhitā. Kammaṃ khettaṃ, viññāṇaṃ bījaṃ, taṇhā sineho. Avijjānīvaraṇānaṃ sattānaṃ taṇhāsaṃyojanānaṃ paṇītāya dhātuyā viññāṇaṃ patiṭṭhitā, patthanā patiṭṭhitā. Evaṃ āyati punabbhavābhinibbatti hoti.*

which is *taṇhā*. Among the three classifications of *taṇhā*-s, the term *bhava* occupies a fitting place with the term *bhava-taṇhā*. This term also includes various mental defilements such as *bhava-saṃyojana* (fetter of becoming) which has been completely abandoned by an arahat. Many *Sutta*-s define an arahat in relation to *bhava-saṃyojana*. See further discussion on this in the section "*Bhava-saṃyojana* and Its Functions."

In conclusion of this section, we would like to cite passages from the *Taṇhā-saṃyojana Sutta* of the *Itivuttaka,* the *Anamatagga-saṃyutta* of the *Nidāna Vagga* in SN, and the *Bhava Sutta* of the *Tika Nipāta* in AN to illustrate that all these *Sutta*-s contain alternative explanations of *taṇhā-saṃyojana* in regard to both existential as well as psychological aspects regarding *saṃsāra* and *bhava.* These two terms show two distinct connotations of fetter: (a) psychological and (b) existential. Earlier (see 2.5.1), it has shown that the term *bhava* is included in *taṇhā*. According to Davids and Stede (1993, 330), "*taṇhā* binds a man to the chain of *Saṁsāra*, of being reborn & dying again & again until Arahantship or Nibbāna is attained." Here the notion of *bhava* seems to be existential rather than psychological. But, Bhikkhu Thanissaro (2008) points out, *bhava* is fully psychological which is something produced by the activity of our minds. He says:

> *Bhava* is included in a variety of lists describing mental states that an arahant—a fully awakened person—has overcome. Thus it is one of the three *āsavas*, or effluents; one of the four *oghas*, or floods; one of the four *yogas*, or burdens; and one of the seven *anusayas*, or obsessions. Although it does not occur in the standard list of ten *sanyojanas*, or fetters, a standard formula describing the arahant states that he/she has "destroyed the fetter of becoming" (Thanissaro, 2008, 14).

This statement is analogous to the foregoing section where *bhava-saṃyojana* (fetter of becoming) is discussed.

2.6.3 Bhava-saṃyojana and Its Functions

The reference to *bhava-saṃyojana* (fetter of becoming) here strongly suggests a dynamic consequence of the term in the Pāli Canon. It is with this term that the highest spiritual stage known as arahatship is defined. For example, the *Arahanta Sutta* of the *Khandha Vagga* in SN states that one could trace the definition of arahat with the destruction of taints and fetter of becoming:

> He is called a monk who is an arahat, whose taints are destroyed, who has lived the holy life, done what had to be done, put down the burden, reached the highest goal, completely destroyed the fetter of becoming [*parikkhīṇa-bhava-saṃyojana*], fully liberated through final knowledge (SN III 161; SN I 71; V 145, 236, 273, 302, 326, 327; DN III 83, 132; MN I 477, 522, II 41, III 4, 30, 81; AN I 144, III 376, IV 362, 370).[27]

The above passage is the standard definition of arahat, also found in many *Sutta*-s. Most *Sutta*-s (SN I 191) also define final liberation by the removal of fetters and bonds (*saññojana-bandhanacchidā*). Final liberation is occasionally defined through the cutting off craving, removal of fetter, and by completely breaking conceit (*acchecchi taṇhāṃ, vāvattayi saṃyojanaṃ, sammā mānābhisamayā*) (AN II 165), and also all fetters (*sabba-saññojana*) (AN III 346 & 354). However, in the *Sutta*-s there are other phrases that define arahat without pronouncing the extinguishment of taints and fetter of becoming. For example: "Birth is devastated, the holy life has been lived, what had to be done had been done, there is nothing more for the sake of state of being" (SN IV 76).[28] Significantly, in this passage although

[27] *bhikkhu arahaṃ khīṇāsavo vusito katakaraṇīyo ohitabhāro anuppattasadattho parikkhīṇa-bhavasaṃyojano sammadaññāvimuttoti.*

[28] *khīṇā jāti, vusitaṃ brahmacariyaṃ, kataṃ karaṇīyaṃ, nāparaṃ itthattāyāti abbhaññāsi.*

taints and fetters were not mentioned, they are understood to have been eliminated. Otherwise the spiritual stage of arahatship could not be attained.

The above statements are repeated in the *Sutta*-s of the first four *Nikāya*-s. According to the foregoing passages, it is evident that the arahatship refers to the stage where *bhava-saṃyojana* is completely destroyed. But here the key question would be to discern what is *bhava-saṃyojana* and how many they are. In response to this question, a detailed exposition is given through the investigation into the *Sutta*-s and Commentaries.

Bhava and *saṃyojana* were used together in the earlier version of the *Sutta*-s, and the term *bhava-saṃyojana* became a later formulation of the standard description of spiritual breakthrough. This description is worth noting because this exhortation occurs throughout the first four *Nikāya*-s of the *Sutta Piṭaka*. In these *Nikāya*-s, *bhava-saṃyojana* was not further defined into several categories. This would imply that monks constantly focus on their goal to obtain final liberation by destroying *bhava-saṃyojana*. Although, *bhava-saṃyojana* appears on its own in the *Sutta*-s, the Commentary to the *Mūlapariyāya Sutta* of MN defines it with the *Abhidhamma* list of ten fetters. For example:

> The fetter of becoming [*bhava-saṃyojana*] is the ten fetters: the fetter of sensual desire, fetter of repulsion, fetter of conceit, fetter of view, fetter of doubt, fetter of clinging to rules and vows, fetter of desire for becoming, fetter of envy, fetter of selfishness, and fetter of ignorance (Ps VRI 21).[29]

This passage represents the commentators' attempts to explain the *Sutta* with *Abhidhamma* materials. Such

---

[29] *bhavasaṃyojanānīti dasa saṃyojanāni–kāmarāga-saṃyojanaṃ paṭigha-māna-diṭṭhi-vicikicchā-sīlabbataparāmāsa-bhavarāga-issā-macchariyasaṃyojanaṃ, avijjā-saṃyojanaṃ.*

interpretations distinctly demonstrate dominance of the commentators' own interpretation over the *Sutta*-s. Here, we argue that the *Abhidhamma* list of ten fetters is an alternative for the term *bhava-saṃyojana* found in the *Sutta*-s (DN III 254; AN IV 7).

In this order, it is essential to discuss another fetter called *rūpa-saññojana* (fetter of form) which has a close relation to *bhava-saṃyojana*. The term *rūpa-saññojana* is documented in the *Devaputta-saṃyutta* of the *Sagāthā Vagga* in SN. The *Sutta*, in a verse, contains this fetter, as follows:

> One who abstains from sensual perception, overcomes the fetter of form, and destroys delight and lust, he does not sink in the deep (SN I 53).[30]

The Commentary (Spk VRI 52) to the verse explains sensual perception (*kāma-saññā)* as the five lower fetters: personality-belief, doubt, clinging to rules and vows, sensual desire, ill-will. The fetter of form (*rūpa-saññojana*) implies the five higher fetters: desire for form, desire for formlessness, conceit, restlessness, and ignorance. The delight and lust *(nandi-rāga)* implies the three kinds of *kammic* volitional formations *(tayo kammābhisaṅkhāra)*, or alternatively, sense-sphere (*kāma-saññā*). The fetter of form (*rūpa-saññojana)* implies the form-sphere, and formless-sphere.[31]

---

[30] *virato kāmasaññāya rūpāsaññojanātigo / Nandirāgaparikkhīṇo so gambhīre na sīdatīti.*

[31] *nandīrāgaparikkhīṇoti parikkhīṇanandīrāgo. Nandīrāgo nāma tayo kammābhisaṅkhārā. Iti imāya gāthāya kāmasaññāgahaṇena pañcorambhāgiyasaṃyojanāni, rūpāsaṃyojana-gahaṇena pañca uddhambhāgiyasaṃyojanāni, nandīrāgena tayo kammābhisaṅkhārā gahitā. Evaṃ yassa dasa saṃyojanāni tayo ca kammābhisaṅkhārā pahīnā, so gambhīre mahoghe na sīdatīti. Kāmasaññāya vā kāmabhavo, rūpasaṃyojanena rūpabhavo gahito, tesaṃ gahaṇena arūpabhavo gahitova, nandīrāgena tayo kammābhisaṅkhārā gahitāti evaṃ yassa tīsu bhavesu tayo saṅkhārā natthi, so gambhīre na sīdatītipi dasseti.*

This summarizes Part Two on the discussion of the fetters *chanda-rāga, nandi, taṇhā,* and *bhava*. Referring to the Commentarial interpretation of the above verse, we consider *kāma-saññā* and *rūpa-saññojana* constitute *bhava-saṃyojana*, and *nandi-rāga* implies the fetter of *chanda-rāga, nandi,* and *taṇhā*. Therefore, it would not be an exaggeration to say that the implication of term *saṃyojana* was different from context to context and it has played various roles in the Buddha's teachings.

Part Three

2.7 *Gihi-saṃyojana* and Its Expositions

In a previous chapter (see 1.1), we have referred to a discussion on fetter by Analāyo (2006) who says there are considerable variations in the meanings of the term in the Pāli Canon. Reviewing his statement, we have listed several kinds of fetter used to denote intra-psychic binding, existential binding and householder binding. In this chapter, we have already examined the first two bindings—the intra-psychic and the existential. This section now will show the fetter that binds a householder only appears in two *Sutta*-s (the *Tevijjavacchagotta Sutta* and the *Potaliya Sutta*) of MN.

The *Tevijjavacchagotta Sutta* contains the function of *gihi-saññojana* (fetter of householder).[32] According to this *Sutta*, once a wanderer, Vacchagotta, asks the Buddha:

> O Gautama! is there any householder (laity) who, not giving up the fetter of householder, on the dissolution of the body has made an end of suffering (MN I 482)?[33]

[32] The *Kathāvatthu* (VRI 115) of the *Abhidhamma Piṭaka* also discusses the function of *gihi-saññojana*.

[33] *atthi nu kho bho gotama koci gihī gihīsaññojanaṃ appahāya kāyassa bhedā dukkhass-antakaro'ti.*

In response to this question, the Buddha says:

> Vaccha! There is no householder who, not giving up the fetter of householder, on the dissolution of the body has made an end of suffering (MN I 482).[34]

But the Buddha further said, without abandoning the fetter of householder many householders can enjoy heavenly contentment (MN I 483). Here the statement made by the Buddha and Vacchagotta represent a conceptual variation of fetter. Before dealing with this, it is necessary to look at what *gihi-saññojana* means? Though the *Sutta* refers to *gihi-saññojana,* nothing is recorded in the *Sutta* about its features. The Commentary (Ps VRI 67) to the *Sutta* states *gihi-saññojana* denotes worldly affairs that are bondage of a householder (*gihībandhanaṃ gihīparikkhāra*). However, the Commentary does not specify which are the worldly affairs. Further the Sub-commentary gives a supplementary explanation that worldly affairs are clothes, ornaments, and wealth.[35]

The *Potaliya Sutta* gives an additional illumination on "worldly affairs". The *Sutta* records once the householder Potaliya has approached the Buddha and said, for the sake of perceptual happiness he has given up all kinds of his worldly affairs such as wealth, grain, silver, and gold to his heir. In contrast to his assertion, the Buddha has said, the cutting off worldly affairs of a householder is a different thing than a Noble One. By saying so, the Buddha has listed the eight fetters which are worldly affairs of a Noble One. These fetters are categorized as:

---

[34] *natthi kho vaccha koci gihī gihīsaññojanaṃ appahāya kāyassa bhedā dukkhassantakaro'ti.*

[35] Tevijjavacchasuttavaṇṇanā, 186 in *MṬ*: *vatthābharaṇādidhanadhaññādigihiparikkhāra.*

1. Killing living beings (*pāṇātipāta*),
2. Stealing (*adinnādāna*),
3. False speech (*musāvāda*),
4. Malicious speech (*pisunāvācā*),
5. Rapacious greed (*giddhilobha*),
6. Spiteful scolding (*nindārosa*),
7. Angry irritation (*kodhūpāyāsa*), and
8. Arrogance (*atimāna*).

The Buddha has said in the code of disciplines of noble disciples that all these fetters were cut off by them (MN I 359). According to the Buddha, these eight fetters can be cut off in eight ways, as follows:

1. By means of the support of the non-killing of living beings, the killing of living beings can be abandoned,
2. By means of the support of taking only what is given, the taking of what is not given can be abandoned,
3. By means of the support of true speech, false speech can be abandoned.
4. By means of the support of unslanderous speech, slanderous speech can be abandoned.
5. By means of the support of refraining from rapacious greed, rapacious greed can be abandoned.
6. By means of the support of refraining from hurtful reprimand, hurtful reprimand can be abandoned.
7. By means of the support of refraining from angry despair, angry despair can be abandoned.
8. By means of the support of non-arrogance, arrogance can be abandoned. (MN I 360).[36]

The Commentary (Ps VRI 15) to the *Sutta* further divides these eight restraints into three categories:

---

[36] 1. *apāṇātipātaṃ nissāya pāṇātipāto pahātabbo*, 2. *dinnādānaṃ nissāya adinnādānaṃ pahātabbaṃ*, 3. *saccaṃ vācaṃ nissāya musāvādo pahātabbo*, 4. *apisunaṃ vācaṃ nissāya pisunā vācā pahātabbā*, 5. *agiddhilobhaṃ nissāya giddhilobho pahātabbo*, 6. *anindārosaṃ nissāya nindāroso pahātabbo*, 7. *akodhūpāyāsaṃ nissāya kodhūpāyāso pahātabbo*, 8. *anatimānaṃ nissāya atimāno pahātabbo*.

1. The killing, and taking of what is not given are to be discarded by bodily virtue;
2. The false speech, and hateful speech are to be discarded by verbal virtue; and
3. The covetous greed, angry irritation, and superciliousness are to discarded by mental virtue, and the unpleasant reprimand is to be discarded by both bodily and verbal virtue.[37]

The Commentary (Ps VRI 15) also notes the killing of living beings, though not falling under the scheme of ten fetters and five hindrances, may also be called a fetter on account of binding into the cycle of existence, *saṃsāra*. And a hindrance on account of its obstruction to obtaining the true benefit.[38] The *Potaliya Sutta,* furthermore, includes the Buddha's teachings on the barriers of sensual desire of the Noble Ones, and threefold knowledge (*tevijjā*) of them. The threefold knowledge is: (1) recollection of the manifold past lives, (2) divine eye which perceives beings passing away and reappearing, and (3) knowledge of the destruction of the taints. Interestingly, the *Tevijjavacchagotta Sutta* also contains this threefold doctrine. Comparing both *Sutta*-s, it is evident that the Buddha willingly conveyed such doctrine either for asserting the cogency of his teachings or boosting the confidence of lay people in the Buddha, the Dhamma, and the Saṅgha. Both *Sutta*-s describe how after the Buddha's talk, both householders rejoiced and delighted in his words, even Potaliya became a lay follower of the Buddha for the rest of his life.

---

[37] *tesāhaṃ saṃyojanānaṃ pahānāyāti imasmiṃ pade iminā dinnādānasaṅkhātena kāyikasīlasaṃvarena, saccavācāsaṅkhātena vācasikasīlasaṃvarena, apisuṇāvācāsaṅkhātena vācasikasīlasaṃvarena, agiddhilobhasaṅkhātena mānasikasīlasaṃvarena, anindārosa-saṅkhātena kāyikavācasikasīlasaṃvarena, akodhupāyāsasaṅkhātena mānasikasīla-saṃvarena, anatimānasaṅkhātena mānasikasīlasaṃvarena pahānatthāya samucchedanatthāya paṭipannoti.*

[38] *vaṭṭabandhanaṭṭhena hi hitapaṭicchādanaṭṭhena ca saṃyojanantipi nīvaraṇantipi vuttaṃ.*

As shown in the foregoing discussion, the concept of fetter was differently employed from context to context in the Pāli Canon. In the *Potaliya Sutta* fetter can be linked to the five precepts—abstaining from killing, stealing or taking what is not given, sexual misconduct, false speech, and taking intoxicant, because the Buddha uses the concept of "fetter" to educate householders on the Buddhist path.

2.8 The Concept of Fetter in the Context of *Jhāna* States

This section discusses the usage of the term "fetter" which is substantially different from other previous sections. Here the concept of fetter is used in association with the *jhāna* states. They are *lokāmisa-saññojana* (fetter of lure of the world), *āneñja-saññojana* (fetter of imperturbability), *ākiñcaññāyatana-saññojana* (fetter of base of nothingness) and *nevasaññānāsaññāyatana-saṃyojana* (fetter of base of neither-perception-nor-non-perception). In the entire *Sutta Piṭaka*, these *jhāna* states with fetter are only mentioned in the *Sunakkhatta Sutta* (MN II 252–61). Before dealing with fetter in relation to the *jhāna* states, it is important to understand the context of *jhāna*. According to Henepola Gunaratana:

> After reaching the first *jhāna* the ardent meditator can go on to reach the higher *jhānas*, this is done by eliminating the coarser factors in each *jhāna*... Beyond the four *jhānas* lies another fourfold set of higher meditative states which deepen still further the element of serenity developed in the *jhānas*. These attainments, known as the immaterial states (*āruppa*)... are the base of boundless space [*ākāsānañcāyatana*], the base of boundless consciousness [*viññānañcayatana*], the base of nothingness [*ākincaññāyatana*], and the base of neither-perception-nor-non-perception [*nevasaññānāsaññāyatana*] (Gunaratana, 1980, 16).

From the above passage, it should be noted that the higher meditative states *ākiñcaññāyatana* and *nevasaññānāsaññāyatana* are called "fetters" in the *Sunakkhatta Sutta.* Though Gunaratana specifically examines the doctrines related to *jhāna*-s, in his discussion he has ignored the term *saṃyojana* in association with *jhāna* states. In the *Sutta*, out of four fetters, two are higher meditative states *ākiñcaññāyatana* and *nevasaññānāsaññāyatana.* The term *lokāmisa* is explained in the *Sunakkhatta Sutta* as the lure of world which denotes the five kinds of sensual pleasure. The term *āneñja* is still subject to examination. According to Ñāṇamoli and Bodhi (1995, 1309, see note 1000), *āneñja* is a technical term used to denote the meditative attainments of *jhāna*. They say, while the *Sunakkhatta Sutta* records the immaterial attainments of the base of nothingness and the base of neither-perception-nor-non-perception, *āneñja* refers to other immaterial attainments that are not contained in the *Sutta*. The next *Sutta* of the text, the *Āneñjasappāya Sutta* (MN II 106), gives further explanation of the term *āneñja* in relation to the meditative attainments of *jhāna*.

The *Sunakkhatta Sutta* explains in detail the significance of liberation from worldly material things to *Nibbāna*. Here the worldly material things are connected to sensual desire and lust generated by five strings of sensual pleasures. These five strings arise dependent on the five sense objects—forms, sounds, odors, flavors, and tangibles. These five objects are cognizable by their respective sense bases—eye, ear, nose, tongue and body. Surprisingly, the *Sutta* excludes the sense base mind and its object mental phenomena. According to the *Sutta*, through cutting off desire and lust associated with all of these five strings, one understands the worldly material things. When he understands worldly material things, he escapes from there and he reaches the state of imperturbability. Again relinquishing the state of imperturbability, he reaches the base of nothingness. Further relinquishing the base of nothingness, he reaches the base of neither-perception-nor-non-perception, and further detaching from the base of neither-perception-nor-non-perception, he attains complete *Nibbāna*. In this *Sutta* all other bases, except *Nibbāna*,—the worldly material things, the imperturbability, the base of nothingness, and the base of neither-perception-nor-non-perception—are themselves defined as fetters. Here we argue that the interpretation of these fetters is highly hypothetical as the *Sutta* explains them differently from other fetters.

The *Sutta* is distinctive as it does not provide any particular reference to fetter except the five strings of desire and lust. Examining the contents of the *Sutta* (MN II 255–56), we opine that the S*utta* mainly refers to the meditative experience through the eradication of various defilements that are linked to the respective sense-sphere, form-sphere, and formless-sphere realms. The *Sutta* itself also says that the five strings are connected to the desire and lust which are worldly materials, and abandoning worldly materials one reached imperturbability. Further abandoning imperturbability one reaches the base of nothingness, and then base of neither-perception-nor-non-perception, then abandoning the base of neither-perception-nor-non-perception, one attains *Nibbāna*.

Because the *Sutta* does not provide further explanation of the fetter in association with meditative attainment states, one may find it difficult to understand the fetter in relation to imperturbability, base of nothingness, and base of neither-perception-nor-non-perception. The Commentary to this *Sutta* does not clarify this point, either. But, the *Cūllaniddesa*, the Commentary to the *Pārāyana Vagga* and the *Khaggavisāna Sutta*, explains the verse 1115 of the *Posālamāṇava Pucchā* in Sn in which the fetter of delight (*nandi-saṃyojana)* occurs in related to the base of nothingness (*ākiñcaññāyatana-saññojana)*. The verse is:

> Knowing the origin of the base of nothingness that delight is a fetter; thus understanding it, he gains insight into it, this is the knowledge of that Brāmaṇa who is truly liberated (Sn 216).[39]

The *Cūllaniddesa* (Nidd II VRI 91) equates the fetter of delight as the desire for formless existence (*nandi-saṃyojanaṃ vuccati arūparāgo*). The Commentarial explanation seems to be a later interpretation of *nandi-saṃyojana* which is applied to define the base of nothingness (*ākiñcaññāyatana*). At this point Wynne says:

> '[U]nderstanding it [the fetter that is the origin of nothingness] thus [i.e. as delight]'. I presume, describes the state of insight (*vipassati*) that arises after one has grasped that delight [*nandi*] is the origin of the state of nothingness. The passage thus states that someone who has attained the meditative state of nothingness, and has applied his meditative state of mind to the practice of mindfulness, must understand something about the meditative state, namely, that its existence in one's experience depends upon desire (Wynne, 2007, 91).

Although Wynne's clarification is insightful, the role of fetter of delight (*nandi-saṃyojana*) could not be sufficient to understand fetters of meditative states occurred in the *Sunakkhatta Sutta*. Hence, an attempt is made here to clarify the function of fetter *āneñja, ākiñcaññāyatana*, and *nevasaññānāsaññāyatana* in the following section.

The purpose of the function of *saṃyojana* in this *Sutta* is to describe the defilements which still remain in a person who is in the state of material and immaterial attainments. These defilements may refer to five hindrances: sensualdesire, malice, torpor-drowsiness, restlessness, and doubt. These defilements constitute the obstacle for noble path, and with detachment from that one reaches spheres to spheres. Further abandoning spheres one reaches *Nibbāna*. Thus, it could be concluded that the concept of *saṃyojana*

---

[39] *ākiñcaññā sambhavaṃ ñatvā nandi saṃyojanaṃ iti / etaṃ ñāṇaṃ tathaṃ tassa brāhmaṇassa vusīmatoti.*

in the *Sunakkhatta Sutta* refers mainly to psychological disposition of a meditator who is still in the *jhāna* states, whereat he cuts off all these defilements at the root. Finally, cutting off all subtle fetters, the person attains *Nibbāna*.

Part Four

2.9 A Comparison between the Vedic Term *Pāśa* and *Saṃyojana*

Though the study of the Vedic term *pāśa,* (Pāli: *pāsa*) is not the main focus of this thesis, this section explores how *pāsa* (fetter) occurs in the *Sutta*-s to denote defilement. The central role of *pāsa* functions like the term *bandhana* and *saṃyojana* in the *Sutta*-s. There are few studies on *pāsa* in modern Buddhist scholarship. However, many Vedic scholars, such as A.A. Macdonell and A.B. Keith (1995), and Surendranath Dasgupta (1991) have contributed scholarship on the concept *pāśa* in Indian philosophical thoughts. This section recognizes that *saṃyojana* is not traced outside Buddhist philosophical schools. But there is record of some traces of parallelism between the Upaniṣadic and the early Buddhist conception of *pāsa*.

The word *pāsa* is used to denote the fastening or tying as pointed out by Macdonell and Keith:

> *Pāśa* denotes in the Rigveda and later a 'rope' used for fasting or tying up. Rope and knot (*granthi*) are mentioned together in the Atharvaveda. *Pāśa* is in the Śatapatha Brāhmaṇa used of the rope by which Manu's ship was fastened to the mountain. It is often employed metaphorical of the 'fetter' of Varuṇa (Macdonell and Keith, 1995, 523).

In the Pāli Canon, the term *pāsa* denotes the fetter of Māra in the *Mārasaṃyutta* (SN I 105–06) and in both *Mārapāsa Sutta*-s of the *Saḷāyatanasaṃyutta* (SN IV 91–93). In *Sutta*

Nipāta, *pāsa* refers to the "fetter of death" (*maccupāsa*) (verse no.166).

Through investigation into the *Sutta*-s, it is evident that the concept *saṃyojana* denotes the notion of binding efficacy of defilement, similar to the meaning of the word *pāsa.* Though its function is not the same, *pāsa* has a similar role of *saṃyojana* in the *Sutta*-s. For example, the first and second *Pāsa Sutta*-s of the *Mārasaṃyutta* (SN I 105–06) say that once Māra[40] approached the Buddha and told him he is bound by Māra's fetter and bondage in both celestial and human spheres. In answer to Māra's claim, the Buddha told Māra he is freed from all kinds of the Māra's fetter and bondage in both celestial and human spheres.[41] The Commentary (Spk VRI 78) to both *Sutta*-s clarifies the term *Mārapāsa* as the fetter of the defilement of sensual pleasure in both human and celestial realms.[42]

It is worth noting that here *mārapāsa* refers to the psychological infatuation which arises based on sense bases and their objects. Both *Mārapāsa Sutta*-s of the *Saḷāyatanasaṃyutta* in SN contain the concept of *pāsa* as the whole psychological defilement. According to the *Sutta*:

---

[40] The concept of Māra has various meanings. Robert (2003, 13) in *The Handbook of Tibetan Buddhist Symbols* categorizes the concept "Māra" into four. The first of these is the *Khandhamāra*, the evil of the five aggregates, the second is *Kilesa-māra*, the evil of emotional defilement, the third is *Maccu-māra*, the evil of death, and the fourth is *Devaputta-māra*, the evil of son of god. Nyanatiloka (1952, 184) in the *Buddhist Dictionary*, lists the fivefold Māra, including the earlier category of fours, and the additional one is named *Kamma-māra*, the evil of the karma-form-action.

[41] Māra—*Baddho'si mārapāsena ye dibbā ye ca mānusā/ Mārabandhanabaddhosi na me samaṇa mokkhasīti.* Bhagavā—*Muttohaṃ mārapāsena ye dibbā ye ca mānusā/ Mārabandhanamuttomhi nihato tvamasi antakāti.* It is worth noting that both *Pāsa Sutta*-s were preached soon after the Buddha's first rains retreat at the Deer Park in Isipatana. It shows that the *Sutta* is earlier doctrine in the Pāli Canon.

[42] *mārapāsenāti kilesapāsena. Ye dibbā ye ca mānusāti ye dibbā kāmaguṇasaṅkhātā mānusā kāma-guṇasaṅkhātā ca mārapāsā nāma atthi.*

> There are forms cognizable by the eye that are desirable, lovely, pleasant, enjoyable, sensually enticing, tantalizing. If then a monk seeks delight in them, welcomes them, and remains holding to them, he is called a monk who has entered Māra's world, come under the control of Māra, and tied by the fetter of Māra [*mārapāsa*] (SN IV 91–93).[43]

In a similar way, when there are sounds, odors, tastes, tangible objects, and mental phenomena cognizable by the ear, nose, tongue, body and mind respectively, and one delights, welcomes, and remains holding to them, he is tied by the fetter of Māra. On the contrary, if he does not seek delight in them he is not tied by the fetter of Māra in both human and celestial spheres.

Using the above passages, this section now sets out to determine the doctrinal setting of *pāsa* and *saṃyojana*. In the passage, the function of *pāsa* implies "intrapsychic binding" which has close connection to the contents of the *Migajāla Sutta* of the *Saḷāyatana Vagga* in SN. According to the *Sutta,* when there are forms cognizable by the eye which are delightful, tantalizing, etc., and a monk delights, welcomes and remains holding to them delight arises. Being delight there is passion. Being passion there is bondage, bound by the fetter of delight (*nandi-saṃyojana*).

By doing a comparison between two *Sutta*-s, it is further noticed that *nandi* has been replaced by *māra*, and *pāsa* has been replaced by *saṃyojana*, while the rest of the doctrines are similar in terms of their settings. But, through the eradication of fetter of delight (*nandi-saṃyojana*) the notion of liberation is defined, no mention about the notion of liberation was made about eradicating *māra-pāsa* in the

[43] *santi bhikkhave sotaviññeyyā saddā iṭṭhā kantā manāpā piyarūpā kāmūpāsaṃhitā rajanīyā, tañce bhikkhu abhinandati abhivadati ajjhosāya tiṭṭhati, ayaṃ vuccati bhikkhave bhikkhu āvāsagato mārassa, mārassa vasaṅgato, paṭimukkassa mārapāso, baddho so mārabandhanena yathākāmakaraṇīyo pāpimato.*

Sutta-s. Besides, though *mārapāsa* implies the fetter of Māra (*kilesa* or defilement), it was not given much importance in the development of Buddhist doctrine. Up to this point, we have examined the Canonical passages available. Yet no comprehensive study of the term *pāsa* has been made to illuminate in Buddhist studies.

A number of scholars has extensively studied the concept *pāśa* under the *Śaiva* System. Among them, K. Sivaraman (2001, 21–22) says the real meaning of *pāśa* is a bond that "yokes man from whose conditions he seeks freedom". He further elaborates the concept *pāśa* in the following way. The world is a bondage and freeing from it is liberation. Freeing from *pāśa* is the higher reaches of knowledge which means one unites with God. The Śaiva System has three philosophical frameworks, namely: *Pati, Paśu* and *Pāśa*. *Pati* is the Transcendent Spirit or God, *paśu* is self whose destiny is to realize *pati* by cutting off all *pāśa*-s. These are three kinds of *pāśa*, namely: *mala, karma,* and *māya*. *Māya* is further divided into two kinds: *māyā-śuddha* and *aśuddha*. These four 'species' of *pāśa* together with *paśu* and *pati*, Śaivism is constituted as six "eternals" of philosophical system. Following up on the above description of *pāśa*, Surendranath says:

> The *pāśa* is the energy of Śiva manifesting itself as *prakṛti* which evolves the material world, the subjective world, as well as pleasures and pains, which fetter the universal soul, the *paśu*, appearing as many under different conditions and circumstances (Surendranath, 1991, 111).

Muller-Ortega (1989, 27), moreover, cites the *Śvetāśvatara Upaniṣad*, a text dated around the 5–6 century BCE, Which contains extensive references to *pāśa* as spiritual bondage which binds beings into existence, and the liberation from such signifies the final release. The *Śvetāśvatara Upaniṣad* says:

> The Lord, *Isa*, supports all this which is a combination of the perishable and the imperishable, the manifest, the effect and the unmanifest, the cause. The same Lord, the Supreme Self, devoid of Lordship, becomes bound because of assuming the attitude of the enjoyer. The *jiva* by realizing the Supreme Self is freed from all fetters. (*Svetasavatara Upanisad* 1.8, translated by Sethumadhava, 9).[44]

Citing Pope's assumption that the doctrine *pāśa* of Śaiva philosophy has close similarity with the doctrines *Āṇava, Karma*, and *Māya-mala* of Jainism, Helmuth Von. Glasenapp (1999, 498) says Pope's deliberation is not correct due to insufficient knowledge in Jainism. Glasenapp further alleges one cannot deny the Karma-theory of Jainas that is based on *Āṇava, Karma*, etc. but he further remarks the problem between these two systems needs more examination and clarification.

It is noteworthy that, in the *Sutta*-s, the word *pāsa* takes place with Māra—*mārapāsa*—to denote the binding notion of defilement. Though the *Sutta*-s do not further classify *māra-pāsa* into various defilements, it denotes the cord of sensual pleasures which is a synecdoche for unwholesome things. The word *māyā* (deceit) which appears under the category of *pāśa* in Śaiva philosophy, is also found in the *Vatthupamā Sutta* (MN I 36–40). The *Sutta* (MN I 36–37) contains a list of sixteen defilements,[45] under which *māyā* is

---

[44] *saṃyuktam etat kṣaram akṣaraṃ ca vyaktāvyaktaṃ bharate viśvam īśaḥ / anīśaś cātmā badhyate bhoktṛbhāvāj jñātvā devaṃ mucyate sarvapāśaiḥ.*

[45] 1. Covetousness and unrighteous greed (*abhijjhāvisamalobha*), 2 Ill-will (*byāpāda*), 3. Anger (*kodha*), 4. Hostility (*upanāha*), 5. Contempt (*makkha*), 6. Presumption (*paḷāsa*), 7. Envy (*issā*), 8. Selfishness (*macchariya*), 9. Deceit (*māyā*), 10. Fraud (*sāṭheyya*), 11. Callousness (*thamba*), 12. Impetuosity (*sārambha*), 13. Conceit (*māna*), 14. Arrogance (*atimāna*), 15. Pride (*mada*), and 16. Negligence (*pamāda*). Among them *issā* and *macchariya* are found in the *Abhidhamma* list of ten fetters, *byāpāda* and *māna* are found in the traditional list of ten fetters, and *avijjā* is found in both lists.

listed as a defilement of the mind (*māyā cittassa upakkileso*) (MN I 36). Pande (1999, 119) believes the *Vatthupamā Sutta* is one of the earliest *Sutta*-s in the *Majjhima Nikāya*. The *Nikāya* evidence and scholar opinions demonstrate that *māra-pāsa* and *māra-bandhana* were employed in Buddhist teaching in the earlier phase of Buddhist history when *bandhana* was developed as a set of defilement, and *pāsa* was dropped. The term *māyā* which denotes defilement also falls into disuse later in the history of Buddhist teaching. There is no doubt that the term *pāsa* was introduced to define the defilement of sensual pleasure in terms of fettering in both human and celestial realms. There is a possibility that the term has close relation to the technical terms *bandhana* and *saṃyojana*. Looking at the Buddhist doctrine and other philosophical systems, we believe the term *pāsa* was introduced to Buddhist teaching to illustrate a binding potency of defilement, although it was not employed as widely as in Vedic philosophical systems. However, it must be noted that the function of *pāśa* used in Upaniṣad is very different from the Pāli Canon.

2.10 Conclusion

This chapter has argued that the concept *saṃyojana* is regarded as defilement which refers to binding. This binding was categorized into three main sections: intra-psychic, existential and householder bindings. The intra-psychic binding as defined with the fetter *chanda-rāga* is likely to the earlier appearance of the concept of fetter in the Pāli Canon.

Secondly, the "existential binding" was examined in a chronological order with the three fetters: *nandi, taṇhā*, and *bhava-saṃyojanas*. Among them, it was shown that the function of *nandi-saṃyojana* denotes both intra-psychic and existential bindings. Each of these fetters was examined by taking evidence from the *Sutta*-s. These evidence suggest that in the earlier phase of Buddha's teachings liberation was defined through abandoning each of these fetters, later it was defined by classifications of into various lists of fetter. We therefore show the concept of fetter was enlarged from context to context in the Pāli Canon.

Thirdly, the worldly material binding was shown with the fetter of householder who is bound by his/her grain, wealth, clothes. In this category, there are eight fetters which are different interpretation than the previous two. Apart from them, it has further encountered the term *saṃyojana* was also employed in association with the several *jhāna* states which are completely different from other cited categories. In conclusion, the *Sutta* descriptions of fetter with these differences indicate that the fetter may not be a fixed set. In the following two chapters, we will attempt to show the concept of fetter based on the *Sutta* and the *Abhidhamma Piṭaka*-s.

Chapter 3 – **Different Methods for Achieving Liberation in the First Four *Nikāya*-s**

3.1 Introduction

This chapter is in three parts. Part one shows the four stages of enlightenment with the method "fetter". Different methods for achieving the four stages have been explained in the first four *Nikāya*-s in diverse ways and different contexts. There is no doubt that one could attain liberation by all these methods. However, this chapter investigates why the Pāli tradition mainly accepts the method with the traditional list of ten fetters to describe the four stages, although different methods are available. By studying the first four *Nikāya*-s, this chapter aims to show that the method with the list of ten fetters does not entirely describe the four stages in the *Sutta*-s, it was later developed in the *Abhidhamma*. The *Sutta*-s, for example, the *Purisagati Sutta* of the *Sattaka Nipāta* (AN IV 70), say a non-returner has to cut off the three latent tendencies (*anusaya*)—*bhava-rāga, māna,* and *avijjā*—to attain final liberation. On the other hand, scholars such as Walshe (1995, 26–27) and Nyanatiloka (1952, 49–50) who follow the Pāli tradition say a non-returner has to cut off the five higher fetters (*saṃyojana*)—*rūpa-rāga*, *arūpa-rāga*, *māna*, *uddhacca*, and *avijjā*—to attain final liberation. This section will show the weakness of the scheme of five higher fetters in the *Sutta*-s. To support this view, it will refer to Somaratne (1999, 144) who says the term *uddhacca* (restlessness) in the list of five higher fetters is later replaced by earlier redactors or copiers. This section will also show an interpretation by the *Vibhaṅga*, the *Puggalapaññatti* and the *Kathāvatthu* of the *Abhidhamma Piṭaka* that the divisions of "lower fetters" and "higher fetters" correspond to the "internal fetters" and "external fetters".

Part two deals with a comparison between the terms *anusaya* (latent tendency) and *saṃyojana*, in reference to AN which contains the two different lists of seven fetters and the list of seven latent tendencies. This section will explore that these lists significantly influenced the composers of the *Dhammasaṅgaṇi* to set up a different list of ten fetters in the *Abhidhamma*.

Part three shows the one central method for attaining liberation. This will be followed by the four stages of liberation as a whole without mentioning the method of fetter. The section will argue that the methods without fetters are used to define the four stages in this very life, and the method with fetters mainly describes rebirth into the three existential realms. It then proposes that the method with fetters is prevalent in the Pāli Canon to describe the existential concept "rebirth".

Part One

3.2 *Dasa-saṃyojanāni* and Its Functions

Two schemes of ten fetters (*dasa-saṃyojanāni*) are found in the Pāli Canon. One scheme is found in the *Sutta*-s, and the other one is documented in the *Dhammasaṅgaṇi* and the *Vibhaṅga* of the *Abhidhamma Piṭaka,* and the *Niddesa* of the *Khuddhaka Nikāya*. But, this section only discusses the scheme of ten fetters and its functions recorded in the *Sutta*-s. Scholars such as Nyanatiloka (1952, 300–01) and W.G. Weeraratne (2003, 683–84) in the Pāli tradition readily accept this scheme as the traditional and standard scheme which describes the four stages. This scheme does not entirely describe the four stages in the *Sutta*-s, but does so in the *Abhidhamma*. It then will be argued that the entire description of the four stages with the method of ten fetters was a later interpretation or development in the *Abhidhamma*.

The *Saṃyojana Sutta* of the *Dasaka Nipāta* in AN contains the scheme of ten fetters (*dasa-saṃyojanāni*). In this *Sutta* the ten fetters are divided into two main categories: (1) *orambhāgiyāni saṃyojanāni* (five fetters belonging to low [lower existence], or the lower fetters) and (2) *uddhambhāgiyāni saṃyojanāni* (five fetters belonging to high [higher existence], or the higher fetters). The *Sutta* lists:

> The five lower fetters: personality belief, doubt, clinging to rules and vows, sensual desire, and ill-will; the five higher fetters: desire for form, desire for formlessness, conceit, restlessness, and ignorance. (AN V 17)[1]

The path to achieve liberation is categorized into the four stages described as the four paths: stream-entry, once-returning, non-returning, and arahatship. These paths produce the four fruits. Those who attain these fruits are called the Four Noble Persons (*ariya*). They are:

1. The stream-enterer (*sotāpanna*)
2. The once-returner (*sakadāgāmin*)
3. The non-returner (*anāgāmin*)
4. The worthy-one (*arahat*)

In the *Cūlasīhanāda Sutta* (MN I 63) and the *Samaṇa Sutta* (AN II 238), these four persons are named *samaṇo* (ascetic): an ascetic, a second ascetic, a third ascetic, and a fourth ascetic. According to those *Sutta*-s, these four ascetics are only referred to in the Buddha's teachings: "only here is an ascetic, only here a second ascetic, only here a third ascetic, only here a fourth ascetic" (*idha samano, idha dutiyo samaṇo, idha tatiyo*

---

[1] *pañcorambhāgiyāni saṃyojanāni: sakkāyadiṭṭhiṃ, vicikicchā sīlabbataparāmāso, kāma-chando, byāpādoti. Imāni pañcorambhāgiya saṃyojanāni. Pañcuddhambhāgiyāni saṃyojanāni: rūparāgo, arūparāgo, māno, uddhaccaṃ, avijjā, imāni kho pañcuddhambhāgiyāni, saṃyojanāni.*

samaṇo, idha catuttho samaṇo, suññā parappavādā samaṇehi aññe'ti) (MN I 63; AN II 238). Wen (2009, 30) states the four ascetics are peculiar to the Buddha's teachings, which cannot be found outside Buddha's dispensation. Wen builds his arguments by consulting parallel passages in both the Pāli *Sutta*-s and the Chinese *Āgama*-s. He says, some corresponding passages recorded the four ascetics in the *Sutta*-s (MN I 64) are parallel with the *Āgama*-s (MĀ 103 at T 1, 590b). He further comments that these four ascetics are "attributed to early Indian Buddhist schools other than the Theravāda" (Wen, 2009, 30).

In the *Saṃyojana Sutta* of the *Duka Nipāta* (AN II 88–89), moreover, the Four Noble Persons are described with interesting names, as follows: the stream-enterer as the unshaken ascetic (*samaṇamacala*), the once-returner as the white-lotus ascetic (*samaṇapuṇḍarīka*), the non-returner as the blue-lotus ascetic (*samaṇapaduma*), and the arahat as the graceful-lotus ascetic (*samaṇasukhumāla*). It is said that *sotāpanna* will have up to a maximum seven births before the attainment of final enlightenment. *Sakadāgāmin* will return one more time to the human realm before attaining arahatship, and *anāgāmin* will have the last birth in the Pure Abode, while an *arahat* who has eliminated all defilements will not be reborn (Ñāṇamoli and Bodhi, 1995, 42–43). It is worth noting that in the Nidd I (VRI 216), with giving up of the fetters and the latent tendencies, the stage of stream-entry, the once-returning, the non-returning and the arahatship are named the first boundary (*paṭhamā sīmā*), the second boundary (*dutiyā sīmā*), the third boundary (*tatiyā sīmā*), and the fourth boundary (*catutthā sīmā*) respectively.

Walshe (1995, 26–27) summarizes the Theravāda tradition as: at the first stage, one becomes a stream-enterer by discarding three of the five lower fetters: (1) personality belief, (2) doubt, and (3) clinging to rules and vows. At the second stage, one becomes a once-returner, in whom the fourth and fifth lower fetters are greatly weakened: (4) sensual desire, and (5) ill-will. At the third stage, one becomes a non-returner, in whom the fourth fetter (sensual desire), and the fifth fetter (ill-will) are completely destroyed. Finally, at the fourth stage, one becomes an arahat, by the destruction of the five higher fetters: (6) desire for form, (7) desire for formlessness, (8) conceit, (9) restlessness, and (10) ignorance.

Now it is necessary to examine how the four stages with fetters are interpreted in the *Sutta*-s. Before dealing with this topic, let us discuss an additional point. The above-mentioned *Saṃyojana Sutta* of the *Dasaka Nipāta* defines the term *dasa-saṃyojanāni* into two categories, apart from that, it does not elaborate their purpose. The term *dasa-saṃyojanāni* is not repeated in the first four *Nikāya*-s, only a few *Sutta*-s refer to the schemes of lower and higher fetters. For example, the *Saṅgīti Sutta* (DN III 232) lists both the schemes of lower and higher fetters. Walshe (1995, 615) says the *Saṅgīti Sutta* is undoubtedly a late *Sutta*. As he says, it is associated with DN 29 with the time immediately following the death of Nigaṇṭha Nātaputta, the Jain leader. He claims "part of the inspiration of DN 34 may have come from the Buddha's words at DN 29.17." Hinüber (1996, 33) says the last two *Sutta*-s, the *Saṅgiti Sutta* and the *Dasuttara Sutta,* which are said to have been spoken by Sāriputta, arranged the number of items by following the system of AN. He also says, though *Sutta*-s preached by Sāriputta, many materials in both *Sutta*-s could have been inserted at a later period. If we accept their assumptions, it is also obvious that the lists of lower fetters and higher fetters together have been inserted in this *Sutta*.

Several *Sutta*-s, including the *Maggasaṃyutta* of the *Mahā Vagga* (SN V 61–62), also contain the list of higher fetters but those *Sutta*-s simply show how the higher fetters can be abandoned through the cultivation of the Noble Eightfold Path, through the development of the seven factors of enlightenment, etc. The discussion here suggests that though the division of lower and higher fetters are recorded in the *Sutta*-s, the texts only present the function of lower fetters in relation to the first three stages while the role of higher fetters is entirely omitted in the *Sutta*-s. The above reference was made by Walshe summarizing the Four Noble Persons with the traditional list of ten fetters. However, in the entire first four *Nikāya*-s the stages of once-returning and arahatship are not traced as Walshe observes. Now it is important to examine how the four stages with fetters are described in the *Sutta*-s.

A passage from the *Mahāli Sutta* of DN is quoted below to show the stages of liberation with the method of fetters. According to the *Sutta*, the Buddha is said to have taught his disciples how fetters have to be removed for the sake of liberation. The Buddha says:

> Here, a monk who has abandoned the three fetters, becomes a stream-enterer, no longer bound to the states of woe, firmly set on the path to enlightenment. Again, a monk who has abandoned the three fetters, and with the diminishing of greed, hatred and delusion, becomes a once-returner who, having returned to this world only one time, will make an end of suffering.
>
> Again, a monk who has abandoned the five lower fetters takes a spontaneous rebirth, will there attain liberation without returning from that world. Again, a monk through the destruction of taints, in this very life, reaches the taintless liberation of mind, the liberation through wisdom, realizing it himself by own insight with direct knowledge. (DN I 156)[2]

After analyzing the above passage, at this point, it is noticed that the three fetters mentioned in defining stream-enterer and once-returner are called *sakkāya-diṭṭhi* (personality belief),

---

[2] *idha...bhikkhu tiṇṇaṃ saṃyojanānaṃ parikkhayā sotāpanno hoti avinipātadhammo niyato sambodhi-parāyaṇo. puna ca'paraṃ..., bhikkhu tiṇṇaṃ saṃyojanānaṃ parikkhayā rāgadosamohānaṃ tanuttā sakadāgāmī hoti sakideva imaṃ lokaṃ āgantvā dukkhassantaṃ karoti.*

puna ca'paraṃ..., bhikkhu orambhāgiyānaṃ saṃyojanānaṃ parikkhayā opapātiko hoti tattha parinibbāyī anāvattidhammo tasmā lokā. puna ca'paraṃ..., bhikkhu āsavānaṃ khayā anāsavaṃ cetovimuttiṃ paññāvimuttiṃ diṭṭheva dhamme sayaṃ abhiññā sacchikatvā upasampajja viharati.

These stages of enlightenment in relation to the fetters sometimes together, and sometimes separately are defined in the *Sutta*-s. This method is recorded in the following *Sutta*-s: DN 26, 18, 19, 28, 29; MN 6, 22, 68; SN V 379, etc.

vicikicchā (doubt), and *sīlabbata-parāmāsa* (clinging to rules and vows). These fetters come under the list of five lower fetters. In the above passage, the once-returner is not defined as one in whom the fourth and fifth lower fetters are greatly weakened. Rather, he is defined as having abandoned the three fetters, together with greatly diminishing greed (*rāga*), hatred (*dosa*) and delusion (*moha*). The five lower fetters in defining the non-returner comes under the traditional list of ten fetters. In addition to the first three fetters, the two fetters of sensual desire (*kāma-rāga*) and ill-will (*vyāpāda*) are added. The taints through the destruction of which the stage of arahatship is defined, are the taint of sensuality (*kāma-āsava*), the taint of becoming (*bhava-āsava*), and the taint of ignorance (*avijjā-āsava*).[3] Among the above-mentioned Four Noble Persons, it is demonstrated that arahat is not defined with the utter destruction of five higher fetters in the first four *Nikāya*-s. The arahat is described through the destruction of taints.

Besides, in other passages, the stage of arahatship is sometimes defined through the destruction of taints and the destruction of fetter of becoming (*parikkhīṇa-bhava-saṃyojana*) together. For example, the *Khandhasaṃyutta* of the *Khandha Vagga* in SN says whoever understood the five aggregates as they really are in terms of—

> ...[T]he origin and the passing away, the indulgence, the danger, and the deliverance in the group of the five aggregates of clinging, then he is called a monk who is an arahat, whose taints are destroyed, lived the holy life, done what had to be done, put down the burden, reached his own goal, completely destroyed the fetter of becoming, and is liberated through direct knowledge (SN III 161).[4]

---

[3] Wen (2009, 32) says the list of four *āsava*-s is recorded in the following *Sutta*-s: "DN II 81, 84, 91, 94, 98, 123, 126; AN I 165." But these texts record only three *āsava*-s: *kāma-āsava*, *bhava-āsava*, and *avijjā-āsava*. The taint of view (*diṭṭhi-āsava*) is later added in the *Dhammasaṅgaṇi* (Dhs VRI 134).

[4] *...samudayañca atthagamañaca assādañca ādīnavañca nissaraṇañca yathābhūtaṃ viditvā anupādo vimutto hoti. Ayaṃ vuccati bhikkhave, bhikkhu arahaṃ khīṇāsavo vusito katakaraṇīyo bahitabhāro anuppattasadattho parikkhīṇabhavasaṃyojano sammadaññāvimuttoti.*

Citing the above *Nikāya* passages, here it is evident that the description of the Four Noble Persons with the method of traditional list of ten fetters does not exclusively serve to define them. Therefore, we propose the method to define the four stages with the list of ten fetters developed in the *Abhidhamma*. With the evidence from the *Abhidhamma Piṭaka*, it will be illuminated in Chapter 4.

3.2.1 Internal and External Fetters vs. Lower and Higher Fetters

This section is a comparison between the internal and the external fetters, and the lower and the higher fetters. Though no comparison was made in any *Sutta*, it is important to show that they have a close connection with regard to the spiritual stages. First, let us discuss the internal and external fetters.

According to the *Duka Nipāta* of AN, one time Venerable Sāriputta gave a talk to a group of monks on the internal and external fetters which define the once-returner and the non-returner internally and externally. Sāriputta says:

> Friend! Here, a monk who is virtuous, resides self-possessed by the *Pātimokkha*, accomplishes of good conduct and recourse, seeing danger in little faults, trains in training rules. After dissolution of the body, he is reborn in a certain plane of devas. Passing away from there, he is a returner, one who returns to this world. He is called the person fettered internally, who is a returner, one who returns to this world (AN I 63).[5]
>
> Friend! Here, a monk who is virtuous, resides self-possessed by the *Pātimokkha*, accomplishes good conduct and recourse, seeing danger in little faults, trains in the training rules. He enters upon a peaceful mind, and dwells in it. After dissolution of the body, he is reborn in a certain plane of devas. Passing away from there, he is a

[5] *idhāvuso bhikkhu sīlavā hoti pātimokkhasaṃvarasaṃvuto viharati ācāragocarasampanno aṇumattesu vajjesu bhayadassāvī samādāya sikkhati sikkhāpadesu. So kāyassa bhedā parammaraṇā aññataraṃ devanikāyaṃ upapajjati. So tato cuto āgāmī hoti āgantā itthattaṃ. Ayaṃ vuccatāvuso ajjhattasaññojano puggalo āgāmī āgantā itthattaṃ.*

non-returner, one who does not return to this world. He is called the person fettered externally, who is a non-returner, one who does not return to this world (AN I 64).[6]

In the same context, furthermore, Sāriputta says, undertaking the training rules, when a monk practices to detach from the sensual world, destroy craving and greed, after dissolution of the body, he is reborn in a certain plane of devas. Passing away from there, he is a non-returner, one who does not return to this world. He is called the person fettered externally. From the above passages, it is worth noting that the *Sutta* does not mention any fetter that is cut off by both once-returner and non-returner. But the third passage shows that the person practices to be detached from sensual pleasure, and to destroy craving and taints.

Additionally, the internal and external fetters indicate that they are similar guidelines as the practice of *satipaṭṭhāna* through which a practitioner cuts off the fetters internally and externally. But the above passages demonstrate that these internal and external fetters bind the once-returner and the non-returner which is different from the practice of *satipaṭṭhāna*. In the *Nikāya*-s, no *Sutta* explains the fettered internally and fettered externally. It seems that there are two divisions of internal and external worlds in which once-returner and non-returner are reborn. To support this argument, reference is made to the *Vibhaṅga* (VRI 215), the *Puggalapaññatti* (VRI 15) and the *Kathāvatthu* (VRI 215) of the *Abhidhamma Piṭaka* which associates the internal fetters with the five lower fetters, and the external fetters with the five higher fetters. For instance, the *Vibhaṅga* states:

---

[6] *idhāvuso bhikkhu sīlavā hoti. Pātimokkhasaṃvarasaṃvuto viharati ācāragocarasampanno aṇumattesu vajjesu bhayadassāvī, samādāya sikkhati sikkhāpadesu. So aññataraṃ santaṃ cetovimuttiṃ upasampajja viharati. So kāyassa bhedā parammaraṇā aññataraṃ devanikāyaṃ upapajjati so tato cuto anāgāmī hoti anāgantā itthattaṃ ayaṃ vuccatāvuso bahiddhāsaññojano puggalo anāgāmī anāgantā itthattaṃ.*

> Five fetters belonging to lower existence are internal fetters, and the five fetters belonging to higher existence are external fetters. (Vibh, VRI 215)[7]

The Commentary to AN gives the same classification as the *Vibhaṅga* but further expands the internal fetters to include sense spheres, and the external fetters to include the form and formlessness spheres (Mp VRI 14).[8] Bodhi compares the *Sutta* with the Chinese *Āgama*, and states:

> It is striking that the Chinese parallel MĀ (at T448c23–25) interprets these two persons in a way diametrically opposite to the Pāli version: In the world there are two kinds of people. Which two? The persons with an internal fetter, the non-returner, who does not come back to this world. And the person with an external fetter, one who is not a non-returner but comes back to this world (Bodhi, 2012, 1627).

Comparing both the Pāli and the Chinese versions, Bodhi shows two different interpretations which are opposite understanding of the once-returner and the nonreturner with the method of internal and external fetters. Scrutinizing the *Sutta*-s, it is also observed that although the internal and external fetters have not been further classified in the *Sutta*-s, the *Abhidhamma* categorizes them into the lower and the higher fetters. For example, the *Vibhaṅga* treats the internal fetters which bind a person in the "internal world" as the same as the "lower world". On the other hand, the external fetters bind a person in the "external world" which is the same as the "upper world". Comparing the *Sutta*-s and the *Vibhaṅga*, it is noticed that the doctrines which are not clear in the *Sutta*-s, the *Abhidhamma* explains them in a proper way for clear understanding. Then the Commentaries take the *Abhidhamma* clarification to explain the *Sutta*-s. For example, in the previous chapter (see 2.4) it

---

[7] *pañcorambhāgiyāni saṃyojanāni– ajjhattasaṃyojana. Pañcuddhambhāgiyāni saṃyo-janāni—bahiddhā-saṃyojana.*

[8] *ajjhattanti kāmabhavo. Bahiddhāti rūpārūpabhavo.*

was shown that the Commentaries have taken the *Abhidhamma* materials to describe the (*Mahā*)-*satipaṭṭhāna Sutta*-s.

By examining the *Sutta*-s, it seems that the *Dhammasaṅgaṇi* develops the ten fetters to describe the four stages and the *Vibhaṅga* mainly divides the scheme of ten fetters into lists of lower and higher fetters in its *Pañcakaniddesa*. According to the text:

> Therein what are five lower fetters belonging to lower [world]? Personality-belief, doubt, clinging to rules and vows, sensual pleasure, ill-will. These are five lower fetters belonging to lower [world]. Therein what are five higher fetters belonging to upper [world]? Desire for form, desire for formlessness, conceit, restlessness, ignorance. These are five higher fetters belonging to upper [world] (Vibh, VRI 228).[9]

Resulting from the above discussion, we propose that earlier the scheme of lower fetters could have been listed as the *pañca-samyojanāni* (five fetters) in the *Sutta*-s which is more consistent than following the *tīni-saṃyojanāni* (three fetters) and *satta-saṃyojanāni* (seven fetters). Since the *Sutta*-s do not describe the non-returner with the remaining five "higher fetters", there is less significance to the term "lower" or "lower world". Of course, it does not mean that the function of five fetters (five lower fetters) is less important. The following section will show how the *Sutta*-s explain the existence of non-returner with the "three latent tendencies", but not the "five higher fetters".

3.3 Stage of Non-returning with the Three *Anusaya*-s

This section shows that the five kinds of non-returners are born in the Pure Abodes due to not having cut off the three "latent tendencies". This section will argue that the scheme of higher fetters was given less significance in the *Nikāya*-s. Before

---

[9] *tattha katamāni pañcaorambhāgiyāni saṃyojanāni? Sakkāyadiṭṭhi, vicikicchā, sīlabbataparāmāso, kāmacchando, byāpādo–imāni pañcaorambhāgiyāni saṃyojanāni. Tattha katamāni pañcuddhambhāgiyāi saṃyojanāni? Rūparāgo, arūparāgo, māno, uddhaccaṃ, avijjā–imāni pañcuddhambhāgiyāni saṃyojanāni.*

dealing with the topic, it is required to discuss the five kinds of non-returners.

In many *Sutta*-s, the non-returner is classified into five levels. For example, the *Saṅgīti Sutta* of DN lists the five classifications of non-returner, as follows:

1. Attainer of *Nibbāna* in the interval (*antarā-pyarinibbāyin*),
2. Attainer of *Nibbāna* upon landing (*upahacca-parinibbāyin*),
3. Attainer of *Nibbāna* without exertion (*asaṃkhāra-parinibbāyin*),
4. Attainer of *Nibbāna* with exertion (*sasaṅkhāra-parinibbāyin*), and
5. One bound upstream, heading towards the Akaniṭṭha sphere (*uddhaṃsoto-akaniṭṭhagāmin*) (DN III 238).[10]

Now let us discuss how the *Sutta*-s deal with the above listed five kinds of nonreturner. In the *Sutta*-s, several methods are applied to describe them. For example, the *Dutiya Vitthāra Sutta* of the *Mahā Vagga* in SN applies the method of five spiritual faculties. The *Sutta* (SN V 201) says one who has accomplished and fulfilled the five faculties becomes an arahat. If they are weaker then he becomes an attainer of *Nibbāna* in the interval, if still weaker an attainer of *Nibbāna* upon landing, if still weaker an attainer of *Nibbāna* without exertion, etc. Another alternative method for attaining the five kinds of non-returner is found in the *Dutiya Phala Sutta* of the same *Vagga*. According to the *Sutta*, on the basis of the four spiritual bases (*iddhipāda*) some attain the sub-stages of non-returning. The four spiritual bases are:

1. Concentration due to desire and volitional formations of endeavoring
2. Concentration due to energy and volitional formations of endeavoring,

[10] Somaratne (1999, 123) lists the ten non-returners including the above five plus five more: the second *antarāparinibbāyin,* the third *antarāparinibbāyin, kāyasakkhin*, *diṭṭhippatta*, and *saddhāvimutta*.

3. Concentration due to mind and volitional formations of endeavoring, and
4. Concentration due to investigation and volitional formations of endeavoring (SN V 285).[11]

In this *Sutta*, all of these non-returners are defined with the five lower fetters. For example, the *Dutiya Phala Sutta* says when one develops these four spiritual bases he either attains final liberation early in this very life; if not he attains liberation at the time of dissolution of the body. If he does not attain final liberation in this very life, or at the time of dissolution of the body, "then with the utter destruction of the five lower fetters he becomes an attainer of *Nibbāna* in the interval...an attainer of *Nibbāna* upon landing...an attainer of *Nibbāna* without exertion...an attainer of *Nibbāna* with exertion...one bound upstream, heading towards the Akaniṭṭha realm" (SN V 285).[12]

It is noteworthy that in this definition though the passage describes the five kinds of non-returner by applying the method of the five lower fetters, no *Sutta* defines their existence by showing their remaining higher fetters. In that gap, the *Purisagati Sutta* of the *Sattaka Nipāta* (AN IV 70) specifies their existence is due to the remaining three defilements called *anusaya*-s (latent tendencies): desire for becoming (*bhava-rāga*), conceit (*māna*), and ignorance (*avijjā*). According to the *Sutta*:

> He is not delighted to becoming; not delighted to origination. He sees the highest state which is peaceful through the right wisdom, yet he has not fully achieved that state. He has not completely abandoned the latent tendency of conceit, not completely abandoned

[11] 1. *chanda-samādhi-padhāna-saṅkhāra*, 2. *viriya-samādhi-padhāna-saṅkhāra*, 3. *citta-samādhi-padhāna-saṅkhāra*, 4. *vīmaṃsā-samādhi-padhāna-saṅkhāra.*

[12] *atha pañcannaṃ orambhāgiyānaṃ saṃyojanānaṃ parikkhayā antarā parinibbāyī hoti, upahacca parinibbāyī hoti, asaṅkhāraparinibbāyī hoti, sasaṅkhāraparinibbāyī hoti, uddhaṃsoto hoti akaniṭṭhagāmī. Imesaṃ kho bhikkhave, catunnaṃ iddhipādānaṃ bhāvitattā bahulīkatattā ime sattaphalā sattānisaṃsā pāṭikaṅkhāti.*

> the latent tendency of desire for becoming, not completely abandoned the latent tendency of ignorance. With the abandonment of the five lower fetters he becomes an attainer of *Nibbāna* in the interval (AN IV 70–71).[13]

The *Sutta* (AN IV 71–72) similarly describes the remaining non-returners[14] who take birth in the Pure Abodes due to not having completely abandoned the latent tendencies of desire for becoming, conceit, and ignorance. Then the *Sutta* (AN IV 70–71) gives a simile of a heated iron bowl to describe their spans of existence in those realms.

The *Saṃyojana-puggala Sutta* of the *Catukka Nipāta* (AN II 133–35) describes the *uddhaṃsoto-akaniṭṭhagāmin* due to not having cut off the fetter that brings rebirth (*uppatti-paṭilābhika-saṃyojana*) or due to not having cut off the fetter bringing becoming (*bhava-paṭilābhika-saṃyojana*), and the *antarāparinibbāyin* who has already abandoned the *uppatti-paṭilābhika-saṃyojana,* yet needs to cut off the *bhava-paṭilābhika-saṃyojana.* By examining these two types of non-returners with their remaining fetters, Somaratne (1999, 123–24 & 143) has shown the weakness of the traditional list of ten fetters, especially the five higher fetters because the above-mentioned two fetters are not listed in the list of higher fetters. He has also found it problematic to understand the various types of non-returners taking the traditional list of ten fetters as a basis. Somaratne says:

> If we assume that the desire for form and the desire for formless states constitute the rebirth fetters [*uppatti-saṃyojana*], then there still remains the problem of identifying the existence fetters [*bhava-*

---

[13] *so bhave na rajjati. Sambhave na rajjati. Atthuttariṃ padaṃ santaṃ sammappaññāya passati. Tañca khvāssa padaṃ na sabbena sabbaṃ sacchikataṃ hoti. Tassa na sabbena sabbaṃ mānānusayo pahīno hoti. Na sabbena sabbaṃ bhavarāgānusayo pahīno hoti. Na sabbena sabbaṃ avijjānusayo pahīno hoti. So pañcannaṃ orambhāgiyānaṃ saññojanānaṃ parikkhayā antarā parinibbāyī hoti.*

[14] The *Sutta* divides non-returner so called "attainer of *Nibbāna* in the interval" into three categories: (1) attainer of *Nibbāna* in the interval, (2) attainer of *Nibbāna* in the interval, and (3) attainer of *Nibbāna* in the interval.

> *saṃyojana*]. Conversely, if we were to understand existence fetters to be the desire for form [rūpa-rāga] and the desire for formless [arūpa-rāga], then the problem of identifying the rebirth fetters would remain unsolved. We have seen that A II 133–34 states that for non-returners there still remain the fetters that bring existence (*bhava-paṭilābhika-saṃyojana*) (Somaratne, 1999, 143–44).

From the foregoing passages, it is evident that the Buddha describes the existence of non-returners differently. However, if the explanation of the *Purisagati Sutta* is considered, one can say that the seven-types of non-returners (including the *uddhaṃsoto-akaniṭṭhagāmin)* are defined as not having completely abandoned the three latent tendencies, but not the higher fetters. Davids and Stede claim that the stage of non-returning does not mean the abandoning defilements, but the cultivation of certain good mental habits such as the *anatta* doctrines and the five *indriya*-s. Davids and Stede say:

> [I]n the oldest passages referring to these 4 stages, the description of the third does not use the word anāgāmin (D i.156; ii.92; iii.107; M ii.146) and anāgāmin does not mean the breaking of bonds [*saṃyojana*], but the cultivation of certain specified good mental habits (S iii.168, the *anatta* doctrine; S v.200–02, the five *Indriyas*; A i.64, 120, cultivation of good qualities, ii 160; v.86, 171=S 149). We have only two cases in the canon of any living persons being called anāgāmin. Those are at S v.177 and 178. The word there means one who has broken the lower five of the ten bonds, & the individuals named are laymen (Davids and Stede, 1993, 39).

Their discussion shows that they have emphasized the other methods to describe the stage of non-returning. Although the *Sutta*-s with other methods do not often describe the future existence of non-returners, but with the fetter, the *Purisagati Sutta* says the non-returner is born due to not having cut off three defilements. But the Theravāda tradition says, they are born due to not having cut off the five higher fetters. From the *Sutta* and Somaratne's explanations it is obvious that the non-returner is not described by not having cut off the five fetters. The definition of non-returning with the five higher fetters is a later interpretation given by the Ābhidhammikas. Here, to support our opinion, we refer to Davids and Stede's explanation:

> At It 96 there are only 3 stages, the worldling, the Anāgāmin, and the Arahant; and the *Saṁyojanas* are not referred to. It is probable that already in the *Nikāya* period the older, wider meaning was falling into dis-use. The *Abhidhamma* books seem to refer only to the *Saṁyojana* explanation; the commentaries, so far as we know them, ignore any other. See Ps ii.194; Kv. Tr.74; Dhs. Tr.302 n; Cp.69 (Davids and Stede, 1993, 39).

3.3.1 Weakness of the Scheme Pañc'uddhambhāgiyāni Saṃyojanāni

In the foregoing section, it was shown that the non-returner is born in the Pure Abode due to not having completely abandoned the latent tendencies of *bhava-rāga, māna*, and *avijjā*. If we take the *Sutta*'s explanation, one could question the validity of the scheme of higher fetters in the *Sutta*-s. Here this fact is discussed by consulting Somaratne's opinion. According to him, the fetter *uddhacca* (restlessness) should not be in the list of higher fetters. He (1999, 144) opines one should get rid of the fetter of "restlessness" in the first two stages of stream-entry, and once-returning. About the higher fetters, Somaratne comments:

> It seems to me that the listing of "restlessness" (*uddhacca)* among the five higher fetters was first a textual corruption and then slipped into the tradition to become part of the standard list. In the place of "restlessness", it is better to read the fetter called "desire for existence". It is also possible that in the original list there were three fetters (desire for form, desire for formless, and desire for existence), and then the early redactors or copiers who understood the first two fetters as a division or expansion of the last deliberately replaced the last with restlessness (Somaratne, 1999, 144).

Included in the above passage, his argument agrees with the *Purisagati Sutta* which includes the three latent tendencies as a basis in which the "desire for existence" occurs. His argument clearly shows the weakness of the five higher fetters in the

Sutta-s. It is also possible that the copiers have divided the term *bhava-rāga* [*bhava-saṃyojana*] into two categories: *rūpa-rāga* and *arūpa-rāga*. The term *kāma-rāga* (*kāma-bhava*) appears in the list of lower fetters. As the fetter of sensual desire is destroyed by the non-returner, the two more categories of *bhava-rāga*—*rūpa-rāga* and *arūpa-rāga*—appear in the list of higher fetters.

If we take the *Purisagati Sutta*'s explanation, however, it is evident that the term *bhava-rāga* occurs to denote the existence of non-returners. From the *Sutta* evidence and Somaratne's argument, therefore, it is clear that the list of five higher fetters is modified to make a standard list of ten fetters. If it is thus, we assert that the *Saṃyojana Sutta* of the *Dasaka Nipāta* in AN which contains the ten fetters including the higher and lower schemes was later interpolated, when the standard definition of the four stages was established with the list of ten fetters. In this connection, it is possible that the doctrines of the *Dhammasaṅgaṇi* and the *Vibhaṅga* have influenced the *Sutta*-s. The *Dhammasaṅgaṇi* explains the stage of arahatship with giving up of the five defilements, in the traditional list called the five higher fetters but some scholars such as Bhikkhu Sujato and Bhikkhu Brahmali, after examining the context of the *Vibhaṅga*, say there is no *Abhidhammic* influence on the *Sutta*-s:

> Texts such as the *Vibhaṅga* of the *Abhidhamma* make it particularly clear what was the direction of these developments. The *Vibhaṅga* is divided into two parts: an analysis according to the *Suttas* and one according to the *Abhidhamma*. The *Sutta* analysis is similar to the EBTs [Early Buddhist Texts], whereas the *Abhidhamma* analysis is a new development. Since the *Sutta* material forms part of the *Abhidhamma* but the *Abhidhamma* material is not, or very rarely, found in the *Suttas*, the direction of development is unambiguous (Sujato and Brahmali, 2014, 113).

Sayadaw U Thittila says:

> It [*Vibhaṅga*] follows a particular plan but is arranged in such a way that it shows how the categories enumerated in *Dhammasaṅgaṇi* are to be applied (Thittila, 1969, xii).

From Tittila's opinion, however, we can discuss that the doctrines which are enumerated in the *Dhammasaṅgaṇi*, were further analyzed by the *Vibhaṅga*. We would say the *Vibhaṅga*'s interpretation further influenced the *Sutta*-s, especially how to define the list of ten fetters. One could assert that the doctrine of "ten fetters" was first developed in the *Dhammasaṅgaṇi*, and the *Vibhaṅga* takes them for analysis. Chapter 4 will show how the *Dhammasaṅgaṇi* describes the stage of arahatship through the eradication of five defilements (five higher fetters).

3.4 *Tīni-saṃyojanāni* and Its Functions

Tīni-saṃyojanāni is a unique term in the Pāli Canon. Throughout the Canon the term repeatedly occurs as *tīni-saṃyojanāni* (DN III 217; SN V 357; etc.). The term is defined with the three fetters: *sakkāya-diṭṭhi* (personality belief), *vicikicchā* (doubt) and *sīlabbata-parāmāsa* (clinging to rules and vows), which are listed in the traditional list of ten fetters. In the texts, the term *tīni-saṃyojanāni* describes the stage of stream-entry, and non-returning. It seems that the term receives much more attention with the stream-entry, and the non-returning than other methods for attaining them. For example, the *Tatiya Giñjakāvasatha Sutta* of the *Mahā Vagga* in SN says, the Buddha is said to have taught the stage of stream-entry, and oncereturning with the scheme of three fetters, as follows:

> With abandoning three fetters, one becomes a stream-enterer, no longer bound to the states of woe, firmly set on the path to liberation.
>
> With abandoning three fetters, and with the diminishing of greed, hatred and delusion, one becomes a once-returner who, having returned to this world only one time, will make an end of suffering (SN V 357).[15]

---

[15] *tiṇṇaṃ saṃyojanānaṃ parikkhayā sotāpanno hoti avinipātadhammo niyato sambodhi-parāyaṇo. tiṇṇaṃ saṃyojanānaṃ parikkhayā rāgadosamohānaṃ tanuttā sakadāgāmī hoti sakideva imaṃ lokaṃ āgantvā dukkhassantaṃ karoti.*

In the above passages, the three fetters are included in both stream-entry and once-returning but the once-returner is one who has reduced greed (*lobha*), hatred (*dosa*) and delusion (*moha*) along with the complete destruction of the three fetters. The *Ekaka Nipāta* of AN divides the stream-enterer with the three fetters into the three sub-categories:

> With abandoning three fetters, one becomes an attainer seven lives-at-most, after transmigrating and wandering on among devas and human, makes an end of suffering. With abandoning three fetters, one becomes an attainer in clan-to-clanner, after transmigrating and roaming on among good families two or three times, makes an end of suffering. With abandoning three fetters, one becomes one-seed attainer, after being re-becoming in human realm one more time, makes an end of suffering (AN I 233 & IV 381).[16]

In the *Ekabīji Sutta* of the *Mahāvagga* (SN V 204) the one-seed attainer (*ekabījī*) is described as one who has completed and fulfilled the five faculties of faith, energy, mindfulness, concentration, and wisdom. Comparing both *Sutta*-s, it is evident the seed-attainer is defined not only with the fetters, but also with the five faculties. But the discrepancy remains with the numbers of existence. The *Sutta*-s also do not show how many defilements, a one-seed attainer has to reduce together with the destruction of the three fetters for future existence. The passage also shows a one-seed attainer to be very similar to once-returner as he also takes birth one more time in this world. In this regard, Wen has compared the one-seed attainer and once-returner with the *Sutta*-s and the *Abhidharmakośaśāstra*. Wen says:

> The *Abhidharmakośaśāstra* (Jushe-lun) (T 29, no.1558) includes the one-seeder in the category of the once-returner, and allows it a higher status than the once-returner in general. Thus, it seems to me

[16] *so tiṇṇaṃ saṃyojanānaṃ parikkhayā sattakkhattuparamo hoti: sattakkhattu-paramaṃ deve ca manusse ca sandhāvitvā saṃsaritvā dukkhassantaṃ karoti. So tiṇṇaṃ saññojanānaṃ parikkhayā kolaṅkolo hoti: dve vā tīṇi vā kulāni sandhāvitvā saṃsaritvā dukkhassantaṃ karoti. So tiṇṇaṃ saññojanānaṃ parikkhayā ekabījī hoti: ekaññeva mānusakaṃ bhavaṃ nibbattetvā dukkha-ssantaṃ karoti.*

> that the way the Sarvāstivāda understands the relationship between once-returner and one-seeder is more logical than Pāli sources (Wen, 2009, 35).

Numerous *Sutta*-s (DN I 156, II 93, 200, 252, III 107, etc.; MN I 34, 141, 227, etc.; SN V 357, 360, 406, etc.) also define the stage of stream-entry through the eradication of three fetters. In the Pāli Canon, this definition becomes a standard formula.

3.5 *Sabba-saṃyojanāni* and Its Functions

Several *Sutta*-s (SN I 251, 191; MN II 199) contain the term *sabba-saṃyojanāni* (all fetters)[17] to describe final liberation but, the term is rarely found in the prose version of the *Nikāya*-s, only in verse. For example, the *Patta Sutta* of the *Sagātha Vagga* in SN includes *sabba-saṃyojanāni* in a verse, as follows:

> When one is detached, secure,
> He has gone beyond all fetters [*sabba-saṃyojana*];
> Though Māra and his army seek him everywhere
> They do not find him (SN I 112).[18]

According to the verse, the term *sabba-saṃyojana* refers to one who has cut off all fetters. The Commentarial explanation of all fetters refers to the ten kinds of fetters (Sv, Vāseṭṭhasuttavaṇṇana, 458),[19] but the Commentary does not give any further elaboration. If we take the Commentarial explanation into account, the ten fetters are either traditional, or the *Abhidhamma* list of ten fetters.[20] Referring to the *Sutta*-s in which the term appears, one may propose that the term may

---

[17] The term occurs in the *Brāhmaṇa Vagga*, Verse 26 of the *Dhammapada*, in the *Hemavata Sutta*, the *Sammāparibbājaniya Sutta*, the *Vāseṭṭha Sutta* of Sn, and in several verses contained in the *Thera Gāthā*, i.e., verse in the *Vasabhatthera Gātha*, the *Bhāradvājatthera Gāthā*, the *Kātiyānatthera Gāthā*, etc.

[18] *evaṃ virattaṃ khemattaṃ sabba-saṃyojanātigaṃ / anvesaṃ sabbaṭhānesu mārasenāpi nājjhagāti.*

[19] *sabbasaṃyojananti dasavidhasaṃyojanaṃ.*

[20] The *Kathāvatthu* (VRI 128) of the *Abhidhamma Piṭaka* says the all fetters are "ten fetters" which are enumerated in the *Abhidhamma*.

have been used in the earlier phase of the Buddha's teachings, because it appears in some verses of Sn and the *Sagātha Vagga* of SN. Several scholars have pointed (see 2.3.1) out that some *Sutta*-s of Sn and *Sagātha Vagga* are earlier doctrines and have a close relationship with each other. The term only describes final liberation regardless of any spiritual stages. It seems that the Buddha did not refer to any particular list of fetters, but all other unwholesome things are connected to the fetters.

3.6 Interpretation of the Concept of Rebirth with Fetters

The above discussion has shown the attainment of spiritual stages with giving up fetters in the *Nikāya*-s. When the methods for attaining the spiritual stages without fetters are available, why is the method with fetter prevalent throughout the Pāli Canon? Investigating the *Nikāya*-s, now an attempt is made to illuminate the topic.

It seems that the method for achieving the stages of enlightenment with giving up fetters is to illustrate the Buddhist ideas of rebirth. According to Buddhism, rebirth takes place in the three realms—desire, form, and formlessness. These realms commonly define those people who take birth after death. In the *Sutta*-s, their births are due to the fetters yet to be cut off before attaining final liberation. To support this opinion, an interpretation of Hirakawa is referred to:

> It combined religious practice with Buddhist ideas of rebirth and the three realms (desire, form, and formless) into which a person might be reborn. Doctrines were thus arrived at that would accommodate those people who could not realize enlightenment during their current lifetimes (Hirakawa, 1990, 58).

There are numerous *Sutta*-s in the *Nikāya*-s where the example of rebirth into the three realms occurs. The texts have given a very clear explanation of how fetters are connected to rebirth. Many *Sutta*-s contain passages when people have died, the Buddha declared their future destinations based on the degree of their fetters. For example, the *Giñjakāvasatha Sutta* of the

Mahāvagga in SN says the Buddha describes the future destinations of a monk named Sāḷha, a nun named Nandā, a male lay follower named Sudatta, and a lay female follower named Sujāta who have died. On one occasion Venerable Ānanda approached the Buddha and asked him the destinations of the above listed people. In reply, the Buddha said:

> Ānanda! The monk Sāḷha who has died, through the destruction of the taints, in this very life he had arrived and dwelt in the taintless liberation of mind, liberation by wisdom, realizing it for himself by insight with direct knowledge. The nun Nandā who has died, with abandoning the five lower fetters, had become one of the spontaneous rebirth, will there attain *Nibbāna* without returning from that world.
>
> The male lay follower Sudatta who has died, with abandoning three fetters, and with weakening of greed, hatred, and delusion, had become a once-returner, who after coming back to this world only one more time, will make an end of suffering. The female lay follower Sujātā who has died, abandoning the three fetters, had become a stream-enterer, no longer bound to the states of woe, firmly set on the path to enlightenment (SN V 356–57).[21]

This passage is also recorded in the *Mahāparinibbāna Sutta* of DN 16, II 92. It seems that the *Giñjakāvasatha Sutta* of SN and DN 16 share similar contents and model of the passages becomes a common formula to define the future destinations of departed people.

In the above passages, however, one may ask why the Buddha so willingly declared the future destinations of departed people. The *Janavasabha Sutta* of DN is consulted as an

[21] *Sāḷho Ānanda, bhikkhu kālakato, āsavānaṃ khayā anāsavaṃ cetovimuttiṃ paññāvimuttiṃ diṭṭheva dhamme sayaṃ abhiññā sacchikatvā upasampajja vihāsi. Nandā ānanda, bhikkhunī kālakatā pañcannaṃ orambhāgiyānaṃ saṃyojanānaṃ parikkhayā opapātikā tattha parinibbāyinī anāvattidhammā tasmālokā.*

Sudatto ānanda, upāsako kālakato tiṇṇaṃ saṃyojanānaṃ parikkhayā rāgadosamohānaṃ tanuttā sakadāgāmī sakideva imaṃ lokaṃ āgantvā dukkhassantaṃ karissati. Sujātā ānanda, upāsikā kālakatā tiṇṇaṃ saṃyojanānaṃ parikkhayā sotāpatti avinipātadhammā niyatā sambodhiparāyaṇā.

example. According to the *Sutta* (DN II 200), on one occasion the Buddha declared the rebirth of numerous people of Kāsi and Kosala, Vajji and Malla, Nādikā, etc. on the basis of their level of remaining fetters. Later, when this news reached the ears of the devotees in Nādikā they were pleased to know their relatives' achievement of such and such spiritual stages. Moreover, in the *Sarākāni Sutta* of the *Mahā Vagga* (SN V 375–78), even the Buddha is said to have taught that if any person does not possess confirmed confidence in the Buddha, the Dhamma, and the Saṅgha, but he has sufficient faith in the Tathāgata, sufficient devotion to him, and has the five spiritual faculties of faith, energy, etc., he will attain the fruit of stream-entry and will not go to any states of woe.

From the foregoing passages, it is note-worthy that the Buddha has declared the future destinations of those who have obtained at least one spiritual stage. Thus, the Buddha has willingly delivered such doctrine either for emphasizing the strength of his teachings or boosting the confidence of lay people in the Buddha, the Dhamma, and the Saṅgha through which people can develop their thoughts to be enlightened. That seems a reason why the Buddha has declared the future destinations of departed people with the degree of their remaining fetters.

Out of curiosity, moreover, Ānanda sometimes approached the Buddha to ask the future destinations of departed people. As Ānanda has gone to the Buddha to ask the future destinations of people again and again, the Buddha experienced physical stress and rebuked him. Afterwards, the Buddha taught the Dhamma to Ānanda saying that if any noble person possesses confirmed confidence in the Buddha, the Dhamma and the Saṅgha, and cut off certain extent of fetters, then if he wishes he himself can declare his spiritual attainment (SN V 375–78). The evidence of self assertion of people's existence can be found in the *Vesālika-ugga Sutta* of the *Aṭṭhaka Nipāta* in AN.

The *Sutta* states a householder Ugga declares his spiritual maturity himself, saying:

> The five lower fetters taught by the Blessed One, I don't see any of that I haven't given up. Bhante! This is the eighth amazing and marvelous characteristic found in me (AN IV 211).[22]

3.6.1 Upādisesa and Saṃyojana in the Context of Rebirth

This section discusses the concepts of *upādisesa* (residue remaining) and *saṃyojana* both of which are reasons for rebirth in Buddhist teachings. It seems that the interpretation of the concept of rebirth with fetters has grown from the concept of *upādisesa*. Before dealing with this topic, let us discuss what *upādisesa* refers to. Hwang clarifies the term *upādisesa* in the context of *Nibbāna*, as follows:

> If we take *upādi* in *upādisesa* to mean 'fuel', the objective meaning of *upādāna*, we can easily understand what *upādisesa* means in the context of nirvana. What is called nirvana with a remainder of clinging [*saupādisesa*] is, as mentioned before, the state where the above triple fire [greed, hatred, and delusion] is extinguished yet the fuel, the aggregates, is still remaining; whereas nirvana without a remainder of clinging [*anupādisesa*] is the state where there is no more fuel, the aggregates, left. Since there are no more rebirths in this state, it can also be regarded as going out or extinction (Hwang, 2006, 20).

Keeping aside the above clarification of the term *upādi* as the object meaning of *upādāna*, in this study, we take it as residue or alternative term as defilement. As many *Sutta*-s describe the future destinations of people with residue remaining which still needs to be cut off to attain final liberation. For example, the *Satisūpaṭṭhita Sutta* of the *Pañcaka Nipāta* (AN III 143) says if any monk or nun develops and cultivates five things, he will attain final knowledge in this very life or, if there is a residue

---

[22] *bhagavatā desitāni pañcorambhāgiyāni saṃyojanāni, nāhaṃ tesaṃ kiñci attani appahīnaṃ samanupassāmīti. Ayaṃ kho me bhante, aṭṭhamo acchariyo abbhuto dhammo saṃvijjati.*

remaining (*upādisesa*) he will attain the state of non-returning. In the *Sutta*-s, the five things are:

1. Establishment of mindfulness for gaining the wisdom that perceives the arising and passing away of phenomena (*ajjhattaṃ yeva sati sūpaṭṭhitā hoti, dhammānaṃ udayatthagāminiyā paññāya*),
2. Contemplation on the unattractiveness of the body (*asubhānupassī kāye viharati*),
3. Perceiving the repugnance of food (*āhāre paṭikkkūlasaññi*),
4. Perceiving non-delight in the entire world (*sabbaloke anabhiratasaññī*), and
5. Contemplation to the impermanence in all conditioned phenomena (*sabbasaṃkhāresu aniccānupassī*).

In the *Sopādisesa Sutta* of the *Navaka Nipāta* (AN IV 378–82) the Buddha is said to have described nine types of Noble Persons with *sa-upādisesa* (with residue remaining). The nine types of Noble Persons are: the five sub-divisions of non-returner—*antarāparinibbāyin*, *upahaccaparinibbāyin*, *asaṅkhāra-parinibbāyin*, *sasaṅkhāraparinibbāyin* and *akaniṭṭha-gāmin*; a once-returner; and three kinds of stream-enterer—*ekabījin*, *kolaṅkola* and *satta-khattuparama*. However, the way in which the *Sopādisesa Sutta* is presented has a great significance as it identifies *saupādisesa* with *saṃyojana*. According to the *Sutta,* once Venerable Sāriputta had a conversation with other sects of wanderers (*paribbājakā*). During the conversation, the wanderers asked Sāriputta:

> Friend! one who passes away with a residue remaining is not freed from hell, the animal realm, or the realm of tormented spirits, the plane of misery, the bad destination, and the state of affliction (AN IV 378).[23]

[23] *yo hi koci āvuso sopādiseso kālaṃ karoti sabbo so aparimutto nirayā, aparimutto tiracchāna-yoniyā, aparimutto pettivisayā, aparimutto apāya duggati vinipātāti.*

It is worth noting that upon listening to the wanderers' statement, Sāriputta neither enjoyed nor rejected the statement. Sāriputta then went to the Buddha and repeated the same assertion. In response, the Buddha said the nine persons, after passing away with residue remaining, were freed from hell, the animal realm, the realm of tormented spirits, etc. According to the *Sutta*, the nine persons are the five sub-divisions of non-returner, a once-returner, and three sub-divisions of stream-enterer. The *Sutta* says the residue remaining is similar to the fetters, as follows:

> When a person accomplishes the virtues and concentration, and cultivates wisdom to a certain reasonable extent, then with the abandonment of the five lower fetters, he is an attainer of *Nibbāna* in the interval. This is the first person, passing away with a residue remaining, who is freed from hell, the animal realm, or the realm of tormented spirits, the plane of misery, the bad destination, and the state of affliction (AN IV 380).[24]

The *Sutta*, moreover, describes the other eight types of Noble Persons with the method of fetters in a similar way. From the above passage it is clear that the residue remaining is identical with fetters. However, it is worth noting that the *Sutta* ends with an interesting statement which says, the Buddha had not been inclined to give this *dhamma* exposition to the monks, nuns, male lay followers, and female lay followers. The Buddha gives the following reasons:

> I was concerned that upon hearing this *dhamma* exposition, they may take to the ways of carelessness. Sāriputta! However, I have spoken this *dhamma* exposition for answering your question (AN IV 381–82).[25]

---

[24] *ekacco puggalo sīlesu paripūrakārī hoti, samādhismiṃ paripūrakārī, paññāya mattasokārī so pañcannaṃ orambhāgiyānaṃ saññojanānaṃ parikkhayā antarā parinibbāyī hoti. Ayaṃ sāriputta, paṭhamo puggalo sopādiseso kālaṃ kurumāno parimutto nirayā, parimutto tiracchānayoniyā parimutto pettivisayā parimutto apāyaduggativinipātā.*

[25] *māyimaṃ dhammapariyāyaṃ sutvā pamādaṃ āhariṃsūti, api ca mayā sāriputta dhamma-pariyāyo pañhādhippāyena bhāsitoti.*

To sum up the above discussion, we would like to say that the concept of fetters in reference to the stages of liberation mainly expand from the concept of residue remaining. The conclusion of the *Sutta* indicates that the Buddha had not taught such *dhamma* exposition to anyone, it was only spoken in answer to Sāriputta's question. Comparing the explanations (3.6) with (3.6.1), it seems to me that in the earlier phase of the teachings, the Buddha did not reveal the future destinations of departed people with reference to the remaining fetters. Later, in certain periods the statement was very common as the Buddha willingly declared the future destination of people. Not only the Buddha himself, but he also taught Venerable Ānanda that anyone can declare their future destinations depending on the degree of remaining fetters. The earlier concept of fetters could have been discussed with residue remaining which relates to the concept of rebirth. Later when the concept of fetters became very common, it was used to describe rebirth into various spheres.

In this regard, it could be a probable reason that in the *Sutta*-s, the attainment of the stage of arahatship is defined through the destruction of the taints. This definition emphasizes the fact that an arahat is enlightened in this very life, whereas the other stages are presented with fetters. This method pinpoints those who are still in certain planes of existence after their death. By saying so, we conclude that the method for attaining spiritual stages with giving up fetters mainly establishes the existential binding of rebirth. However, the four stages in this very life with fetters can also be described as psychologically binding for those who have become an arahat through the stage by stage.

Part Two

3.7 A Comparison between *Saṃyojana* and *Anusaya*

Referring to the *Purisagati Sutta* in AN, the non-returner who has completely destroyed the five lower fetters is to be born in the Pure Abodes due to not having completely cut off the three latent tendencies (*anusaya*). As the fetters and latent tendencies play a crucial role in the stage of non-returning, this section reviews them together to illuminate their relationship. This section will show how the *Abhidhamma* has set up another list of ten fetters based on the two lists of seven fetters (*satta-saṃyojanāni).* Before dealing with this topic, it is important to discuss how the *Sutta*-s discuss the functions of fetters and latent tendencies.

In the *Mahāmāluṅkya Sutta* of MN, the Buddha explains the notion of *saṃyojana* and *anusaya*[26] differently. According to this *Sutta* (MN I 433–34), when the five defilements (fetters), personality-belief, doubt, clinging to rules and vows, sensual pleasure, and ill-will, exist in an infant, they are at a latent level. On the other hand, when the five defilements exist in a mature person, they are fetters. Why are they fetters? Because an ordinary person when untaught, has no regard for Noble Persons, has no regard for true men and is undisciplined in the Dhamma, abides by the personality-belief, and he does not understand it, does not escape from the arisen personality-belief, and when the personality-belief has become habitual and is uneradicated it is called fetter of personality-belief. Similarly, the other remaining four fetters of the five lower fetters are described.

From the discussion, it is evident that there is a specific distinction between the notion of "fetter" and "latent tendency". But it should be understood that the latent tendencies in a child are only present in a latent state and they become active only as he grows up and circumstances are conducive for their appearance at a grosser level. From the example, it is understood that a non-returner's desire of becoming, conceit and ignorance are at latent level. Their latent tendencies will not be intensified because they have completely eradicated the five lower fetters. It is worth noting that the *Mahāmāluṅkya Sutta* refers to the five lower fetters as five latent tendencies when these are at a

[26] Etymologically, *anusaya* is derived from anu + √*si* ('lie down', or 'sleep'). According to Dhammajoti (2015, 366), "[T]he function of *anusaya* is growing or intensifying in accord with an impure object."

latent level. However, the traditional scheme of *anusaya*-s consists of a list of seven latent tendencies in which the term *sīlabbata-parāmāsa-anusaya* (latent tendency of clinging to rules and vows) is omitted. That could be a reason that the function of *sīlabbata-parāmāsa* is included in *sakkāya-diṭṭhi* or *diṭṭhi-anusaya* as both exist due to wrong view.

According to the *Anusaya Sutta* of the *Anusaya Vagga* (AN IV 8), there are seven *anusaya*-s (latent tendencies). They are: (1) sensual desire (*kāma-rāga*), (2) hatred (*paṭigha*), (3) view (*diṭṭhi*), (4) doubt (*vicikicchā*), (5) conceit (*māna*), (6) desire for becoming (*bhava-rāga*), and (7) ignorance (*avijjā*).

A similar set of seven fetters are found in the *Satta-saññojana Sutta* of the *Sattaka Nipāta* in AN which are identical to the list of seven latent tendencies. For example: (1) compliance / lust (*anunaya*), (2) hatred (*paṭigha*), (3) views (*diṭṭhi*), (4) doubt (*vicikicchā*), (5) conceit (*māna*), (6) desire for becoming (*bhava-rāga*), and (7) ignorance (*avijjā*) (AN IV 7).[27] According to the *Sutta,* the list of seven fetters defines liberation, as:

> Monks! When a monk has abandoned the fetter of compliance... hatred...views...doubt...conceit...desire for becoming... ignorance, uprooted them, made like a palm stump, demolished them so that there is no more subject to future arising, he is then called a monk who has cut off craving, stripped off the fetter, and by completely breaking through conceit, made an end of suffering (AN IV 8).[28]

The *Saññojana Sutta* and the *Macchariya-saṃyojana Sutta* in AN also record another scheme of seven fetters: (1) compliance /

---

[27] The list is also found in the *Saṅgīti Sutta* at DN III 254. The reference to this scheme is also found in the *Vibhaṅga* of the *Abhidhamma Piṭaka* (Vibh VRI 2015).

[28] *yato ca kho bhikkhave bhikkhuno anunayasaññojanaṃ... paṭighasaññojanaṃ... diṭṭhi-saññojanaṃ... vicikicchāsaññojanaṃ... mānasaññojanaṃ... bhavarāgasaññojanaṃ...avijjās aññojanaṃ pahīnaṃ hoti ucchinnamūlaṃ tālāvatthukataṃ anabhāvakataṃ āyati anuppādadhammaṃ, ayaṃ vuccati bhikkhave, bhikkhu acchecchi taṇhaṃ, vāvattayi saññojanaṃ, sammā mānābhi-samayā antamakāsi dukkhassāti.*

lust (*anunaya*),[29] (2) hatred, (3) views, (4) doubt, (5) conceit, (6) envy (*issā*), and (7) selfishness (*macchariya*) (AN IV 8).[30]

Scrutinizing the above two lists of seven fetters, one point is important to add. Though the function of the scheme of seven fetters has great significance with regard to the attaining of liberation, the *Sutta*-s give less attention to it but the *Abhidhamma* gives them more value as among the ten fetters of the *Abhidhamma* list, the nine fetters are parallel with the above first list of seven fetters and two more fetters, envy (*issā*), and selfishness (*machariya*), from the second list. Only the fetter of clinging to rules and vows (*sīlabbata-parāmāsa)* is excluded. The *Abhidhamma* (Dhs VRI 166) list of ten fetters is given, for example: The fetters of sensuality (*kāma-rāga)*, hatred (*paṭigha)*, conceit (*māna)*, view (*diṭṭhi)*, doubt (*vicikicchā)*, clinging to rules and vows (*sīlabbata-parāmāsa*), desire for becoming (*bhava-rāga)*, envy (*issā)*, selfishness (*macchariya*), and ignorance (*avijjā*).

Moreover, it seems that the Sanskrit *Abhidharma* set up the list of nine fetters based on the schemes of seven fetters recorded in AN. It is worth noting that, the *Abhidharma* maintains the term *anunaya-saṃyojana* in its list. For example:

> The fetters of lust (*anunaya*), hostility, conceit, ignorance, views, irrational adherence (*parāmarśa*), doubt, jealousy and avarice (Dhammajoti, 2015, 367).

Hirakawa (1990, 202–03) says, from the *anusaya*-s the list of nine fetters was developed in the Sarvāstivāda *Abhidharma* but when we compare both lists of seven fetters, it is clear that the Sarvāstivāda *Abhidharma* list of nine fetters has a closer

[29] The fetter of compliance (*anunaya-saññojana)* recorded in both lists is an unusual fetter as it does not come under any of other lists of fetters. Referring to the Commentarial explanation on the *Sutta,* Bodhi (*Numerical Discourses of the Buddha*, 1772) says the term *anunaya-saññojana* has equal meaning as *kāma-rāga-saṃyojana* (fetter of sensual desire). But, the term *anunaya-saññojana* is used instead of *kāmarāga-saṃyojana* in the Sanskrit *Abhidharma* list of nine fetters, (Dhammajoti, 2015, 367).

[30] *issā* and *macchariya* fetters are also referenced by passing in the *Sakkapañha Sutta* (DN II 277).

connection with both traditional lists of seven fetters than the list of latent tendencies.

Comparing the Pāli and Sanskrit *Abhidharma*-s, it is evident that the lists of seven fetters recorded in the *Sutta*-s are important in the formation of the lists of fetters in the Pāli *Abhidhamma* and the Sanskrit *Abhidharma* respectively. It seems that there is a doctrinal similarity between the Pāli *Abhidhamma* and the Sanskrit *Abhidharma* with regard to the concept "fetter". More on the fetters and latent tendencies will be discussed under the discussion on fetters in the *Paṭisambhidāmagga* in Chapter 4.

Part Three

3.8 The Central Method for Achieving Liberation

In this chapter, part one has surveyed the method for attaining liberation with giving up fetters. This part shows how an ordinary person could attain liberation by exercising different methods, without applying the method "fetter". There are numerous *Sutta*-s in the *Nikāya*-s where the four stages are shown without fetters. Taking examples from the *Sutta*-s, it would be demonstrated that the methods without fetters are awakening techniques mainly emphasizing the four stages of final liberation in this very life, and the method with giving up fetters is mainly describing rebirth. Before dealing with this topic, it is necessary to examine how liberation is defined in Buddhism.

Liberation requires an understanding of suffering (*dukkha*), the First Noble Truth, in the broadest sense of the term. From the outset, Buddhism is explicit about liberation, *Nibbāna*, which is free from all *dukkha*-s. The freeing from *dukkha*-s means the eradication of craving (*taṇhā*), which is identified as the root cause of suffering. This is the central method for achieving liberation presented in the early discourses of the *Nikāya*-s. For example, the *Dhammacakkappavattana Sutta*[31] of the *Mahāvagga* in SN states:

[31] According to Sujato (2012, 37), the *Dhammacakkappavattana Sutta* is the first discourse among others in Buddhist teachings. See previous chapter (see 2.5.1).

> This is the noble truth of the origin of suffering: the craving which leads to future becoming, accompanied by delight and lust, seeking delight here and there; that is, craving for sensual pleasures, craving for becoming, craving for non-becoming (SN V 421).[32]

The following passage explains ways leading to the cessation of suffering known as the "Middle Path" (*majjhimā paṭipadā*) which is eightfold: right view (*sammā-diṭṭhi*), right thought (*sammā-saṅkappa*), right speech (*sammā-vācā*), right action (*sammā-kammanta*), right livelihood (*sammā-ājīva)*, right effort (*sammā-vāyāma*), right mindfulness (*sammā-sati*), and right concentration (*sammā-samādhi*). Though liberation occurs when all eightfold path factors, some *Sutta*-s in the *Nikāya*-s, for example, AN II 220 contains a tenfold path. In addition to the eightfold path, two extra things, right knowledge (*sammā-ñāṇa*) and right liberation (*sammā-vimutti*) are added. In the *Mahācattārīsaka Sutta* (MN III 76), the Buddha mentions these two things saying that when in one of right concentration is established, right knowledge comes into being, and when in one of right knowledge is established, right liberation comes into being. According to the same *Sutta*, the path of the disciple in higher training possesses eightfold path, and the arahat possesses tenfold path. About the tenfold path, however, scholars give different opinions. For example, in the *Encyclopedia of Indian Philosophies*: *Abhidharma Buddhism to 150 A.D.* Vol VII, Karl H. Potter says the tenfold enumeration occurs over sixty times in the first four *Nikāya*-s of the *Sutta Piṭaka*, mostly in AN. Potter summarizes his discussion:

> The eightfold path concludes with "right concentration," i.e. cultivation of the meditative states *via* tranquility, whereas this tenfold listing seems to suggest that insight is the ultimate spiritual cultivation. One passage states specially that this tenfold path is the path of the arahat and is superior to the eightfold path, which is the path of the learner (Potter, 1996, 55).

In contrast, Christopher W. Gowans (2003, 162) in his *Philosophy of the Buddha*: *An Introduction*, says, "these

[32] *idaṃ..., dukkhasamudayaṃ ariyasaccaṃ: yāyaṃ taṇhā ponobhavikā nandirāgasahagatā tatra tatrā-bhinandinī, seyyathīdaṃ: kāmataṇhā bhavataṇhā vibhavataṇhā.*

additional steps do not seem to add anything of great substance, and the Buddha almost always spoke of the eight." Moreover, Mun-keat Choong in the *The Fundamental Teachings of Early Buddhism: A Comparative Study*, comments:

> This difference does not represent a doctrinal divergence, since other discourses show that cultivation of the noble eightfold path and the elimination of craving are identified in both collections as means to the cessation of feeling of suffering (Choong, 2000, 118).

Besides, the content of the above-eightfold path is summarized as the threefold training (*tisso sikkhā*): training in the higher virtuous behavior (*adhisīla-sikkhā*), training in the higher mind (*adhicitta-sikkhā*), and training in the higher wisdom (*adhipaññā-sikkhā*) (AN I 231). The *Cūḷavedalla Sutta* (MN I 301) categorizes the eightfold path into threefold aggregates (*tayo-khandhā*), as follows:

1. The aggregate of virtue (*sīla-khandha*): right speech, right action, and right livelihood;
2. The aggregate of concentration (*samādhi-khandha*): right effort, right mindfulness, and right concentration; and
3. The aggregate of wisdom (*paññā-khandha*): right view and right intention.

The *Mahāparinibbāna Sutta* of DN records that while the Buddha was staying at Koṭigāma, he gave a comprehensive discourse on virtue (*sīla*), concentration (*samādhi*), and wisdom (*paññā*). The Buddha says:

> This is virtue, this is concentration, this is wisdom. When concentration is fully developed by virtue, it brings great fruit and profit. When wisdom is fully developed by concentration, it brings great fruit and profit. When the mind is fully developed in wisdom, it becomes completely free from the taint of lust, the taint of becoming, taint of ignorance. (MN II 91)[33]

---

[33] *iti sīlaṃ, iti samādhi, iti paññā sīlaparibhāvito samādhi mahapphalo hoti mahānisaṃso. Samādhiparibhāvitā paññā mahapphalā hoti mahānisaṃsā. Paññāparibhāvitaṃ cittaṃ sammadeva āsavehi vimuccati, seyyathīdaṃ: kāmāsavā bhavāsavā avijjāsavā'ti.*

From the above passage, it is obvious that through the training of *sīla, samādhi* and *paññā* one could gradually attain liberation. This threefold scheme is identical to the Eightfold Path (including the scheme of Four Noble Truths) and subsumes the entire teaching of the Buddha, ranging from the analysis of the unsatisfactory condition of human existence to liberation. In the same *Sutta*, the Buddha says one can attain final liberation by understanding and penetrating the Four Noble Truths. With this method, the Buddha delineates liberation as "craving of becoming has been cut off, the renewed becoming has been destroyed, there is no more re-becoming" (MN II 90).[34]

From the above discussion, by understanding and penetrating the Four Noble Truths, final liberation can be understood. With this method though final liberation is clearly explained, the methods for achieving the four hierarchical stages of liberation are contextually different. These are elaborated in the following section.

3.9 Different Methods to Attain the Four Stages without Fetters

According to the *Kāyagatāsati Vagga* of the *Ekaka Nipāta* in AN, the Buddha is said to have described whoever develops and cultivates mindfulness (*sati*) can achieve one of the four stages:

> The mindfulness is the one thing that, when one developed and cultivated, leads to realization of the fruit of stream-entry... to realization of the fruit of once-returning...to realization of the fruit of non-returning...to realization of the fruit of arahatship (AN I 44–45).[35]

Another explanation of the four stages is given in the *Macchariya Sutta* of the *Pañcaka Nipāta* in AN. Having

[34] *ucchinnā bhavataṇhā, khīṇā bhavanetti. Natthidāni punabbhavo'ti.*

[35] *kāyagatā sati...ekadhammo bhāvito bahulīkato sotāpattiphala-sacchikiriyāya saṃvattati...sakadāgāmi-phalasacchikiriyāya saṃvattati...anāgāmiphala-sacchikiriyāya saṃvattati...arahatta-phalasacchikiriyāya saṃvattati.*

abandoned five things of selfishness (*macchariya*) with regard to dwellings (*āvāsa*), families (*kula*), gains (*lābha*), praise (*vaṇṇa*), and the Dhamma (*dhamma*) "one realizes the fruit of stream-entry... the fruit of once-returning...the fruit of non-returning... the fruit of arahatship" (AN III 273).[36] In the *Anicca*, *Dukkha*, *Anatta Sutta*-s, and the *Nibbāna Sutta* of the *Chakka Nipāta* in AN, it is said that insight into the impermanent, suffering and non-self nature of all conditioned phenomena, and considering *Nibbāna* to be happiness, one could attain the four stages:

> When a monk considers all conditioned phenomena to be impermanent...to be suffering...to be non-self...*Nibbāna* to be happiness, he will possess a conviction in accordance [with them]. When he possesses a conviction in accordance [with them], he will enter upon the fixed course of rightness. When he will enter upon the fixed course of rightness, he will realize the fruit of stream-entry or the fruit of once-returning or the fruit of non-returning, or the fruit of arahatship (AN III 441–43).[37]

Yet in the *Indriyasaṃyutta* of the *Mahāvagga* in SN, a further scheme of the four stages is used to describe the varying strengths of five faculties: faith (*saddhā*), energy (*viriya*), mindfulness (*sati*), concentration (*samādhi*), and wisdom (*paññā*). According to the *Sutta*, with the five faculties one determines the stage where a practitioner is along the path towards liberation.

> One who has accomplished and fulfilled these five faculties he is an arahat. If they are weaker than that, he is an attainer of *Nibbāna* in the interval; if still weaker an attainer of *Nibbāna* upon landing, if

[36] *ime...pañca dhamme appahāya abhabbo sotāpattiphalaṃ sacchikātuṃ... sakadāgāmiphalaṃ sacchikātuṃ...anāgāmiphalaṃ sacchikātuṃ...arahattaphalaṃ sacchikātuṃ.*

[37] *so vata...bhikkhu sabbasaṅkhāraṃ aniccato...dukkhato...anattato...nibbānaṃ sukhato...samanupassanto anulomikāya khantiyā samannāgato bhavissatī'ti ṭhānametaṃ vijjati. Anulomikāya khantiyā samannāgato sammattaniyāmaṃ okkamissatīti ṭhānametaṃ vijjati. Sammattaniyāmaṃ okkamamāno sotāpatti phalaṃ vā sakadāgāmiphalaṃ vā anāgāmiphalaṃ vā arahattaṃ vā sacchikarissatīti ṭhānametaṃ vijjatīti.*

still weaker an attainer of *Nibbāna* without exertion; if still weaker an attainer of *Nibbāna* with exertion; if still weaker he is bound upstream towards the Akaniṭṭha realm; if still weaker a non-returner; if still weaker a once-returner; if still weaker a stream-enterer; if still weaker a Dhamma-follower; if still weaker a faith-follower (SN V 201).[38]

The above passage represents the methods for attaining final liberation. It should be noted that the four stages here are not defined with giving up "fetters", but rather with some awakening methods. The following section will show some other passages from the *Nikāya*-s which discuss the methods for attaining liberation through the destruction of the taints (*āsava*). In the *Mahāsīhanāda Sutta* of MN, the Buddha is said to have defined liberation through the destruction of taints:

> Sāriputta! I understand *Nibbāna*, and the path and way leading to *Nibbāna*. I also understand how one has entered this path, by realizing for himself with direct knowledge, here and now enter upon and abide in the liberation of mind, liberation by wisdom that are taintless with the destruction of taints (MN I 73–74).[39]

In the *Sutta*-s, one way to eliminate taints is presented through the practice of *jhāna*-s. For example, the *Aṭṭhakanāgara Sutta* of MN says:

> Here is the case when a monk quite secluded from sensual pleasures, secluded from unwholesome states, he enters upon and remains in the first *jhāna*, which is accompanied by direct thought and evaluation, with rapture and pleasure. He considers this and

---

[38] *pañcannaṃ indriyānaṃ samattā paripūrattā arahaṃ hoti. Tato mudutarehi antarā parinibbāyī hoti. Tato mudutarehi upahacca parinibbāyī hoti. Tato mudutarehi asaṅkhāra parinibbāyī hoti. Tato mudutarehi sasaṅkhāra parinibbāyī hoti. Tato mudutarehi uddhaṃsoto hoti akaniṭṭhagāmī. Tato mudutarehi sakadāgāmī hoti. Tato mudutarehi sotāpanno hoti. Tato mudutarehi dhammānusārī hoti. Tato mudutarehi saddhānusārī hotīti.*

[39] *nibbānañcāhaṃ sāriputta pajānāmi nibbānagāminñca maggaṃ nibbānagāmininīca paṭipadaṃ. Yathāpaṭipanno ca āsavānaṃ khayā anāsavaṃ cetovimuttiṃ paññāvimuttiṃ diṭṭheva dhamme sayaṃ abhiññā sacchikatvā upasampajja viharati, tañca pajānāmi.*

> understands it thus: this first *jhāna* is conditioned and volitionally produced. Now whatever is conditioned and volitionally produced is impermanent and subject to cessation. Standing upon there, he attains the destruction of taints (MN I 350).[40]

The *Sutta* (MN I 350–51), moreover, teaches the methods of the second *jhāna,* the third *jhāna*, and the fourth *jhāna* "with the stilling of applied and sustained thought," "with the padding away as well as rapture," and "with the abandoning of pleasure and pain," a monk attains liberation through the destruction of taints. The *Chabbisodhana Sutta* (MN III 36) similarly states through the development of the four *jhāna*-s there arises the knowledge of destruction of the taints which leads to liberation.

Now we shall discuss the attainment of the spiritual stage of stream-entry in various ways without fetters. The *Khandhasaṃyutta* of the *Khandha Vagga* in SN says whoever understands the five aggregates as they really are in terms of the "arising and the passing away, the gratification, the danger, and the deliverance in the group of the five aggregates of clinging, he is called a noble disciple who is a stream-enterer" (AN III 160–61).[41] In the *Indriyasaṃyutta* of the *Mahāvagga* in SN, the stream-enterer is presented through the six faculties including eye, ear, nose, tongue, body, and mind. The *Sutta*-s state when a noble disciple understands "as they really are the gratification, the danger, and the deliverance in the case of these six faculties, he is called a noble disciple who is a stream-enterer" (SN V 205).[42]

---

[40] *idha...bhikkhu vivicceva kāmehi vivicca akusalehi dhammehi savitakkaṃ savicāraṃ vivekajaṃ pītisukhaṃ paṭhamaṃ jhānaṃ upasampajja viharati. So iti paṭisañcikkhati. Idampi kho paṭhamaṃ jhānaṃ abhisaṅkhataṃ abhisañcetayitaṃ, yaṃ kho pana kiñci abhisaṅkhataṃ abhisañcetayitaṃ tadaniccaṃ nirodhadhammanti pajānāti. So tattha ṭhito āsavānaṃ khayaṃ pāpuṇāti, no ce āsavānaṃ khayaṃ pāpuṇāti.*

[41] *ariyasāvako imesaṃ pañcannaṃ upadānakkhandhānaṃ samudayañca atthagamañaca assādañca ādīnavañca nissaraṇañca yathābhūtaṃ pajānanti. Ayaṃ vuccati bhikkhave, ariyasāvako sotāpanno.*

[42] *imesaṃ channaṃ indriyānaṃ samudayañca atthagamañca assādañca ādīnavañca nissaraṇañca yathā-bhūtaṃ pajānāti. Ayaṃ vuccati bhikkhave, ariyasāvako sotāpanno.*

According to the *Sāriputta Sutta* of the *Mahā Vagga* in SN, the stage of stream-entry is explained with the Noble Eightfold Path as: "One who possesses the Eight Noble Path is a stream-enterer..." (SN V 348).[43] In the *Rāja Sutta* of *Sotāpattisaṃyutta* of the *Mahā Vagga* (SN V 343), the Buddha is said to have taught his disciples that the four factors of stream-entry in such a way that whoever possesses these factors could declare himself a stream-enterer. The four factors are: who possesses confirmed confidence in the Buddha, the Dhamma, the Saṅgha, and the virtues dear to noble ones. In addition, numerous *Sutta*-s of the *Sotāpatti-saṃyutta* of the *Mahā Vagga* in SN present alternative methods for attaining stream-entry. For example, when one develops and cultivates four practices he becomes streamenterer. The four practices are: "association with superior persons (*sappurisasaṃseva*), hearing the true *Dhamma* (*saddhammassavana*), careful attention (*yonisomanasikāra*), practice in accordance with the *Dhamma* (*dhammānudhammappaṭipatti*)" (SN V 410).[44] This passage also claims that these four practices lead to the stage of non-returning "when these four things are developed and cultivated one leads to the realization of the fruit of non-returning" (SN V 410).[45] Similarly this phrase also defines the fruit of once-returning, and the fruit of arahatship. According to the same *Sutta* (SN V 112), these qualities not only lead to all four fruits of the spiritual stages, but also they bring one to the fulfilment of the various potentialities of wisdom.

The foregoing passages have surveyed different methods for attaining the four stages of liberation without fetters. They have shown different qualities and characteristics of the four stages. In summary, we opine that there are many different methods for attaining final liberation in the *Nikāya*-s. But,

---

43 *iminā ariyena aṭṭhaṅgikena maggena samannāgato. Ayaṃ vuccati sotāpanno.*

44 *sappurisasaṃsevo saddhammasavanaṃ yonisomanasikāro dhammānudhammapaṭipatti.*

45 *ime kho..., cattāro dhammā bhāvitā bahulīkatā sakadāgāmiphalasacchikiriyāya saṃvattant ti.*

regardless of other methods shown in the above sections, the method with giving up fetters is prevalent throughout the Pāli Canon. This method mainly describes the rebirth of people on the basis of their level of remaining fetters.

In the above section, we have shown evidences to support our opinion. The other methods are the awakening techniques by which one can destroy all defilements including fetters, bonds, taints, etc. But the Theravāda tradition mainly accepts the method with fetters to define the four stages of liberation to show the existential binding. This binding has been systematically presented by applying fetters in the *Abhidhamma*. The next chapter will show how the *Abhidhamma* present the four stages with the method of ten fetters.

3.10 Conclusion

This chapter has shown the methods for attaining the spiritual stages with fetters and without fetters. The methods without fetters are connected to the understanding and penetration of the Four Noble Truths including the Eightfold Path, development and cultivation of mindfulness, abandoning the five things of selfishness (*macchariya*), accomplishment of the five spiritual faculties, insight into the five aggregates, insight into the impermanent, suffering and non-self nature, etc.

The method with fetters are connected to liberation through eradication of the list of three fetters, the list of five lower fetters, and the list of seven fetters. The method with the list of seven fetters is taken as a whole to describe the highest spiritual stage. Comparing this list with another list of seven fetters, and seven *anusaya*-s it is found that these lists have played an important role to set up the Pāli *Abhidhamma* scheme of ten fetters, and the Sanskrit *Abhidharma* scheme of nine fetters.

It was observed that method with fetters is more prevalent in the *Nikāya*-s than other methods listed above. In this connection, it was argued that the methods without fetters mainly emphasize the realization of the four stages in this very life. On the other hand, the method with fetters mainly concerns rebirth into various realms according to the degree of remaining fetters.

The doctrinal background to the methods with fetters shows that the traditional list of ten fetters does not entirely describe the four stages of liberation in the first four *Nikāya*-s. It was shown the stage of arahatship is described either through the utter destruction of taints (*āsava*) alone, or together with the fetter of becoming (*bhava-saṃyojana*). It was also shown that the non-returner is born in the Pure Abode due to not having cut off the three latent tendencies: *bhava-rāga-anusaya, māna-anusaya,* and *avijjā-anusaya.* The function of the higher fetters in the *Sutta*s is therefore insufficient. To support this view, reference was made to the *Purisagati Sutta* in AN, and Somaratne, Davids and Stede' opinions on the fetters. By doing so, finally, it has been proposed only the *Abhidhamma* interprets the four stages of enlightenment entirely with the traditional list of ten fetters to define the spiritual maturity of a person and the concept of rebirth in the cycle of existence, *saṃsāra*. The *Abhidhammic* interpretation of fetters will be discussed in the following chapter.

Chapter 4 – **The Development of the Concept of Fetter in the *Abhidhamma*: An Analysis**

4.1 Introduction

This chapter shows how the *Abhidhamma* has developed the traditional list of ten fetters to describe the four stages of enlightenment. To establish this argument, the discussions are arranged in the order of the *Dhammasaṅgaṇi*, the *Vibhaṅga*, the *Puggalapaññatti* and the *Kathāvatthu* of the *Abhidhamma Piṭaka*; the *Niddesa* and the *Paṭisambhidāmagga* of the *Khuddaka Nikāya*, and the *Abhidhammattha Saṅgaha*. Several scholars such as Hirakawa (1990, 128) say the *Niddesa* and the *Paṭisambhidāmagga* are "a literary stage between the *Nikāya*-s and the works of the *Abhidhamma-piṭaka*," that would make these two texts forerunners of the *Abhidhamma* literature. This study will claim that both texts, as a whole, could have not been composed before the *Abhidhamma*, but over a period of time. Although they share the *Sutta* and the *Abhidhammic* materials both texts are later *Abhidhammic*. In this study, the *Dhātukathā*, the *Yamaka*, and the *Paṭṭhāna* of the *Abhidhamma Piṭaka* are not consulted, because they do not contain much considerable descriptions about the development of fetter.

This chapter is in two parts, the first part is a brief review on the *Sutta*-s and scholars' explanations on the four stages with fetters. It aims to show that the *Dhammasaṅgaṇi* mainly develops the ten fetters to describe and systematize the four stages, stage by stage following the order of the defilements: *lobha*, *dosa*, and *moha*, or following the order of the notion of *bhava* (becoming): *kāma-bhava*, *rūpa-bhava*, and *arūpa-bhava*, on the basis of which the *Abhidhamma* doctrines have been elaborated. The text first ever describes the stage of once-returning with diminishing sensual desire (*kāma-rāga*) and ill-will (*vyāpāda/paṭigha*), and the stage of arahatship through abandoning the five defilements (higher fetters), these explanations were not found in the *Sutta*-s. This part will argue that the *Dhammasaṅgaṇi* list (*Abhidhamma* list) of ten fetters was compiled before the traditional list of ten fetters (*Sutta* list). This part will also argue that although the *Dhammasaṅgaṇi* develops the ten fetters to describe the spiritual stages, the description of them was heterogeneous with the *Sutta*-s and the *Dhammasaṅgaṇi*'s materials in the *Puggalapaññatti*. It is the *Kathāvatthu* that defines the four stages based on the *Dhammasaṅgaṇi*'s exposition and discounts the *Sutta*-s' explanation. Also, it is in that text that the functions of the "five lower fetters" and the "five higher fetters" were first together shown.

The discussion then goes on to the *Niddesa* and the *Paṭisambhidāmagga* which describe the four stages with giving up of the ten fetters and the seven latent tendencies (*anusaya*) together. It will be shown that the *Visuddhimagga* has shared the *Paṭisambhidāmagga*'s composition of the description of four stages. The discussion goes on to the *Abhidhammattha Saṅgaha* (Abhidh-s) which describes in detail the four stages with the five lower and five higher fetters. This study will propose that scholars in the Pāli tradition widely accept the Abhidh-s' explanation to define the four stages with the list of ten fetters, which I will name as the "traditional list". It will also be shown a similarity between the list of nine fetters recorded in the Abhidh-s, and the list of nine fetters found in the *Sarvāstivāda Abhidharma*.

By consulting the *Sutta* and the *Abhidhamma Piṭaka*-s together, part two shows how fetters and other defilements are synonymous. It then provides a hypothesis on why the term "fetter" is prevalent to describe the four stages, when other "terms" denoting defilements are available. This chapter ends with a discussion on how to cut off fetters to attain final liberation. Particular emphasis is given on ignorance (*avijjā*), being a root of not understanding the Four Noble Truths, and why it is placed as the last of the two lists of ten fetters.

Part One

4.2 The Four Stages with the List of Ten Fetters: A Review

Chapter 3 has examined the four stages with the method of fetters, and has proposed that the four stages with the method of fetters developed in the *Abhidhamma* period. Now this chapter turns to the *Abhidhamma* to examine how the method of fetters was used to describe the four stages. Before dealing with this topic, it is important to give a brief review on the *Sutta*-s, the *Dhammasaṅgaṇi*, and how scholars treat the four stages with fetters.

The List of Ten Fetters in AN V 17

The Five Lower Fetters	The Five Higher Fetters
(1) Personality-belief (*sakkāya-diṭṭhi*), (2) doubt (*vicikicchā*), (3) clinging to rules and vows (*sīlabbata-parāmāsa*), (4) sensual desire (*kāma-chanda*), and (5) ill-will (*vyāpāda*)	(6) desire for form (*rūpa-rāga*), (7) desire for formlessness (*arūpa-rāga*), (8) conceit (*māna*), (9) restlessness (*uddhacca*), and (10) ignorance (*avijjā*)

The Explanation in the *Sutta*-s (i.e. the *Mahāli Sutta*, DN I 156)

The stream-enterer	Through the eradication of personality-belief, doubt, and, clinging to rules and vows
The once-returner	Through the eradication of personality-belief, doubt, and clinging to rules and vows, and greatly diminishing lust (*rāga*), hatred (*dosa*), and delusion (*moha*)
The non-returner	Through the eradication of personality-belief, doubt, clinging to rules and vows, sensual desire, and ill-will
The arahat	Through the destruction of taints (*āsava*)

The Explanation in the *Dhammasaṅgaṇi* of the *Abhidhamma Piṭaka*

The stream-enterer	[R]elinquishing of the wrong view of Personality or Self, *sakkāya diṭṭhi*. In addition to *sakkāya diṭṭhi*, all other *akusala dhammas* which tend to lead to the realm of misery and woe are also simultaneously eliminated by this *Sotāpatti-magga-ñāṇa*.
The once-returner	The second stage, the *Sakadāgāmi-magga-ñāṇa*, weakens sensuous desire [*kāma-rāga*] and ill will [*vyāpāda*]. This *magga ñāṇa* also has the effect of weakening the remaining defilements as well.
The non-returner	The third stage, namely, the *Anāgāmi-magga-ñāṇa* completely roots out sensuous desire and ill will.
The arahat	The final stage, *Arahatta-magga-ñāṇa*, eradicates completely the remaining five defilements, viz., desire for the Fine Material Sphere [rūpa-rāga], desire for the Non-material Sphere [*arūpa-rāga*], conceit [*māna*], restlessness [*uddhacca*] and ignorance [*avijjā*].

Online source: *Introduction to Dhammasaṅgaṇi* (1995), See also Dhs VRI 55–56.

Nyanatiloka (1952, 49–50) States

The stream-enterer	[O]ne 'becomes' free (whereas in realizing the fruition, one 'is' free) from the first 3 fetters (*saṃyojana*, q.v.) which bind beings to existence in the sensuous sphere, to wit: (1) personality-belief (*sakkāya-diṭṭhi*; s. *diṭṭhi*), (2) Skeptical doubt (*vicikicchā*, q.v.), (3) attachment to mere rules and rituals (*sīlabbata-parāmāsa*; s *upādāna*)

The once-returner	[O]ne becomes nearly free from the 4th and 5th fetters, to wit: (4) sensuous craving (*kāma-cchanda=kāma-rāga*; s. *rāga*), (5) ill-will (*vyāpāda =dosa*, s. *mūla*)
The non-returner	[O]ne becomes fully free from the above-mentioned 5 lower fetters
The arahat	[O]ne further becomes free from the 5 higher fetters, to wit: (6) craving for fine material existence (*rūpa-rāga*), (7) craving for immaterial existence (*arūpa-rāga*), (8) conceit (*māna*, q.v.), (9) restlessness (*uddhacca*, q.v.), (10) ignorance (*avijjā*, q.v.)

After analysing the above-mentioned interpretations, it is observed that the traditional list of ten fetters was not entirely used to describe the four stages in the *Sutta*-s. It is the *Dhammasaṅgaṇi* which first defines the once-returner as one who has greatly weakened sensual desire (*kāma-rāga*) and ill-will (*vyāpāda*). The *Dhammasaṅgaṇi* (Dhs VRI 55–56) says the second path (once-returning) has greatly diminished sensual desire and ill-will (*kāma-rāga-vyāpādānaṃ patanubhāvāya*); whereas the third path (non-returning) has completely put away sensual desire and ill-will (*kāma-rāga-vyāpādānam anavasesappahānāya*). On the other hand, the *Sutta*-s describe the once-returner as one who has greatly weekend lust (*rāga*), hatred (*dosa*), and delusion (*moha*) together with the complet abandoning of the first three fetters. In this regard, Hwang (2006) says the explanation of the Four Noble Persons with the traditional list of ten fetters was entirely developed in the *Abhidhamma*. According to Hwang:

> [E]xplaining the four noble persons entirely in terms of their giving up of the traditional ten fetters is a later development, within the *abhidhamma*. It is in the *Dhammasaṅgaṇi* that a once returner was first explained in this sense. It says that one attains

> the second path, a once returner, while diminishing sensual desire and ill-will (*kāmarāgavyāpādānaṃ patanubhāvāya*); whereas one attains the third path, a non-returner, while giving up sensual desire and ill-will without any remainder (*kāmarāgavyāpādānam anavasesa-ppahānāya*). This new interpretation was later applied in the *Puggalapaññatti* and also appeared in the *Dharmaskandha* in the Chinese *abhidharma* (Hwang, 2006, 27).

Observing the *Dhammasaṅgaṇi,* moreover, it is found that the text not only defines the once-returner with the diminishing sensual desire and ill-will, but also defines arahat through putting away of the five defilements called fetters. The *Dhammasaṅgaṇi* defines the fourth path (the arahatship) as one who has completely put away the desire for form (*rūpa-rāga*), desire for formlessness (*arūpa-rāga*), conceit (*māna*), restlessness (*uddhacca*), and ignorance (*avijjā*) (Dhs VRI 56).[1] But, the *Sutta*-s describe the arahat as one who has completely destroyed the taints (*āsava*).

Ven. Nyanatiloka describes the four stages with the lower and higher fetters. As will be shown below, this study proposes that although the description of four stages with giving up of the traditional ten fetters was developed in the *Abhidhamma Piṭaka*, it is the Abhidh-s which describes the four stages as Nyanatiloka observes. Regarding his explanation of the four stages, more elaboration will be given in the section "Interpretation of the Four Stages with the Ten Fetters in the *Abhidhammattha Saṅgaha*". Now it is important to examine how the *Dhammasaṅgaṇi* elaborates the concept "fetter".

4.3 Reflection on the Concept of Fetter in the *Dhammasaṅgaṇi*

The *Dhammasaṅgaṇi* is the first text among other *Abhidhamma* treatises, which develops the description of the spiritual stages with the ten defilements (fetters). This text

[1] *rūparāga-arūparāga-māna-uddhacca-avijjāya anavasesappahānāya.*

describes the stage of non-returning with the weakening sensual desire (*kāma-rāga*), and ill-will (*vyāpāda*), and the stage of arahatship with completely putting away the five defilements, or the higher fetters according to the Theravāda tradition. Now we shall discuss how the *Dhammasaṅgaṇi* interprets the four stages. Before dealing with the topic, let us identify the first text of the *Abhidhamma Piṭaka*. Potter says that the *Dhammasaṅgaṇī* is the first among other *Abhidhamma* texts:

> In the list of seven *Abhidharma* treatises accepted by Theravāda tradition the *Dhammasaṅgaṇi* stands at the head. Tradition tells us that the *Dhammasaṅgaṇi* was recited at the Second Council, held around 386 BC according to Warder. This agrees with the date assigned by Mrs. Rhys Davids in T and accepted by many other scholars, a date which would make the *Dhammasaṅgaṇi* about the oldest of the *Abhidharma* texts of either the Theravāda or Sarvāstivāda tradition. There are close connections between portions of these texts and passages in the *Vibhaṅga* and the *Puggalapaññatti*, which leads many scholars to assign all three texts to an early period (Potter, 1996, 137).

Citing the above-passage, we take the *Dhammasaṅgaṇi* as the first text among other *Abhidhamma* treatises, which systematizes the description of the four stages with giving up the defilements (fetters). However, although the text has developed the list of ten defilements (fetters), it does not use the terms *orambhāgiyāni saṃyojanāni* (the fetters belonging to lower), and *uddhambhāgiyāni saṃyojanāni* (the fetters belonging to higher). We have also observed that, apart from the term *tīni-saṃyojanāni* (three fetters) (Dhs VRI 126),[2] the text does not contain the traditional list of ten fetters. Instead, the text introduces a new set of ten fetters which is different from the traditional list. Below are both lists:

---

[2] *katame dhammā dassanena pahātabbā? Tīṇi saṃyojanāni-sakkāyadiṭṭhi, vicikicchā, sīlabbataparāmāso.*

Two Lists of Ten Fetters in the Pāli Canon

Traditional list	(1) personality-belief, (2) doubt, (3) clinging to rules and vows, (4) sensual desire, (5) ill-will, (6) desire for form, (7) desire for formlessness, (8) conceit, (9) restlessness, and (10) ignorance.
Dhammasaṅgaṇi list (Dhs, VRI 166)	(1) sensual desire (*kāma-rāga*), (2) repulsion *paṭigha*), (3) conceit (*māna)*, (4) wrong view (*diṭṭhi*), (5) doubt (*vicikicchā)*, (6) clinging to rules and vows (*sīlabbata-parāmāsa)*, (7) desire for form (*bhava-rāga)*, (8) envy (*issā*), (9) selfishness (*macchariya)*, and (10) ignorance *(avijjā).*

In chapter 3 (see 3.6), it was proposed that the traditional list of ten fetters has been interpolated in the *Abhidhamma*. Now we would like to elaborate that the *Dhammasaṅgaṇi* plays a crucial role in the definition of the four stages with the method of ten fetters. Here are our reasons:

1. In the first four *Nikāya*-s, no *Sutta* exclusively describes the four stages with the traditional list of ten fetters. In chapter 3 (see 3.2), we have referred to the *Purisagati Sutta* (AN IV 70–1) which describes the non-returner as one who has eradicated the five lower fetter, but not realized the highest stage due to not having cut off the three latent tendencies (*anusaya*): *bhava-rāga, māna,* and *avijjā*. No *Sutta* describes the non-returner as one who has not realized the highest stage due to not having cut off the five higher fetters.
2. We have shown above that the *Dhammasaṅgaṇi* first describes the once-returner with diminishing sensual desire and ill-will, the description of which is different from the *Sutta*-s. The stage of arahatship is defined through completely cutting off desire for form, desire for formlessness, conceit, restlessness, and

ignorance, the description of which was not found in the *Sutta*-s.

3. Gethin (cited by Sujato (2012, 105)) points out that many of the *mātikā*-s (matrix) in the *Abhidhamma* are construed with the *Aṅguttara* principle. He has given example of the *Dhammasaṅgaṇi* which is based on a *mātikā* of 22 dyads and 100 triads of *dhamma*-s. He says the *Dhammasaṅgaṇi* is based on the *Aṅguttara-mātikā*, and analyzes this with the *Saṃyutta-mātikā*. We observe in the section *Mātikā*, that the *Dhammasaṅgaṇi* contains the *Āsavagocchakaṃ* (Dhs VRI 134),[3] *Saṃyojanagocchakaṃ*, *Gantha-gocchakaṃ*, *Oghagocchakaṃ*, etc. which further elaborates by reference to all taints, knots and floods found in the *Sutta*-s. For example, to elaborate the taints the *Dhammasaṅgaṇi* refers to *kāma-āsava, bhava-āsava, diṭṭhi-āsava,* and *avijjā-āsava* (except *diṭṭhi-āsava,* the other three *āsava*-s are found in the *Sutta*-s). But in the *Saṃyojanagocchakaṃ*, the text does not contain the traditional list of ten fetters as appeared in AN V 17, not even the scheme of lower and higher fetters. Instead, the text introduces its own list of ten fetters which is different from the traditional list. Which means, if the traditional list of ten fetters was developed earlier in the *Sutta*-s, then the *Dhammasaṅgaṇi* would have mentioned them as taints, knots, etc.

Showing the above probable reasons, we propose that the *Dhammasaṅgaṇi* first explains the stage of arahatship with the eradication of defilements—desire for form, desire for formlessness, conceit, restlessness, and ignorance. Later or

---

[3] The text contains the for *āsava*-s: *kāmāsava, bhavāsava, diṭṭhāsava,* and *avijjāsava.* But, the *Sutta*-s, for example, DN II 81, 84, 91, 94, 98, 123, 126; AN I 165, contain three *āsava*-s excluding *diṭṭhi-āsava.* We suggest that *diṭṭhi-āsava* was developed in the *Dhammasaṅgaṇi*.

simultaneously, compilers of the *Vibhaṅga* take the *Dhammasaṅgaṇi*'s explanation of the stage of arahatship, and further name those defilements as fetters. These five fetters together with the five fetters found in the *Sutta*-s so-called lower fetters, the compilers categorize them into two schemes:

> five lower fetters [*pañca-orambhāgiyāni saṃyojanāni*]: personality-belief, doubt, clinging to rules and vows, sensual pleasure, ill will; the five higher fetters [*pañc'uddhabhāgiyāi saṃyojanāni*]: desire for form, desire for formlessness, conceit, restlessness, ignorance (Vibh VRI 228).[4]

It seems that these schemes have been placed in AN V 17, because apart from the listing in the *Sutta*-s, there is no function of higher fetters in the first four *Nikāya*-s. Several scholars say that the *Vibhaṅga* and other *Abhidhamma* texts have taken the *Dhammasaṅgaṇi*'s enumerations and further elaborated them on how to be applied. For example, Thittila says:

> It [*Vibhaṅga*] follows a particular plan but is arranged in such a way that it shows how the categories enumerated in *Dhammasaṅgaṇi* are to be applied (Thittila, 1969, xii).

R.E. Iggleden similarly states:

> So far as *Abhidhamma* as a whole is cornered the analysis of states conducted by *Dhammasaṅgaṇi* is but the beginning of a process, for although it establishes the terminology by which the states it isolates may be identified, their extent and limitation are continued in subsequent volumes (Iggleden, 1997, xi).

However, Sujato (2012, 36 &147) relies on the work of Frauwallner (1995) who says the *Vibhaṅga* is the earliest text among other *Abhidhamma* treatises. Sujato accounts:

---

[4] *tattha katamāni pañcaorambhāgiyāni saṃyojanāni? Sakkāyadiṭṭhi, vicikicchā, sīlabbata-parāmāso, kāmacchando, byāpādo–imāni pañcaorambhāgiyāni saṃyojanāni. tattha katamāni pañcuddhambhāgiyāi saṃyojanāni? Rūparāgo, arūparāgo, māno, uddhaccaṃ, avijjā–imāni pañcuddhambhāgiyāni saṃyojanāni.*

> Earliest discourses: *Dhammacakkappavattana*, *Anattalakkhaṇa*, and *Adittapariyāya Suttas*, and the Request of Brahmā. Earliest Collection: Congruent sections of *Saṃyutta Nikāya*/ *Saṃyukta Āgama*. Earliest *Abhidhamma*: Congruent sections of *Vibhaṅga*/ *Dharmaskandha* / *Śāriputrābhidharma* (Sujato, 2012, 37).

Investigating the *Vibhaṅga*, however, we argue that many materials in the *Vibhaṅga* are taken from the *Dhammasaṅgini*. For example, the list of four taints (Vibh VRI 225–26), the list of ten defilements (Vibh VRI 237), and the *Dhammasaṅgaṇi* list of ten fetters (Vibh VRI 238) are from the *Dhammasaṅgaṇi.* Using these examples, therefore, one could assert that the entire *Vibhaṅga*'s materials would not be the earliest, rather these two texts were compiled simultaneously and shared each other's materials during the compilation process.

It was mentioned in the above discussion that the *Dhammasaṅgaṇi* does not use the terms *orambhāgiyāni saṃyojanāni* (lower fetters) to describe the stage of non-returning, and *uddambhāgiyāni saṃyojanāni* (higher fetters) to describe the stage of arahatship. But, the *Atthasālinī*, the Commentary to the *Dhammasaṅgaṇi,* comments on the stage of arahatship with the method of *pañcuddambhāgiyāni saṃyojanāni* (five higher fetters), as follows:

> At the stage of four [arahatship]—desire for form, desire for formlessness, conceit, restlessness, and ignorance—these five fetters belonging to higher (existence) [*pañcannaṃ uddhambhāgiyasaṃyojanānaṃ*] are completely destroyed without any remaining (As VRI 68).[5]

On the other hand, the above Commentarial elucidation is not found in the Commentaries to the *Sutta*-s which contain the term *uddhambhāgiyāni-saṃyojanāni*. The Commentary to the *Saṃyojana Sutta* (AN V 17), for example, only explains the term as *saṃyojanānīti bandhanāni* (fetter is bondage) and *uddhambhāgiyānīti uparibhāgiyāni* (the

[5] *catutthe rūparāga-arūparāga-māna-uddhacca-avijjā anavasesa-pahānāyāti etesaṃ pañcannaṃ uddham-bhāgiyasaṃyojanānaṃ nissessapajapahanatthāya.*

higher portion is upper portion), or *uddhambhāgiyānīti uparikoṭṭhāsiyāni* (the higher portion is upper part) (Mp VRI *aṭṭhakanipāta-aṭṭhakathā*, 48). Also, the Commentaries to the all *Sutta*-s do not describe the stage of arahatship with the method of higher fetters as the *Atthasālinī* comments. Only in the Commentary to AN (Mp VRI *Dukanipātā-aṭṭhakathā*, 17), when the internal and external fetters are expounded, the lower fetters are used to denote the sensual sphere, and the higher fetters are used to denote the form and formless spheres together. Therefore, if these pieces of evidence are taken into consideration, it is evident that the traditional list of ten fetter was developed during the compilation of the *Abhidhamma*.

4.3.1 Analysing the Once-returning and Arahatship

Now it is necessary to discuss how the *Dhammasaṅgaṇi* defines the stages of once-returning and arahatship. According to the *Purisagati Sutta* (AN V 70–71), without having cut off the three latent tendencies—*bhava-rāga, māna, avijjā*—a non-returner does not realize the highest peaceful stage, arahatship. Here, it seems that the *Dhammasaṅgaṇi* divides the *bhava-rāga* into two categories: *rūpa-rāga* and *arūpa-rāga*. As the non-returner has already destroyed the *kāma-rāga*, it is excluded from the four defilements: *rūpa-rāga*, *arūpa-rāga, māna,* and *avijjā*. Further, the text has included the term *uddhacca* (restlessness) to make the five: *rūpa-rāga*, *arūpa-rāga, māna, uddhacca,* and *avijjā*. In the previous chapter (see 3.2.1), we have quoted Somaratne who says the term *uddhacca* (restlessness) was put in the five higher fetters by the early redactors or copiers. Here this study claims that the compilers of the *Dhammasaṅgaṇi* have added the term *uddhacca* in the list. Examining the *Dhammasaṅgaṇi,* the following section investigates why *uddhacca* was added to the list.

The *Dhammasaṅgaṇi* mainly emphasizes on the psychological approach of human existence. It gives a detailed explanation of the human mind, and material phenomena painstakingly divide them numerically. In regard to this, Iggleden says:

> In any consideration of *Abhidhamma* studies the term to be examined before all others "*mātikā*". The reason for this lies in the method adopted throughout the *Abhidhamma-Piṭaka* of examining the nature and behaviour of the many states, mental and material, which is in accord with the fundamental principles of *anicca*, *dukkha* and *anatta* shown to arise and pass away throughout the whole continuity of process which existence demonstrated to be (Iggleden, 1997, vii).

Analysing the four stages of enlightenment in the *Dhammasaṅgaṇi*, it is observed that the stages are described through the *jhāna* practice. The text (Dhs, VRI 55–56) says, when he cultivates the *jhāna* of the higher meditation (*yasmiṃ samaye lokuttaraṃ jhānam bhāveti*) whereby there is going forth and onward making the end of becoming by cutting off the defilements. According to the *Abhidhammattha Saṅgaha*:

> The *jhānas* are so called because they closely contemplate the objects and because they burn up the adverse states opposed to concentration. The adverse are the five hindrances (*nīvaraṇa*) of sensual desire, ill-will, sloth and torpor, restlessness and worry, and doubt (Bodhi, 1999, 56).

Considering the above explanation, we argue that the *Dhammasaṅgaṇi* categorizes the stages of once-returning and arahatship in the following order:

Stage	*Sutta*-s	*Dhammasaṅgaṇi*
The once-returning	attenuation of *rāga*, *dosa*, and *moha*	attenuation of *kāma-rāga* and *vyāpāda*

Notes: The *Dhammasaṅgaṇi* divides—

1. *Rāga* > *kāma-rāga,*
2. *Dosa* > *vyāpāda*/ *paṭigha*, and
3. *Moha* > *uddhacca*

Stage	*Sutta* (AN V 70–71)	*Dhammasaṅgaṇi*
The arahatship	Having cut off latent tendencies: *bhava-rāga*, *māna*, and *avijjā*	Having cut off *rūpa-rāga*, *arūpa-rāga*, *māna*, *uddhacca*, and *avijjā*

Note: The *Dhammasaṅgaṇi* divides—

1. *Bhava-rāga* > *rūpa-rāga*, and *arūpa-rāga*
2. *Māna* > *māna*
3. *Avijjā* > *avijjā*
4. *Uddhacca* > added

Now it is necessary to discuss why the term *uddhacca* was placed in the list. According to the Abhidh-s, *uddhacca* is rooted in delusion (*moha*). For example, the text says:

> Restlessness [*uddhacca*] is disquietude, mental distraction, or agitation, and the *citta* infected by this restlessness is the second type of consciousness rooted in delusion. According to the *Abhidhamma*, the mental factor of restlessness is found in all twelve unwholesome *cittas*, but in the other eleven *cittas* its force (*satti*) is relatively weak and its function is secondary. However, in this last type of *citta*, restlessness becomes the chief factor; thus this last type alone is described as *consciousness associated with restlessness* (Bodhi, 1999, 38).

From the above passage, it is obvious that the *Dhammasaṅgaṇi* purposely replaces *moha* with *uddhacca* to systematize the stage of non-returning with the fetters. However, about the function of *uddhacca*, the *Abhidhammattha Saṅgha* contends that there is still minor contradiction between the Commentarial explanation and Ledi Sayadaw:

> It should be noted that no qualification in terms of prompted or unprompted is attached to the description of these two *cittas* rooted in delusion... They [the *Vibhāvinī-Ṭīkā* and the *Mahā-Ṭīkā* to the *Visuddhimagga*] state that since these two *cittas* lack natural acuteness, they cannot be described as unprompted; and since there is no occasion when one deliberately tries to arouse

> them, they cannot be described as prompted. Ledi Sayadaw, however, rejects this position, holding these *cittas* to be exclusively unprompted. He contends: "Since these two *cittas* occur in beings naturally, by their own intrinsic nature, they need not to be aroused by any inducement or expedient means. They always occur without trouble or difficulty. Therefore, they are exclusively unprompted, and this should be seen as the reason the distinction by way of prompting is not mentioned here (Bodhi, 1999, 39).

From the above-mentioned passage it seems that although the root cause of *avijjā* is due to *moha*, there is still immense difference between the functions of *avijjā* and *uddhacca*. According to the *Abhidhammattha Saṅgaha* (Bodhi 1999, 83), "*moha* is a synonym for *avijjā*, ignorance. Its characteristic is mental blindness of unknowing (*aññāṇa*)." On the other hand, "Its [restlessness] function is to make the mind unsteady, as wind makes a banner ripple." This could be a reason why the *Dhammasaṅgaṇi* has not put *moha* into *avijjā-anusaya*, rather it has put *moha* with *uddhacca* whose root is delusion. However, it is also proper to state that a practitioner destroys the grosser level of *uddhacca* and *avijjā* while passing through the stages of once-returning, and non-returning.

4.3.2 Dasa-saṃyojanāni and Its Functions

Chapter 2 (see 2.4) has briefly discussed *dasa-saṃyojanāni* (ten fetters) and its functions in the *Abhidhamma*. After investigating the *Abhidhamma Piṭaka*, it was found that it is in the *Abhidhamma*, the *Dhammasaṅgaṇi* that the list of ten fetters was first introduced. Above we have shown that this list is different from the traditional list of ten fetters. In chapter 3 (see 3.6), it was shown that the *Dhammasaṅgaṇi* has set up the list based on the two sets of seven fetters recorded in the *Sattaka Nipāta* of AN. According to Tan (2009), the *Abhidhamma* list of ten fetters is older than the traditional list of ten fetters. Explaining the traditional list above, we agree that the list of ten fetters listed in the *Dhammasaṅgaṇi* is older set. The traditional list of ten fetters was later developed from the *Dhammasaṅgaṇi* when it describes the stages of once-returning and arahatship with giving up the defilements (fetters). The *Abhidhamma* list of ten fetters is also found in the *Vibhaṅga* (VRI 238) and the *Niddesa*. Now let us discuss the possible reasons why the *Dhammasaṅgaṇi* introduces the list of ten fetters. The list of ten fetters in the *Dhammasaṅgaṇi* is:

> (1) Sensual desire (*kāma-rāga*), (2) repulsion (*paṭigha*), (3) conceit (*māna*), (4) view (*diṭṭhi*), (5) doubt (*vicikicchā*), (6) clinging to rules and vows (*sīlabbata-parāmāsa*), (7) desire for form (*bhava-rāga*), (8) envy (*issā*), (9) selfishness (*macchariya*), and (10) ignorance (*avijjā*) (Dhs VRI 166).

It seems that the *Dhammasaṅgaṇi* introduces the ten fetters in the order of greed (*lobha*) followed by hatred (*dosa*) and delusion (*moha*) on the basis of which the *Abhidhamma* doctrines have been elaborated. That is why, the fetter of sensual desire (*kāma-rāga*), which is rooted in greed, is enumerated as the first of the sequence, and the fetter of restlessness and ignorance which are rooted in delusion, are placed at the end. In other words, this list can also be interpreted following the order of *taṇhā*: *kāma* and *bhava*, or *bhava* which is three kinds: *kāma-bhava*, *rūpa-bhava*, and *arūpa-bhava*. In this order, the *Dhammasaṅgaṇi* puts the term *kāma-rāga-saṃyojana* (fetter of sensual desire) to mean *kāma-taṇhā* or *kāma-bhava*, intensified craving for sense desire. This sensual desire in reference to the *satipaṭṭhāna* practice which is dependent on sense bases and sense objects. That could be one reason why the *Dhammasaṅgaṇi* contains detailed enumeration corresponding to all phenomena based on the *satipaṭṭhāna* practice. There is also direct reference to "*saṃyojanā dhammā* (things that fetter)," "*no saṃyojanā dhammā* (things that are not fetter)," and "*saññojaniyā dhammā*" (the things to be fettered) in the section "Saññojanagocchaka" of the "Mātikā," in the

Dhamma-saṅgaṇi. The term "*saññojaniyā dhammā*" is directly connected to the *satipaṭṭhāna* practice recorded in the *Saṃyojana Sutta* of the *Saḷāyatana Vagga* (SN IV 282) on which we have discussed in chapter 2 (see 2.2). Regarding the connection between the *satipaṭṭhāna* and the *Dhammasaṅgaṇi*, Sujato (2012, 190–91 & 329) has extensively discussed in his work *History of Mindfulness*. The Commentaries to the (*Mahā*)-*satipaṭṭhāna Sutta*-s also explain the fetter in the practice of *satipaṭṭhāna* with the *Dhammasaṅgaṇi* list of ten fetters. It seems that the commentator also considers the *Abhidhamma* list of fetter to be more appropriate with regard to senses bases and sense objects which extensively employed in the practice of the *satipaṭṭhāna*. For example:

> In dependence on both [sense bases and sense objects] the fetter arises... There are ten kinds of fetter arise as the fetters of sensual desire, repulsion, conceit, view, doubt, clinging to rules and vows, desire for form, envy, selfishness, and ignorance (Sv VRI 181; Ps VRI 134).[6]

From the above discussion, therefore, we conclude that the *Dhammasaṅgaṇi* introduces the list of ten fetters in the *Abhidhamma* to show the spiritual maturity through the "intra-psychic," and "psychological" binding of fetters with regard to sense bases and sense objects. That could be a reason the *Abhidhamma* list of ten fetters starts with the fetter of sensual desire (*kāma-rāga*) which is most noticeable with the sense bases and sense objects. It is also noteworthy that the Commentaries categorize the Four Noble Persons in accordance with the *Abhidhamma* list of ten fetters, as follows:

> The five kinds of fetters of view, doubt, clinging to rules and vows, envy, selfishness are eradicated through the path of stream-

[6] *yañca tadubhyaṃ paṭiccha uppajjati saṃyojananti.... Kāmarāga-saṃyojanaṃ, paṭigha, māna, diṭṭhi, vicikicchā, sīlabbataparāmāsa, bhavarāga, issā, macchariya, avijjāsaṃyojananti dasavidhaṃ saṃyojanaṃ uppajjati.*

> entry; the two more fetters of sensual desire, repulsion are greatly weakened through the path of once-returning; the two more fetters of sensual desire, repulsion are completely destroyed through the path of non-returning; the fetter of conceit, desire for form, and ignorance are eradicated through the path of arahatship (Sv VRI 181).[7]

According to the foregoing passage, it is evident that the Four Noble Persons can be classified without applying the traditional list of ten fetters. From the Commentarial explanation, it can also be claimed that the traditional list of ten fetters would not be the best to describe the four stages.

4.4 Exposition of the Concept of Fetter in the *Abhidhamma*

The above discussion on fetters was mainly based on the *Dhammasaṅgaṇi*. Now the discussion turns to other *Abhidhamma* texts in which the doctrine "fetter" has been elaborated widely. Earlier in this chapter it was proposed that the *Vibhaṅga* elaborates the higher and lower fetters by taking the *Dhammasaṅgaṇi*'s enumerations. Now it is important to discuss how other texts treat the fetters. In this section, the *Dhātukathā*, the *Yamaka* and the *Paṭṭhāna* are not referred to as they do not contain much material on fetter with regard to its development.

First we would like to consult the *Puggalapaññatti*. According to Rev. Richard Morris (1883, ix), the *Puggalapaññatti* contains materials from the older *Piṭaka* books modelled upon that of the *Sañgīti Sutta* of DN. Robert E. Buswell and Padmanabh S. Jaini (1996, 92) say that the text shares more similarities with the *Sutta*-s than the definitive language of the *Abhidhamma*, and "much of its contents may be traced to the *Aṅguttaranikāya* and *Saṅgītisuttanta* of the *Dīghanikāya*." Scholars' clarification

---

[7] *diṭṭhi-vicikicchā-sīlabbataparāmāsa-issā-macchariya-bhedassa tāva pañcavidhassa saṃyojanassa sotā-pattimaggena āyatiṃ anuppādo hoti. Kāmarāga-paṭigha-saṃyojanadvayassa oḷārikassa sakadāgāmimaggena, aṇusahagatassa anāgāmimaggena, māna-bhavarāga-avijjā-saṃyojanattayassa arahattamaggena āyatiṃ anuppādo hoti.*

can also be traced through the doctrine of fetters. The text defines the ordinary person (*puthujjana*) who has not yet abandoned the first three fetters in the traditional list of ten fetters. Apart from that, the text describes the three sub-categories of stream-enterer which are found in the *Ekaka Nipāta* of AN (see 3.3), the once-returner as recorded in the *Sutta*-s, and all sub-categories of non-returner found in the *Sutta*-s (see 3.2) with the method of fetters. But, the text does not describe the stage of arahatship as recorded in the *Sutta*-s. Instead of the *Sutta*-s exposition on the stage of arahatship, the text takes the *Dhammasaṅgaṇi*'s explanation. It also describes the stage of once-returning as found in the *Dhammasaṅgaṇi*. For example:

> Through diminishing sensual desire, and hatred, a person realizes the fruit of once-returning. I called him "once-returner" one who has diminished the sensual desire and hatred. Through the complete destruction (without any reminding) of sensual desire, and hatred, a person realizes the fruit of non-returning. I called him "non-returner" one who has completely destroyed the sensual desire and hatred.
>
> Through the complete destruction (without any reminding) of desire for form, desire for formlessness, conceit, restlessness, and ignorance, a person realizes the fruit of arahatship. I called him "arahat" who has completely destroyed the desire for form, desire for formlessness, conceit, restlessness, and ignorance (Pp VRI 13).[8]

From the above passages, it is worth noting that the *Puggalapaññatti* describes the stage of arahatship with the

[8] *kāmarāgabyāpādānaṃ tanubhāvāya paṭipanno puggalo sakadāgāmiphalasac-chikiriyāya-paṭipanno. Yassa puggalassa kāmarāgabyāpādā tanubhūtā—ayaṃ vuccati puggalo "sakadāgāmī". kāmarāgabyāpādānaṃ anavasesappahānāya paṭipanno puggalo anāgāmiphalasacchikiriyāya paṭipanno. Yassa puggalassa kāmarāgabyāpādā anavasesā pahīnā—ayaṃ vuccati puggalo "anāgāmī".*

rūparāgaarūparāgamānauddhaccaavijjāya anavasesappahānāya paṭipanno puggalo arahatta-phalasacchikiriyāya paṭipanno. Yassa puggalassa rūparāgo arūparāgo māno uddhaccaṃ avijjā anavasesā pahīnā—ayaṃ vuccati puggalo "arahā".

Dhammasaṅgaṇi's exposition, and excluded the *Sutta*-s description such as, through the destruction of taints a person becomes an arahat. But this text maintains the description of the stage of once-returning applying both *Sutta*-s and *Dhammasaṅgaṇi*'s explanations. But while this text describes the stage of non-returning, it always uses the term *orambhāgiyāni saṃyojanāni* (lower fetters), and the term *uddambhāgiyāni saṃyojanāni* (higher fetters) is not applied to describe the stage of arahatship.

We wish to show that it is in the *Kathāvatthu* the spiritual stages with the method of "lower fetters" and "higher fetters" were first ever clearly divided. In the entire Pāli Canon, this is the first time the function of "lower fetters" and "higher fetters" are properly applied. Now let us discuss how the text describes the spiritual stages with the method of the traditional list of ten fetters. Before dealing with the topic, the composition of the *Kathāvatthu* is given as follows.

According to Sujato and Brahmali, the *Kathāvatthu* is composed in the form of a dialogue where the texts and ideas of the early Buddhist texts are presented and opposing interpretations given. Sujato and Brahmali say:

> The *Kathāvatthu* of the Pali *Abhidhamma* was begun in the time of Asoka, or not long thereafter, which places its beginnings around 150–200 years after the Buddha.... For the *Kathāvatthu*, the EBTs [Early Buddhist Texts] or more precisely the four main *Nikāyas/Āgamas* plus a small part of the *Khuddaka Nikāya*, are always the final authority in settling opposing views, not the *Abhidhamma* or any other Buddhist text. In fact, it argues about practically everything except the actual letter of the text of the EBTs (Sujato and Brahmali, 2014, 35–36).

In the above passage, Sujato and Brahmali claim that the *Kathāvatthu* only discusses materials taken from the early Buddhist texts, mostly *Nikāya*-s, but not *Abhidhamma*. Through the discussion on fetters, however, one could show that the text also heavily relies on the *Dhammasaṅgaṇi*. For example, in the *Puggalapaññatti* it was shown that the text maintains the *Sutta*-s, and the *Dhammasaṅgaṇi*'s explanations of the stage of once-returning: diminishing *rāga*, *dosa*, and *moha* (*Sutta* explanation), and diminishing *kāma-rāga*, *vyāpāda* (*Dhammasaṅgaṇi* explanation). But the *Kathāvatthu* only follows the *Dhammasaṅgaṇi*'s exposition of the stage of once-returning. Now we will show that only the *Kathāvatthu* which describes the four stages with the traditional list of ten fetters. For example, the *Kathāvatthu* (VRI 49–51) says:

> One realizes the fruit of the first path (stream-enterer): one gives up the three of the ten fetters—personality belief (*sakkāya-diṭṭhi*), doubt (*vicikicchā*), and clinging to rules and vows (*sīlabbata-parāmāsa*); One realizes the fruit of the second path (once-returner): One gives up gross sensual desire (*kāma-rāga*), and ill-will (*vyāpāda*);
>
> One realizes the fruit of the third path (non-returner): One completely gives up sensual desire (*kāma-rāga*), and ill-will (*vyāpāda*); One realizes the fruit of the fourth path (arahat): One completely gives up desire for form (*rūpa-rāga*), desire for formlessness (*arūpa-rāga*), conceit (*māna*), restlessness (*uddhacca*), and ignorance (*avijjā*).

In addition to the above explanation, the *Kathāvatthu* also divides the stage of non-returning and arahatships as elaborating that, "the non-returner, for whom five lower fetters are completely destroyed; yet the five higher fetters are not destroyed" (Kv VRI 48).[9] It is worth noting that the *Kathāvatthu* defines the four stages through the eradication of fetters, and the fetters correspond to all defilements.

In summary, the *Dhammasaṅgaṇi* first defines the stage of once-returning with the diminishing of *kāma-rāga*, and *vyāpāda*, and the stage of arahatship through the destruction of the five defilements—*rūpa-rāga*, *arūpa-rāga*, *māna*, *uddhacca*, and *avijjā*. But the text does not mention them

[9] *anāgāmissa puggalassa pañcorambhāgiyāni saṃyojanāni pahīnāni, pañcuddhambhāgiyāni saṃyojanāni appahanīnāni.*

as "fetters", nor any classification of the lower and higher fetters. Following the *Dhammasaṅgaṇi*'s classification, the *Vibhaṅga* divides the traditional list of ten fetters into two categories—lower fetters, and higher fetters. The *Puggalapaññatti* further takes the *Dhammasaṅgaṇi*'s classification to describe the four stages. But this text has traced both the *Sutta*-s and the *Dhammasaṅgaṇi*'s explanation. Later, only the *Kathāvatthu* describes the four stages with the method of ten fetters, and discounts the *Sutta*-s exposition. Citing the above evidences, we claim that the description of the four stages with the method of traditional list of ten fetters was entirely developed in the *Abhidāamma* to systematize the four stages of enlightenment which shows the enlightenment could be achieved through stage by stage.

4.5 The Description of the Four Stages with *Saṃyojana* and *Anusaya* in the *Niddesa* and the *Paṭisambhidāmagga*

As discussed in the above section, the four stages were entirely explained with the method of traditional list of ten fetters in the *Abhidhamma*. Now the discussion turns to the *Niddesa* and the *Paṭisambhidāmagga* (Paṭis) both of which describe the four stages through the abandonment of *saṃyojana* and *anusaya* together.

The *Niddesa* is a Commentarial work which consists of two volumes: the *Mahā-niddesa* (Nidd I) and the *Culla-niddesa* (Nidd II). The Nidd I deals with the sixteen *Sutta*-s of the *Aṭṭhaka Vagga*, and the Nidd II comments on the *Khaggavisāna Sutta* and the *Pārāyana Vagga* of Sn. Though the *Niddesa* and the Paṭis are included in the *Khuddaka Nikāya*, as whole texts, we consider them later *Abhidhamma*, because both of them follow the *Abhidhammic* explanation of the doctrines of fetter. Scholars have different views on the compilation dates of the *Niddesa* and the Paṭis. Some say both texts are pre-*abhidhammic*, and some claim they are later *Abhidhammic*. However, this study argues that both texts are later *Abhidhammic*. Before dealing with this topic, let us discuss how scholars observe the compilation dates of both texts.

Hajime Nakamura (1999, 48) cites Kōgen Midzuno's view, who says the composition of the *Niddesa* is in the reign of King Aśoka or in a period not much remote from him. Nakamura particularly emphasises on the compilation date of the Nidd I and says it "must not have been composed before the 2nd century AD" He also says the Paṭis was composed after King Aśoka. Norman (1983, 87) says the *Niddesa* is before the first century BC. Brace G. Burford (1996, 312) says that the Nidd I is a Commentary of *Abhidhammic*-style to the *Aṭṭhaka Vagga,* its interpretation is in a manner of early text but it consists of a highly *abhidhammic* elaboration that belongs to its own era. Burford agrees that between two *Niddesa*-s, the Nidd I and the Nidd II, there are not great divergence, and by the compilation time of *Niddesa,* they never use the basic *Abhidhammic* terms or classification. Oliver Abeynayake (1984, 156) says while the "tradition counts it as a Canonical text but it is evident that the *Niddesa* is an old Commentary which was included in the Canon in a later period". Hirakawa (1990, 128) says the date of *Niddesa* is 250 BC which is a forerunner of *Abhidāamma* texts.

About the compilation dates of the Paṭis, Frauwallner (1995, 42) says "it is the latest of the *Abhidharma* works and was written at a time when the formation of the canon has been essentially completed." Hinüber (1996, 60) cites the view of Frauwallner and says, if it is so, it could be a forerunner of both the *Vimuttimagga* and the *Visuddhimagga.* On the other hand, Malalasekera (1998, Vol.II, 116) says, "it is possible that, before the development of the extant Abhidhammapiṭaka, it [Paṭis] passed as one of the Abhidhamma treatises." Warder (2000, 299) says that the text is dated 237 to c. 100 BC. Anālayo (2014, 53) agrees and says, "the beginning parts of the *Paṭisambhidāmagga,* a work of *Abhidharma* character found in the fifth *Nikāya-s* of the Pāli canon, appear to be based on extracts from the

Theravāda version of the *Dasuttara-sutta*". Hirakawa (1990, 128) is of a third opinion as he says the Paṭis is a forerunner of *Abhidhamma* literature which was compiled around 250 B.C.E. Fuller (2005, 86) similarly states the text "can be regarded as a form of early *Abhidhamma* in style and content'. Sajato and Brahmali in *The Authenticity of the Early Buddhist Texts*, say:

> According to the Sinhalese chronicle the *Dīpavaṁsa* (5.37 of Oldenberg's translation), the Mahāsāṅghika rejected the *Parivāra* (the last book of the Pali *Vinaya Piṭaka*), the six books of the *Abhidhamma* (six, because this is said to have occurred before the composition of the *Kathāvatthu*), the *Paṭisambhidāmagga*, the *Niddesa*, and some of the *Jātakas* (Sajato and Brahmali, 2014, 137).

Meanwhile, Abeynayake states:

> The *Paṭisambhidā* [*magga*] seems to be a Commentary written on the passages which are taken from the *Vinaya* and from the collections of the *Sutta Piṭaka*. In this respect the text seems to belong to the same class of literature as the *Niddesa* (Abeynayake, 1984, 162).

Abeynayake further suggests that most of the texts in the *Khuddhaka Nikāya* have evidence of later interpolation and development, and the growth of the texts had not completed in the specific period between the great demise of the Buddha and the reign of Emperor Aśoka. Abeynayake identifies the two strata of the *Khuddaka* texts, as follows:

> The texts *Suttanipāta*, *Itivuttaka*, *Dhammapada*, *Therīgathā* (*Theragāthā*) and *Jātaka* belong to the early stratum. The texts *Khuddakapāṭha*, *Vimānavaṭṭhu* [*vatthu*], *Petavatthu*, *Niddesa*, *Paṭisambhidā* [*magga*], *Apadāna*, *Buddhavaṃsa* and *Cariyāpiṭaka* can be categorised in the late stratum (Abeynayake 1984, 113).

Reviewing the above scholars' opinions, we are of the opinion that both the *Niddesa* and the Paṭis could have been produced over a period of time and both texts were composed after

Abhidhammic texts which share the *Abhidhamma* materials in terms of doctrine of fetter, because both the *Niddesa* and the Paṭis contain the *Dhammasaṅgaṇi* and some other *Abhidhamma* texts' exposition of the four stages with the traditional list of fetters. The Nidd II twice uses the *Dhammasaṅgaṇi* list of ten fetters to comment on verse 148 of the *Khaggavisāna Sutta*. The verse is "*sandālayitvāna saṃyojanāni, jālaṃva bhetvā salilambucārī; Aggīva daḍḍhaṃ anivattamāno, eko care khaggavisāṇakappa.*" The Nidd II describes the term *sandālayitvāna saṃyojanāni* (shatter the fetters) by mentioning:

> Shattering fetter means shattering ten fetters: fetter of sensual desire, fetter of hatred, fetter of conceit, fetter of view, fetter of doubt, fetter of clinging to rules and vows, fetter of desire for becoming, fetter of envy, fetter of selfishness, and fetter of ignorance (Nidd II VRI 148).[10]

The Nidd I also shares similar doctrines on fetters found in the *Abhidhamma*. But an interesting point is that the Nidd I and the Paṭis both define the four stages with giving up of the traditional ten fetters as well as with giving up of the seven latent tendencies (*anusaya*) together, which were not found in the *Sutta*-s and the *Abhidhamma*. For example, the Nidd I says:

> Abandoning the fetter of personality-belief, doubt, clinging to rules and vows, and latent tendencies of view and doubt together with the respective defilements, the mind of stream-enterer is secluded. Diminishing the fetter of sensual desire and ill-will, and latent tendencies of sensual desire and ill-will together with the respective defilements, the mind of once-returner is secluded.
>
> Abandoning the fetter of sensual desire and ill-will, and latent tendencies of sensual desire and ill-will together with the respective defilements, the mind of non-returner is secluded. Abandoning the fetter of desire for form, desire for formlessness,

[10] *sandālayitvāna saṃyojanānīti dasa saṃyojanāni kāmarāgasaṃyojanaṃ, paṭigha-saṃyojanaṃ, māna-saṃyojanaṃ, diṭṭhisaṃyojanaṃ, vicikicchāsaṃyojanaṃ, sīlabbata-parāmāsa-saṃyojanaṃ, bhavarāga-saṃyojanaṃ, issāsaṃyojanaṃ, macchariyasaṃyojanaṃ, avijjāsaṃyojanaṃ.*

> conceit, restlessness and ignorance, and latent tendencies of desire for becoming, conceit and ignorance together with all outer objects of defilements and signs, the mind of arahat is secluded (Nidd I VRI 11).[11]

Similarly, the Paṭis states:

> Through the path of stream-entry, three fetters of personality-belief, doubt, clinging to rules and vows are destroyed, and two latent tendencies of view and doubt are ended without any residue. Through the path of once-returning, two fetters of sensual desire and ill-will are weakened, and two latent tendencies of sensual desire and ill-will are reduced.
>
> Through the path of once-returning, two fetters of sensual desire and ill-will are destroyed, and two latent tendencies of sensual desire and ill-will are ended without any residue. Through the path of arahatship, five fetters of desire for form, desire for formlessness, conceit, restlessness and ignorance are destroyed, and three latent tendencies of desire for becoming, conceit, and ignorance are ended without any residue (Paṭis VRI 151).[12]

---

[11] *sotāpannassa sakkāyadiṭṭhiyā vicikicchāya sīlabbataparāmāsā diṭṭhānusayā vicikicchā-anusayā, tade-kaṭṭhehi ca kilesehi cittaṃ vivittaṃ hoti. Sakadāgāmissa oḷārikā kāmarāgasaññojanā paṭighasaññojanā oḷārikā kāmarāgānusayā paṭighānusayā, tadekaṭṭhehi ca kilesehi cittaṃ vivittaṃ hoti.*

Anāgāmissa anusahagatā kāmarāgasaññojanā paṭighasaññojanā anusahagatā kāmarāgānusayā paṭighānusayā, tadekaṭṭhehi ca kilesehi cittaṃ vivittaṃ hoti. Arahato rūpārūparāgā mānā uddhaccā avijjāya mānānusayā bhavarāgānusayā avijjānusayā, tadekaṭṭhehi ca kilesehi bahiddhā ca sabbanimittehi cittaṃ vivittaṃ hoti.

It is worth noting that, in Nidd I (VRI 216), with giving up the fetters and latent tendencies, the stage of stream-entry, once-returning, non-returning and arahatship are named the first boundary (*paṭhamā sīmā*), the second boundary (*dutiyā sīmā*), the third boundary (*tatiyā sīmā*), and the fourth boundary (*catutthā sīmā*) respectively.

[12] *sotāpattimaggena sakkāyadiṭṭhi vicikicchā sīlabbataparāmāso—imāni tīṇi saṃojanāni pahīyanti; diṭṭhānusayo, vicikicchānusayo—ime dve anusayā byantīhonti. Sakadāgāmimaggena oḷārikaṃ kāmarāgasaṃojanaṃ, paṭighasaññojanaṃ-imāni dve saṃojanāni pahīyanti; oḷāriko kāmarāgānusayo paṭighānusayo-ime dve anusaya byantīhonti.*

Anāgāmimaggena anusahagataṃ kāmarāgasaṃojanaṃ, paṭighasaññojanaṃ-imāni dve saṃojanāni pahīyanti; anusahagato kāmarāgānusayo, paṭighānusayo-ime dve anusayā byantīhonti. Arahattamaggena rūparāgo, arūparāgo, māno, uddhaccaṃ, avijjā-imāni pañca saṃojanāni pahīyanti; mānānusayo, bhavarāgānusayo, avijjānusayo- ime tayo anusayā byantīhonti.

Analysing the above-mentioned passages, it seems that there is very clear explanation of the four stages through the eradication of the ten fetters and seven latent tendencies in the Nidd I and the Paṭis. Both texts share the *Abhidhammic* explanation of the four stages, but the explanations of both texts are unique as they employ the latent tendencies together with fetters. This explanation is not found in any *Sutta*-s, not even in the *Abhidhamma*. It seems that both texts were composed based on the *Sutta* and the *Abhidhamma*. In chapter 3 (see 3.6), reference was made to the *Mahāmāluṅkya Sutta* of MN in which the Buddha is said to have explained that the function of latent tendencies for a child was at a latent level, and fetters for a mature person was at a grosser level. It was also shown that, in AN, a list of seven fetters and seven latent tendencies are identical as their names. It was further mentioned that the *Dhammasaṅgaṇi* has set up a list of ten fetters based on the two lists of seven fetters found in the *Sattaka Nipāta* of AN. If we take these examples into consideration, it is obvious that the Nidd I and the Paṭis were composed based on the *Abhidhamma* and the *Sutta*-s expositions with regard to the doctrines of fetters and latent tendencies.

From the above discussion, we claim that the *Niddesa* and the Paṭis are later *Abhidhamma*, but the materials of both texts are from the *Abhidhamma* and the *Sutta*-s. To support this argument, an additional example is that the *Dhammasaṅgaṇi* first categorizes the taints (*āsava*) into four: *kāma*, *bhava*, *diṭṭhi*, and *avijjā* (see 4.2). These four kinds of taints are also shared by the Nidd II (VRI 64): *anāsavāti cattāro āsavā-kāmāsavo, bhavāsavo, diṭṭhāsavo, avijjāsavo*, and the Paṭis VRI 50: *āsavāti katame te āsavā? kāmāsavo, bhavāsavo, diṭṭhāsavo, avijjāsavo*. But in the *Sutta*-s, there are three *āsava*-s, *diṭṭhi-āsava* is not included. The Commentary to the Paṭis expounds on the fetter by taking the list of seven fetters from AN (Paṭis-a, VRI 179) and the list of ten fetters from the *Dhammasaṅgaṇi* (Paṭis-a, VRI 182). This section has referred to Hinüber (1996, 60) who says the Paṭis could be a forerunner of both the *Vimuttimagga* and the *Visuddhimagga.* Supporting his view, this study also argues that the Paṭis is a forerunner of the *Vimuttimagga* and the *Visuddhimagga.* The *Visuddhimagga* also shares some similar doctrines in terms of fetters. For instance, we have shown that the Paṭis define the four stages with giving up the fetters and latent tendencies together. This categorization is also found in the *Visuddhimagga* (Visud I VRI 103, and II VRI 78).

Citing the above evidences, this section concludes that the *Niddesa* and the Paṭis are later *Abhidhamma.* However, it is also true that the compilation date of many Pāli *Nikāya* texts is not accountable of precise determination. Most of the texts are composite which underwent changes or part of the text was composed earlier and some later. Inspecting different hypotheses, we argue that both the *Niddesa* and the Paṭis could have been produced over a long period, and the final composition of them took place after the Pāli *Abhidhamma* texts. In this connection we agree with Kōgen Midzuno and Nakamura (1999, 48) who say the composition of the *Niddesa* is in the reign of King Aśoka or in a period not much remote from him. Nakamura particularly says the Paṭis was composed after King Aśoka. Considering scholars' views, it seems that the Paṭis was compiled in a manner to refute the several Buddhist schools' views outside Theravāda in order to encapsulate the Theravāda Buddhist thoughts. To me, because large number of the doctrines were taken from the *Sutta*-s to compose the Paṭis, it was then placed in the *Khuddaka Nikāya* of the *Sutta Piṭaka.* There is also possibility that in the development of the Pāli Canon, the texts which developed with new materials taken from the *Sutta*-s and the *Abhidhamma*, were not added to the *Abhidhamma Piṭaka*, but added to the *Khuddaka Nikāya* of the *Sutta Piṭaka* instead. Because it was the repository section in the *Sutta Piṭaka* in which both early and late texts were included.

4.6 Interpretation of the Four Stages in the *Abhidhammattha Saṅgaha*

In order to strengthen our argument about the development of concept "fetter", we shall continue to discuss the Abhidh-s which systematically describe the four stages of enlightenment with the schemes of five lower and five higher fetters. We will show that the Abhidh-s' enumeration of the four stages with the traditional list of ten fetters highly influences contemporary scholars in the Pāli tradition. Above in this chapter we have quoted Nyanatiloka's (1952, 49–50) exposition of the four stages and mentioned that it is based on the Abhidh-s. Not only Nyanatiloka, but also Walshe whom we referred to in chapter 3 (see 3.1) follows the Abhidh-s' description of four stages with giving up of the traditional list of ten fetters. Of course, it does not mean that the Abhidh-s has developed the concept "fetter" with regard to the four stages. It is believed that the concept of fetter was enumerated by the Buddha himself, which was recorded in the *Sutta*-s. But, the concept of fetter in relation to the four stages was subsequently developed in the *Dhammasaṅgaṇi* which was followed by other *Abhidhamma* texts. Although the *Abhidhamma* has developed the concept of fetter, it has used the heterogeneous explanations with the *Sutta*-s and the *Abhidhamma* materials. Based on the *Abhidhamma Piṭaka*, the Abhidh-s further describes the four stages with the traditional list of ten fetters. This description became more prevalent in the Theravāda tradition. Now the following section will show how the Abhidh-s' description of fetter is generally accepted by scholars. Before dealing with this topic, it is necessary to discuss why the Abhidh-s was composed.

The Abhidh-s is a compendium of the *Abhidhamma* (*Abhidhamma Piṭaka*) written by Ācariya Anuruddha. The *Encyclopaedia of the Hindu World* Vol I (1992, 102) dates this work, "according to Ceylonese tradition, [it] was written in the 1st century BC, but Winternitz places the work in the 12th century AD". According to Bodhi (1999, 1), the text is "one of the most important and influential textbooks of Theravāda Buddhism...a masterly summary of that abstruse body of Buddhist doctrine called the *Abhidhamma.*"

Now we shall discuss how the Abhidh-s systematically describes the fours stages. According to the text:

> The path consciousness of stream-entry (*sotāpatti-maggacitta*) has the function of cutting off the first three fetters: personality-belief, doubt, and clinging to rules and vows; The path consciousness of once-returning (*sakadāgāmi-maggacitta*) attenuates the grosser forms of fetter of sensual desire, and ill-will;
>
> The path consciousness of non-returning (*sakadāgāmi-maggacitta*) cuts off the fetters of sensual desire, and ill-will; The path consciousness of arahatship (*arahatta-maggacitta*) destroys the five remaining fetters (five higher fetters): desire for form, desire for formlessness, conceit, restlessness, and ignorance (Nārada 1979, 87–88 & Bodhi 1999, 67–68).

From the above example, it is evident that the Abhidh-s systematically describes the four stages with the method of the traditional list of ten fetters. Examining the other enumerations in the *Abhidhamma* treatises, it is observed the above-enumeration is more systematic. The text (Bodhi 1999, 362) also analyses the four spiritual paths as saying that the five fetters, abandoned by the first three paths, are called the lower fetters (*orambhāgiya-saṃyojana*) because they bind beings to the lower world, the sensual sphere of existence. One who has eradicated them is called a non-returner, no longer returns to the sensual sphere, but he is still bound to the round of existence by the five higher fetters (*uddhambhāgiya-saṃyojana*). With the attainment of the path of arahatship, these five higher fetters are also eradicated. We believe this description of the four stages with the cutting of fetters directly influences the scholars.

That is why most scholars summarize the four stages of enlightenment in the following order:

1. The stream-enterer is one who has eradicated the three fetters of the five lower fetters: personality belief, doubt, and clinging to rules and vows.
2. The once-returner is one who has greatly weakened fourth and fifth lower fetters: sensual desire, and ill-will.
3. The non-returner is one who has completely destroyed fourth and fifth lower fetters: sensual desire, and ill-will.
4. The arahat is one who has completely destroyed the five higher fetters: desire for form, desire for formlessness, conceit, restlessness, and ignorance.

It is noteworthy that while the Abhidh-s defines the Four Noble Persons through the eradication of twelve unwholesome consciousness (*akusala-citta*), it does not include the fetter *sīlabbata-parāmāsa*. Comparing Bodhi's (1999) and Narada's (1979) translated volumes of the Abhidh-s, it seems to me that Narada (1979, 43) highlights the point as he says, "*sīlabbata-parāmāsa*-indulgence in wrongful rites and ceremonies, one of the ten Fetters, not mentioned above, is eradicated by a *Sotāpanna*." According to the *Abhidhammattha Saṅgaha* the twelve unwholesome consciousness are:

***Lobha-mūla-cittāni* (Consciousness Rooted in Greed)**

1. One consciousness, accompanied by joy, associated with wrong view, unprompted.
2. One consciousness, accompanied by joy, associated with wrong view, prompted.
3. One consciousness, accompanied by joy, dissociated with wrong view, unprompted.
4. One consciousness, accompanied by joy, dissociated with wrong view, prompted.
5. One consciousness, accompanied by equanimity, associated with wrong view, unprompted.

6. One consciousness, accompanied by equanimity, associated with wrong view, prompted.
7. One consciousness, accompanied by equanimity, dissociated with wrong view, unprompted.
8. One consciousness, accompanied by equanimity, dissociated with wrong view, prompted.

***Dosa-mūla-cittạni* (Consciousness Rooted in Hatred)**

9. One consciousness, accompanied by displeasure, associated with aversion, unprompted.
10. One consciousness, accompanied by displeasure, associated with aversion, prompted.

***Moha-mūla-cittāni* (Consciousness Rooted in Delusion)**

11. One consciousness, accompanied by equanimity, associated with doubt.
12. One consciousness, accompanied by equanimity, associated with restlessness (Bodhi 1999, 32–33, 36 & 37).

The *Abhidhammattha Saṅgaha* (Bodhi 1999, 181) says a stream-enterer eradicates the 1st, 2nd, 6th, 11th types of consciousness as he has destroyed the two fetters: *sakkāya-diṭṭhi*, and *vicikicchā*. A once-returner greatly reduces the potentiality of the 9th and 10th types of consciousness as he has attenuated the two fetters: *kāma rāga,* and *vyāpāda.* A non-returner eradicates the 9th and 10th types of consciousness as he has destroyed the two fetters: *kāma-rāga,* and *vyāpāda.* And, an arahat has eliminated all unwholesome consciousness as he has completely destroyed the five higher fetters: *rūpa-rāga, arūpa-rāga, māna, uddhacca*, and *avijjā*.

At this point, Venerable Narada points out that the text has not referred to the fetter *sīlabbata-parāmāsa* eradicated by the stream-enterer. Though he has not clarified in detail, it is possible that *sīlabbata-parāmāsa* (clinging to rules and vows) is associated with *diṭṭhi* (wrong view) due to which a person undertakes the rules and vows and he believes that through this practice one can attain liberation.

4.6.1 A Comparison between the Nine Fetters in the Abhidhammattha Saṅgaha and in the Sarvāstivāda Abhidharma

This section discusses the list of nine fetters enumerated in the Abhidh-s which is slightly different from any other lists. We have found that this list has close relationship with the list of nine fetters recorded in the Sarvāstivāda *Abhidharma*. Comparing both lists, it would seem that the Abhidh-s and the Sarvāstivāda *Abhidharma* introduce the list of nine fetters not to show existential binding, rather as mental factors as defilements (*kilesa*). Before dealing with this topic, let us list both lists of nine fetters in the Abhidh-s and the Sarvāstivāda *Abhidharma.*

The list of nine fetters, according to the Abhidh-s is: (1) greed (*lobha*), (2) wrong view (*diṭṭhi*), (3) delusion (*moha*), (4) hatred (*vyāpāda/paṭigha*), (5) doubt (*vicikicchā*), (6) conceit (*māna*), (7) restlessness (*uddhacca*), (8) envy (*issā*), and (9) avarice (*macchariya*) (Bodhi, 1999, 270).

The list of nine fetters, according to the Sarvāsitvāda *Abhidharma* is: (1) lust (*anunaya*), (2) hostility, (3) conceit, (4) ignorance, (5) views, (6) irrational adherence (*parāmarśa*), (7) doubt, (8) jealousy, and (9) avarice (Dhammajoti, 2015, 367).

Comparing the above-mentioned two lists, one could observe that both lists are quite similar, and the fetter of becoming (*bhava-rāga*) is excluded from both lists. The term *moha* is used as a synonym of *avidyā*. The function of *dṛṣṭi* and *parāmarśa* can be included in one category. Only the term *uddhacca* is added in the list of the Abhidh-s. If we take these enumerations into account, one could say that the Sarvāstivāda *Abhidharma* enumerates fetters to illustrate defilements, not to show the existential connotation. According to Dhammajoti (2015, 367), the Sarvāstivāda *Abhidharma* also holds the doctrine of the five lower fetters and the five higher fetters. He says the *Abhidharma*

Mahāvibhāṣā Śāstra (MVŚ) later divides the term *anunaya* (lust/greed) into two more categories that denote the fine-material sphere, and the immaterial sphere. Here it seems that the MVŚ follows the Pāli *Dhammasaṅgaṇi*'s enumeration which we have already discussed above.

The Abhidh-s, moreover, refers to the two lists of fetters: one belonging to *Sutta* method, and the other one belonging to *Abhidhamma* method. Comparing both lists, it is evident that although the text refers to the *Sutta* method of ten fetters, the enumeration of the list is different. The list is:

> Ten fetter, according to the *Sutta*: the fetter of (1) sensual desire, (2) desire for form, (3) desire for formlessness, (4) aversion, (5) conceit, (6) wrong views, (7) clinging to rites and ritual, (8) doubt, (9) restlessness, and (10) ignorance (Bodhi, 1999, 268).

From the above list, it seems that the author of the Abhidh-s enumerates the above set following the *Abhidhamma* list of ten fetters. The list is enumerated following *rāga, dosa* and *moha*, or *kāma-taṇhā*, *bhava-taṇhā*, or *kāma-bhava*, *rūpa-bhava*, and *arūpa-bhava*, because the term *kāma-rāga*, *rūpa-rāga*, and *arūpa-rāga* are placed as the first in the sequence.

In summary, we would like to say that it is the Abhidh-s which systematically describe the four stages with the traditional list of ten fetters. This description highly influences scholars in the Pāli tradition, more than other explanations on which we have discussed throughout this study. It is observed that the list of nine fetters in the Abhidh-s is quite similar to the list of nine fetters in the Sarvāstivāda *Abhidharma*. Comparing both lists, it seems that both lists mainly denote mental factors, not the existential setting. It is also observed that the author of the Abhidh-s enumerates the *Sutta* list of ten fetters following the *Abhidhamma* list, which is different from the traditional list of fetters in their sequence. Therefore, we believe throughout the Pāli tradition, the concept "fetter" was interpreted and developed from context to context in order to show the mental infatuation. However, the main development occurred during the compilation of the *Abhidhamma* texts, primarily in the *Dhammasaṅgaṇi*. In discussion of the above development of the concept "fetter", we would like to name the list of ten fetters which systematically describes the four stages as "traditional list", rather than "*Sutta* list". This list is more prevalent in the Pāli tradition.

Up to this part in this study we have shown the development of the concept of fetter. Now in the following part we will show how the fetters and other defilements are synonymous. We will discuss why the term "fetter" is prevalent to describe the four stages, when other "terms" denoting defilements are available. We will also discuss how to cut off the fetters for attaining final liberation. The part will end with a discussion on *avijjā*, being a root of not understanding the Four Noble Truths, how it is placed as the last of the two lists of ten fetters.

Part Two

4.7 The Fetters and Other Doctrinal Terms Denoting Defilement

This part shows the other doctrinal terms denoting defilement: *kilesa* in Pāli and *kleśa* in Sanskrit). According to Dhammajoti, the term *kilesa* is understood in the sense of 'defilement' or 'impurity' which he elaborates as:

> The occurrence of this term is rare in the *sūtra-piṭaka*. Its use was historically preceded by that of *upakleśa*, although subsequently the latter generally came to be understood as 'secondary defilements'—those which proceed from *kleśa*. At this later stage, it is explained that *upakleśa*-s are also the *kleśa*, but they additionally include other defilements which are not called *kleśa*. Examples of these secondary defilements are moral immodesty, avarice and restlessness which are said to be emanations (*niṣyanda*) from greed (*rāga*) (Dhammajoti, 2015, 365).

Many studies have been conducted on defilements in Buddhist studies. For example, Anālayo's *From Craving to Liberation...* (2009), *From Grasping to Emptiness...* (2010), Lee's *Beyond Āsava & Kilesa: Understanding the Roots of Suffering According to the Pāli Canon* (2009) are important scholarly works on defilements. Ow's (2000) PhD dissertation "Ānanda's Path to Becoming an Arahat: How He Overcame the Ten Fetters..." is a worthy work on the traditional list of ten fetters. Ow's research on the "Ten Fetters" contained in "Chapters 4 & 7" which are based on the Abhidh-s. He has not made any Canonical reference in his study. Although his study is relevant to this section, our discussion differs from him in that we show the other defilements are synonymous with fetters. The main focus of this section is to show how when different doctrinal terms to denote the defilements are available in the *Sutta*-s, the term "fetter" is prevalent to describe the four stages. Before dealing with this topic, it is first necessary to list the defilements in the Buddhist teachings. The lists are enumerated from the Abhidh-s, but the reference will also be traced from the *Sutta*-s and the *Abhidhamma*.

The Abhidh-s contains several lists of defilements including the fetter and latent tendencies. The lists of defilement are:

1. Four taints (*āsava*): sensual pleasure (*kāma*), becoming (*bhava*), wrong view (*diṭṭhi*), and ignorance (*avijjā*);
2. Four floods (*ogha*): sensual pleasure (*kāma*), becoming (*bhava*), wrong view (*diṭṭhi*), and ignorance (*avijjā*);
3. Four bonds (*yoga*): sensual pleasure (*kāma*), becoming (*bhava*), wrong view (*diṭṭhi*), and ignorance (*avijjā*);
4. Four knots (*gantha*): covetousness (*abhijjhā*), ill-will (*vyāpāda*), clinging to rules and vows (*sīlabbata-parāmāsa*), dogmatic belief that this alone is the truth (*idaṃ-saccābhinivesa*);

5. Four clinging (*upādāna*): sensual pleasure (*kāma*), wrong view (*diṭṭhi*), rules and vows (*sīlabbata*), doctrine of self (*attavāda*);
6. Six hindrances (*nīvaraṇa*): sensual pleasure (*kāma*), ill-will (*vyāpāda*), sloth and torpor (*thīna-middha*), restlessness and worry (*uddhacca-kukkucca*), doubt (*vicikicchā*), and ignorance (*avijjā*);
7. Seven latent tendencies (*anusaya*): sensual desire (*kāma-rāga*), desire for becoming (*bhava-rāga*), aversion (*paṭigha*), conceit (*māna*), wrong view (*diṭṭhi*), doubt (*vicikicchā*), ignorance (*avijjā*);
8. Ten fetters (*saṃyojana*), according to *Sutta* method: sensual desire (*kāma-rāga*), desire for form (*rūpa-rāga*), desire for formlessness (*arūpa-rāga*), aversion (*paṭigha*), conceit (*māna*), wrong view (*diṭṭhi*), clinging to rules and vows (*sīlabbata-parāmāsa*), doubt (*vicikicchā*), restlessness (*uddhacca*), and ignorance (*avijjā*);
9. Ten fetters (*saṃyojana*), according to *Abhidāamma* method: sensual desire (*kāma-rāga*), desire for becoming (*bhava-rāga*), aversion (*paṭigha*), conceit (*māna*), wrong view (*diṭṭhi*), clinging to rites and rituals (*sīlabbata-parāmāsa*), doubt (*vicikicchā*), envy (*issā*), avarice (*macchariya*) and ignorance (*avijjā*), and
10. Ten defilements (*kilesa*): greed (*lobha*), hatred (*dosa*), delusion (*moha*), conceit (*māna*), wrong view (*diṭṭhi*), doubt (*vicikicchā*), sloth (*thīna*), restlessness (*uddhacca*), shamelessness (*ahirika*), fearlessness of wrongdoing (*anottappa*) (Bodhi, 1999, 263–71).

The above paragraph contains all kinds of defilements from the Abhidh-s. Included in the paragraph, the two lists of ten fetters (the *Sutta* and the *Abhidhamma*), and list of seven latent tendencies (*anusaya*) together with their functions have been discussed in this work. Apart from that, now we will discuss other defilements in the following section.

Āsava is an important term which literally means "outflow". The *Abhidhammattha Saṅgaha* says, the word *āsava* "denotes both pus oozing from an abscess and intoxicants which have been fermented for a long time" (Bodhi, 1999, 265). Dhammajoti elaborates the term:

> Both the AKB [*Abhidharma-kośa-bhāsya*] and the *Avatāra* give three etymologies for *āsrava*: (1) they keep (*āsayanti*) beings in the three spheres of existence; (ii) they cause beings to flow around (*āsravanti*) between the highest state of existence (*bhavāgra*) and the lowest, the Avici hell; (iii) they incessantly discharge (*kṣar*) inexhaustible impurities through the six wound-like entrances—the six sense faculties—of beings (*ṣadbhir āyatanavraṇāih*) (Dhammajoti, 2015, 368).

Earlier in this chapter we have mentioned that the *Sutta*-s only contain the three *āsava*-s, later the *Dhammasaṅgaṇi* added *diṭṭhi-āsava* to make four. The *Vibhaṅga* (VRI 205) also mentions the list of four taints. According to Dhammajoti (2015, 368), there are three *āsava*-s in the Sarvāstivāda *Abhidharma*.

The above-mentioned taints are also called floods. Similarly, they are called bonds (*yoga*). The flood denotes the act of sweeping beings into the ocean of existence, and they are unable to cross. The bond denotes yoking beings to suffering, do not allow them to escape from the cycle of existence. These fourfold floods and bonds are also found in the *Sutta*-s (SN V 59). Similarly, the fourfold clinging and knots are found in the *Sutta*-s (SN V 56 & 60). The hindrances are so called because they constitute the obstacles for the noble path. The six hindrances which are contained in the Abhidh-s are also found in the *Dhammasaṅgaṇi* (VRI 140), but the *Sutta*-s (SN V 60) record only five hindrances. It is the *Dhammasaṅgaṇi* which adds the hindrance of "ignorance" to the list. According to the *Abhidhammattha Saṅgaha*, "the five hindrances are the major obstacles to the attainment of the *jhānas*, the sixth hindrance is the major obstacle to the arising of wisdom" (Bodhi 1999, 267). There is also a list of ten defilements found in the Abhidh-s. The text says, they are called defilements because "they afflict (*kilissanti*) or torment the mind, or because they defile beings by dragging them down to a mentally soiled and depraved condition" (Bodhi 1999, 269). Among the listed defilements, according to Dhammajoti, some defilements are 'secondary defilements' (*upakleśa*-s), i.e. as Dhammajoti illustrates:

> Examples of these secondary defilements are moral immodesty, avarice and restlessness which are said to be emanations (*niṣyanda*) from greed (*rāga*) (Dhammajoti, 2015, 365).

The list of ten defilements is also found in the *Dhammasaṅgaṇi* (VRI 146), which is further enumerated in the *Vibhaṅga* (VRI 206). But, the *Sutta*-s, for example, the *Vatthupamā Sutta* (MN I 36–40) consists a set of sixteen defilements (see 2.8), many of them are not found in the list. It seems that the enumeration of defilements is different from context to context.

Analysing the above-mentioned defilements, it is observed there is no difference between fetters, taints, bonds, etc. in terms of their functions. The difference only lies in the scope of operation. For example, in the *Sutta*-s, the stage of arahatship is attributed as *khīna-āsava*, one who has exhausted the out-flows, which is used as an epithet for an arahat. Sometimes, it is also said the final goal is the destruction of all defilements. Nonetheless, the term "*saṃyojana*" has become very prevalent among other terms to describe final liberation. Somaratne (1999, 129) says "taints" and "fetters" are more or less the same and the difference lies mostly in the terms used rather than in meaning. Lee (2009, 44–45) says, the fetter is proximately related to *āsava* and the all fetters originated in it. We also agree that "taints" and "fetters" are more or less the same in function. But the difference lies in usages. Here we suggest that the term *āsava* is used for denoting an arahat (*khīna-āsava*) in this very life in the Pāli Canon, whereas the term *saṃyojana* is used for describing the spiritual stages to show rebirth through existential binding from this life to another life.

Moreover, although the words "bond" and "yoke" (*yoga*) are quite similar to "fetter" (*saṃyojana*), there are still subtle differences. The term *yoga* and *yojana* are derived from the word *yojayanti* or *yuñjati*, meaning "binding". However, *yojana* is applied with the prefix *saṃ* (*saṃ+yojana*) which means "together," and *saṃyojana* means "binding together," which binds a person from this existence to another existence, or from here to there. The term "yoke" has less impact in terms of its application. The Commentarial (Sv VRI 104) explanation of the term *saṃyojana* equates it with the term *bandhana* (bondage). Dhammajoti (2015, 368) says, "this term [bondage] stresses the aspect of defilement which is the binding of beings to the triple sphere of existence". Three kinds of bondages are mentioned in the *Sutta*-s (SN IV 292): (1) greed-bondage (*rāga-bandhana*), (2) hatred-bondage (*dosa-bandhana*), and (3) delusion-bondage (*moha-bandhana*). About these three bondages, Dhammajoti elaborates:

> The greed-bondage, which comprises all greed, with same characterization as for the lust-fetter; the hatred-bondage, which comprises all hatred, with the same characterization as for the hostility-fetter; and the delusion-bondage, which comprises all delusion, with the same characterization as for the ignorance fetter (Dhammajoti, 2015, 367–68).

Through the above discussion, we intend to say that the term *saṃyojana* is more relevant to show the binding in the sense of existential binding from this existence to another existence. The term can also be used for any kinds of binding, for example, intra-psychic binding, householder binding on which we have discussed in this study. Showing the above examples, we intend to say that *saṃyojana* is a technical term used in the Buddha's teaching for denoting binding. But, in Buddhist teachings, it is always referred to as binding to unwholesome things. Through this study, we come to the conclusion that the term was initially used to denote the "intra-psychic bind" that is dependent on the sense bases and sense objects with regard to the practice of *satipaṭṭhāna*. But, subsequently the term was used for showing the existential binding to establish the concept of rebirth in *saṃsāra*, the cycle of existence.

4.8 How Fetters can be Cut off for Attaining Liberation

Chapter 3 (see 3.8) has discussed several methods for attaining liberation without fetters. It was mentioned that all these methods are awakening techniques for attaining liberation. As far as liberation is concerned, through these techniques one can cut off all fetters as well as all kinds of defilements. Nevertheless, some specific *Sutta*-s are found in the *Nikāya*-s, which contain methods on how to cut off fetters. For example, the *Saññojana-samugghāta Sutta* (SN IV 31–32) says, when one knows and sees the six sense bases as impermanent, the six sense objects as impermanent, the six sense base—consciousness, contact at the six sense bases—fetters are abandoned and true knowledge arises. When one knows and sees as impermanent whatever feeling arises with mind-contact as condition, whether pleasant or painful or neither-painful-nor-pleasant, fetters are abandoned and true knowledge arises. When one knows and sees thus, fetters are abandoned and true knowledge arises.

Another *Saññojana-samugghāta Sutta* (SN IV 31–32) similarly states when one knows and sees the six sense bases as non-self, the six sense objects as non-self, etc., fetters are abandoned and true knowledge arises. The *Iddhipāda Saṃyutta* (SN V 254) of the same *Vagga* says, through the development of mindfulness one can cut off the fetters. The *Ogha Vagga* of the *Sammappadhana Saṃyutta* (SN V 242) says, through the development of the four right striving (non-arising of un-arisen unwholesome states, abandoning of arisen unwholesome states, arising of un-arisen wholesome states, maintenance of arisen wholesome states), one can cut off the fetters. The *Bala Saṃyutta* of *Mahāvagga* (SN V 247) says through the development of the spiritual powers (faith, effort, mindfulness, concentration and wisdom) one can cut off the fetters. Here it is necessary to say that through these methods one not only cuts off the fetters, but also he can cut off all other defilements recorded in the *Sutta*-s and the *Abhidhamma*.

4.9 *Avijjā* and Its Functions

So far this study it has analysed the four stages through the eradication of ten fetters. Ow's (2000) PhD dissertation "Ānanda's Path to Becoming an Arahat: How He Overcame the Ten Fetters..." discusses each of the "Ten Fetters" in its Chapters 4 & 7. Ven. Nyanatiloka's (1980) *The Ten Fetters of Existence* (*Dasa Saṃyojana*) similarly discusses the traditional list of ten fetters. On defilements a number of studies are also available, including Fuller's *The Notion of Diṭṭhi in Theravāda Buddhism* (2005) and Thanissaro Bhikkhu's *The Paradox of Becoming* (2008). However, this section will only show ignorance (*avijjā*), being a root of not understating the Four Noble Truths, how it is placed as the last in the list of ten fetters.

It is common-place in the Buddha's teachings that the root cause of all cravings and consequent sufferings are due to ignorance. The *Kūṭa Sutta* (SN II 262–63) says, "whatever unwholesome things are there, they are all due to ignorance" (*ye keci akusalamūlā sabbe te avijjaṅgamā*). The *Vibhaṅga Sutta* of the *Nidāna Vagga* in SN explains the function of ignorance as follows:

> Monks! Not knowing suffering, not knowing the origin of suffering, not knowing the cessation of suffering, not knowing the way leading to the cessation of suffering. Monks! This is called ignorance (SN II 2–4).[13]

---

[13] *yaṃ kho bhikkhave dukkhe aññṇaṃ, dukkhasamudaye aññṇaṃ, dukkhanirodhe aññṇaṃ, dukkha-nirodhagāminiyā paṭipadāya aññṇaṃ, ayaṃ vuccati bhikkhave, avijjā.*

This explanation also applies to the five aggregates in the *Avijjā Sutta* of the *Khanddha Vagga* (SN III 162–63). This passage shows that ignorance is the basic cause of becoming or *saṃsāric* existence, which is lack of knowledge of the Four Noble Truths, and lack of proper understanding about the five aggregates and the consequent clinging to them give rise to the conceit of 'I' or 'I' ness. Due to lack of proper understanding, the 'I' ness constitutes bondage and, therefore, liberation is said to be the eradication of this conceit of 'I' ness. This 'I' ness is the form of clinging caused by desire or craving for personality-belief (*sakkāya-diṭṭhi*). Therefore, it is quite understandable that liberation is defined through destruction of craving.

In the *Sutta*-s (SN II 72), suffering and its cessation is being defined through the causal condition based on the doctrine of dependent co-arising (*paṭicca-samuppāda*) which contains twelve links. The destruction of one link in the setting of twelve links leads to the destruction of other links. As the Buddha himself points out, through the cessation of ignorance (*avijjā*) other links are extinguished, and there is no future arising. But, sometimes the Buddha is said to have taught: through the eradication of craving, clinging is extinguished, and through the extinction of clinging, the process of becoming is extinguished. Following cessation of the other links in the sequence, finally there is no future becoming.

To say one attains final liberation through the eradication of ten fetters is an abbreviated form to describe liberation. However, ignorance which is a root cause of knowing the 'I' ness or the personality-belief, is placed at the end. One becomes a stream-enterer through the eradication of first three fetters in which the personality-belief (*sakkāya-diṭṭhi*) comes first in the sequence. This is a view produced by clinging to the notion of 'I' ness. The Buddha analyses the total 'I' ness into the five aggregates and says there is nothing permanent (MN I 232–33). In the *Khandha Saṃyutta* of the *Khandha Vagga* (SN III 58–59), the Buddha is said to have taught that the five aggregates are suffering or the five aggregates are subject to clinging of suffering. If we take this example into consideration, it is obvious that though ignorance is placed as the last of the list of ten fetters, a stream-enterer has already removed a grosser level of ignorance (*avijjā*). From the *Khandhasaṃyutta* of the *Khandha Vagga* in SN, it can be traced that one who understands the five aggregates as they really are in terms of the "arising and the passing away, the indulgence, the danger, and the deliverance in the group of the five aggregates of clinging, he is called a noble disciple who is a stream-enterer" (SN III 160–61).[14] The same *Sutta* says having understood the five aggregates a person becomes an arahat.

Although it is understood that a stream-enterer has removed a grosser level of ignorance (*avijjā*) until the attainment of stage of arahatship, he still has to remove ignorance while passing through the stages of once-returning, and non-returning. That is why, it is proper to say that all of the ten fetters are associated with ignorance. To support this argument, a passage from the *Attasālinī*, the Commentary to the *Dhammasaṅgaṇi*, is quoted as follows:

> As long as sensual desire exists, the fetter of ignorance arises with the four fetters of conceit, view, clinging to rules and vows, and ignorance. When avarice exists, the fetter of ignorance arises with the three fetters of envy, selfishness, and ignorance. When the fetter of conceit exists, the fetter of ignorance arises with the fetter of desire for becoming. When there doubt exists, the fetter of ignorance arises with doubt (As VRI 105).[15]

[14] *ariyasāvako imesaṃ pañcannaṃ upadānakkhandhānaṃ samudayañca atthagamañaca assādañca ādīnavañca nissaraṇañca yathābhūtaṃ pajānati. Ayaṃ vuccati bhikkhave, ariyasāvako sotāpanno.*

[15] *kāmarāgo tāva mānasaṃyojanaavijjāsaṃyojanehi ceva, diṭṭhisaṃyojanaavijjāsaṃyojanehi ca, sīlabbata-parāmāsaavijjāsaṃyojanehi ca, avijjāsaṃyojanamatteneva ca saddhinti evaṃ catudhā ekato uppajjati. Paṭigho pana issāsaṃyojanaavijjāsaṃyojanehi ceva, macchariya-saṃyojanaavijjāsaṃyojanehi ca, avijjāsaṃyojanamatteneva ca saddhinti evaṃ tidhā ekato uppajjati. Māno bhavarāgāvijjāsaṃyojanehi saddhiṃ ekadhāva ekato uppajjati. Tathā vicikicchā. Sā hi avijjāsaṃyojanena saddhiṃ ekadhā uppajjati.*

From the above passage, it is evident that although ignorance is placed as the last of the list of ten fetters, the subtle form of ignorance exists until the attainment of the stage of arahatship. That is why, ignorance is placed at the end. However, if someone considers ignorance one of the fetters and it is only destroyed by the stage of arahatship, it would be illogical. Ignorance has to be removed from the stage of stream-entry up to the stage of the arahatship. In that case, ignorance as the latent tendency (*avijjā-anusaya*) is more appropriate than ignorance with the term fetter (*avijjā-saṃyojana*). We have frequently referred to the example of the *Purisagati Sutta* (AN IV 70–71), in which the Buddha is said to have described a non-returner as one who has not yet realized the highest stage of arahatship due to not having cut off the three latent tendencies: *bhava-rāga-anusaya, māna-anusaya*, and *avijjā-anuṣaya*. If we consider this example, it is correct to say that for a non-returner the desire for becoming, conceit, and ignorance still exist at a latent level. Therefore, we find *Purisagati Sutta*'s enumeration (see 3.3) more accurate to understand the four stages of enlightenment with the method of fetters. Considering the traditional list of ten fetters, it would be appropriate to say the five higher fetters are "subtle fetters" or "latent tendencies" in other words.

4.10 Conclusion

This chapter has argued that the description of the four stages of enlightenment with the traditional list of ten fetters was entirely developed in the *Dhammasaṅgaṇi* to show the attainment of enlightenment through the stage by stage sequentially. Although the definition of the spiritual stages with giving up the fetters was contained in the *Sutta*-s, the definition of the stage of once-returning through the attenuation of sensual desire (*kāma-rāga*), ill-will (*vyāpāda*), and the stage of arahatship through the eradication of desire for form (*rūpa-rāga*), desire for formlessness (*arūpa-rāga*), conceit (*māna*), restlessness (*uddhacca*), and ignorance (*avijjā*) never occurs in the first four *Nikāya*-s. This study has shown that the *Dhammasaṅgaṇi* divides *Sutta*-s enumeration of once-returning *rāga* > *kāma-rāga*, *dosa* > *vyāpāda/paṭigha*, and *moha* >*uddhacca*. The term *uddhacca* was placed in the list of higher fetters, and the term *bhava-rāga* is divided into *rūpa-rāga* and *arūpa-rāga,* and made the list of five defilements (five higher fetters): *rūpa-rāga, arūpa-rāga, māna, uddhacca,* and *avijjā*. But, the description of four stages in the *Dhammasaṅgaṇi* is somewhat exceptional as the text does not refer to the schemes of lower and higher fetters, not even the traditional list of ten fetters. Instead, the text introduces a new set of ten fetters which is traditionally known as the *Abhidhamma* list. This study has also shown that the *Abhidhamma* list is older than the traditional list of ten fetters in terms of their compilation. To the best of our understanding, it seems that the *Vibhaṅga* takes the *Dhammasaṅgaṇi*'s enumeration and divides it into two categories: the lower fetters and the higher fetters.

This study has shown that the *Puggalapaññatti* shares the *Dhammasaṅgaṇi*'s enumeration, but combines the definition with the *Sutta*-s, and the *Dhammasaṅgaṇi*. It is the *Kathāvatthu* which describes the spiritual stages based on the *Dhammasaṅgaṇi*'s explanation, and discounts the *Sutta*-s method. This text first shows the traditional usage of the schemes of lower and higher fetters. In this regard, we have reviewed Sujato and Brahmali's (2014) claim that the *Kathāvatthu* only discusses materials taken from the early Buddhist texts, mostly the *Nikāya*-s, but not the *Abhidhamma*. The *Niddesa* and the *Paṭisambhidāmagga* were entirely formed after the *Abhidhamma* literature as both of them share the *Dhammasaṅgaṇi*'s classification of spiritual stages. But, both texts were compiled based on the *Sutta*-s and the *Abhidhamma*. In passing, this chapter has also mentioned that the *Paṭisambhidāmagga*'s exposition of four stages together with the fetters and latent tendencies was shared in the *Visuddhimagga*.

This chapter notes that the Abhidh-s which was composed based on the *Abhidhamma Piṭaka* takes further steps to describe the four stages with the lower and higher fetters. This description is more systematic which directly influences scholars in the Pāli tradition. This study argues the term *saṃyojana* best suits to describe the four stages than the other terms denoting the defilement. It was also argued that initially the term appears to denote the "intra-psychic" bind dependent on sense bases and sense objects, and subsequently it was used to denote to the existential binding of rebirth from existence to existence or from here to there.

This chapter ends by discussing the function of ignorance. This study has shown that although ignorance is placed as the last of the two lists of ten fetters, a practitioner has to remove grosser form of ignorance while passing through the stages of stream-entry, once-returning, and non-returning. Finally, ignorance remains at a latent level which can be called the "latent tendency of ignorance" (*avijjā-anusaya*) or "subtle fetter". This ignorance is completely eradicated when one becomes an arahat.

Chapter 5 – **Conclusion**

Hwang says:

> [E]xplaining the four noble persons entirely in terms of their giving up of the traditional ten fetters is a later development, within the *abhidhamma*. It is in the *Dhammasaṅgaṇi* that a once returner was first explained in this sense.... This new interpretation was later applied in the *Puggalapaññatti* and also appeared in the *Dharmaskandha* in the Chinese *abhidharma* (Hwang, 2006, 27).

Somaratne opines:

> It seems to me that the listing of "restlessness" (*uddhacca*) among the five higher fetters was first a textual corruption and then slipped into the tradition to become part of the standard list (Somaratne, 1999, 144).

Through careful textual analysis of the *Sutta* and the *Abhidhamma Piṭaka*-s, this study has investigated two scholars' above-mentioned valuable perspectives on why the concept of fetter (*saṃyojana*) was given more importance in defining the soteriological aim in Buddhist teachings, when other concepts without fetters are available in the *Sutta*-s. Through the present investigation, this study has found that the *Abhidhamma* only emphasizes one method for achieving liberation, which is through the eradication of fetters or defilements, and discounts the other methods recorded in the *Sutta*-s. It is initially the composers of the *Dhammasaṅgaṇi* who took the initiative to systematize the description of the four stages sequentially with the method of fetters. They first ever described the stage of once-returning through the attenuation of *kāma-rāga*, and *vyāpāda*. They also described the stage of arahatship through the destruction of *rūpa-rāga*, *arūpa-rāga, māna, uddhacca,* and *avijjā*. These descriptions of stages of once-returning and arahatship were not found in the *Sutta*-s. Investigating the *Sutta*-s, it was observed that the concept "fetter" is not only employed to define the four stages, but it also has different variations from context to context throughout the *Sutta* and the *Abhidhamma Piṭaka*-s.

One variation of this concept is prominent in the Pāli Canon and its Commentaries, and among scholars. This variation is in the description of the four stages of enlightenment using the method of fetters. It is said, one who eradicates the first three fetters of the five lower fetters, becomes a stream-enterer. One who weakens the fourth and fifth lower fetters, becomes a once-returner. One who completely destroys the fourth and fifth lower fetters, becomes a non-returner. And, one who gives up the five higher fetters, becomes an arahat. This is one of the standard definitions of the four stages. But, this definition which is applicable to all Four Noble Persons is not found in the *Sutta*-s, because it was developed in the *Abhidhamma.*

To me, the compilers of the *Abhidhamma* have implied that one can attain final liberation going through stage by stage, i.e. stream-entry, once-returning, non-returning, and arahatship, in this very life or after death rather than becoming an enlightened being 'arahat' at a time. This theory suggests the spiritual maturity of an individual is from the perspective of progressive or sequential attainment. That is to say, the Ābhidhammikas have traditionalized or systematized one type of sequential attainment of enlightenment, which is through the eradication of ten fetters only. The Ābhidhammikas seem to present the Buddha's teaching into a perspective of comprehensive visions all-encompassing a system of completeness and with an analytical precision. Through this process, the compilers of the *Abhidhamma* show the existence of a person in different existential realms considering to the level of his or her defilements until the attainment of final liberation. It was shown that the compilers used the concept of fetter to define the spiritual attainment with the method of fetter, that is through the eradication of fetters, rather than other methods referred in the *Sutta*-s. That could be a reason that throughout the Buddha's teaching, the Buddha is said to have taught that the attainment of enlightenment is cessation of suffering. Since the Buddha teaches that suffering is due to our defiled attitudes, mental view points from greed (*lobha*), hatred (*dosa*) and delusion (*moha*), the Ābhidhammikas take this phenomenological psychology of a person that to say that the purification of mind from all kinds of defilement brings about liberation. As all fetters or defilements orient from greed, hatred and delusion, therefore, the *Abhidhamma* texts show that the whole scale of mental purification is emancipation from all fetters or defilements. Therefore, this study proposes that the four stages of enlightenment are the process of emancipation from all defilements which is systematically portrayed with giving up of the traditional ten fetters during the compilation of the *Abhidhamma*, mainly in the *Dhammasaṅgaṇi*.

The development of the concept of fetter was discussed in chapter four. It demonstrates the stages of once-returning and arahatship were first described with the giving up of the traditional fetters in the *Dhammasaṅgaṇi*, the first text of the *Abhidhamma Piṭaka*. As such, it was shown that the terms *rāga, dosa*, and *moha* which were applied to define the once-returner in the *Sutta*-s, were defined in terms of fetters: *rāga* as *kāma-rāga*, *dosa* as *vyāpāda/paṭigha*, and *moha* as *uddhacca* in the *Abhidhamma*. And, the term *bhava-rāga-anusaya* found in AN IV 70 was defined as *rūpa-rāga*, and *arūpa-rāga*. With the *bhava-rāga-anusaya*, *māna-anusaya*, and *avijjā-anusaya*, the stage of non-returner was defined in AN IV 70. It is possible that the composers of the *Dhammasaṅgaṇi* took this reference and divided the term *bhāva-rāga-anusaya* into two kinds—*rūpa*, and *arūpa*—and *māna*, and *avijjā-anusaya*-s were kept without defining. To show the five fetters, the composers added the term *uddhacca* in the sequence right after the terms *rūpa-rāga* and *arūpa-rāga*. The term *uddhacca* was clarified with the term *moha* as saying that the root of "restlessness" is due to "ignorance". The *Dhammasaṅgaṇi* describes the once-returner as one who has weakened *kāma-rāga* and *vyāpāda/ paṭigha*, and the non-returner as one who has completely eradicated *kāma-rāga* and *vyāpāda/ paṭigha.* The text then describes the arahat as one who has given up *rūpa-rāga, arūpa-rāga, māna, uddhacca,* and *avijjā.* Although the text defines the spiritual stages in accordance with the degree of fetter, it does not contain any schemes of lower and higher fetters, not even the traditional list of ten fetters. Instead the text introduces its own list of ten fetters which is different from the traditional list. In this regard, this study has argued that it is the *Vibhaṅga* which takes the *Dhammasaṅgaṇi*'s enumeration and divides it into two categories: the lower and the higher fetters. Of course, the schemes of higher and lower fetters were found in several *Sutta*-s, for example, DN II 232 and AN V 17. But, while the scheme of lower fetters is employed to define the spiritual stages, the scheme of higher fetters is not used at all to define the stage of arahatship. As they were not entirely employed to describe the four stages in the *Sutta*-s, this study has suggested they could be later interpolation in the *Sutta*-s, probably influenced by the composers of the *Dhammasaṅgaṇi* and the *Vibhaṅga.*

Reference was made in chapter 4 (see 4.3) to Thittila (1969) and Iggleden (1997) who claim that the *Dhammasaṅgaṇi*'s enumerations were further taken by the *Vibhaṅga* to show how to *Dhammasaṅgaṇi*'s enumerations were applied. Relying on the work of Frauwallner (1995), some scholars such as Sujato (2012) say the *Vibhaṅga* consists of earlier doctrines, some of which are relevant to the *Dharmaskandha* and the *Śāriputrābhidharma*. In this regard, our study has shown that the *Vibhaṅga* shares many materials from the *Dhammasaṅgaṇi* including the four kinds of taints, the ten defilements, and the *Dhammasaṅgaṇi* list of ten fetters. Therefore, we reveal that the *Vibhaṅga* would not be entirely the earlier work in the *Abhidhamma Piṭaka*, rather it was composed simultaneously with the *Dhammasaṅgaṇi*.

Furthermore, the *Puggalapaññatti* also shares the *Dhammasaṅgaṇi*'s enumeration of the stages of non-returning and arahatship. But the *Puggalapaññatti* follows both the *Sutta*, and the *Abhidhamma* enumerations for describing the spiritual stages with the method of fetters. It was observed that the *Puggalapaññatti* only accepts the *Dhammasaṅgaṇi*'s enumeration to describe the stage of arahatship, and discounts the *Sutta*-s account. It is mainly the *Kathāvatthu* which describes the four stages of enlightenment with one method of fetter. The way the *Kathāvatthu* emphasizes the importance of the traditional list of fetters also reveals the great significance of the schemes of lower and higher fetters because these are duly applied to denote the lower and higher existence. Apart from the *Kathāvatthu*, no text of the *Sutta Piṭaka* and the *Abhidhamma Piṭaka* properly employs the higher and lower fetters.

It was also argued that the *Paṭisambhidāmagga* and the *Niddesa* were not forerunner of the *Abhidhamma*, rather they were produced over a long time and the final compositions took place after the *Abhidhamma*. Through scrutiny, this study has found both texts have shared the *Abhidhammic* interpretation of the concept of fetter. Additionally, it was shown that both texts were composed based on the *Sutta* and *Abhidhamma* materials. Citing the above sources, this study comes to conclusion that the schemes of higher and lower fetters are historical construction in the *Abhidhamma*.

On the basis of the *Abhidhamma Piṭaka*, the *Abhidhammattha Saṅgaha* takes further steps to define the four stages with the traditional list of ten fetters. To our observation, the *Abhidhammattha Saṅgaha*'s interpretation is more systematic, and is adopted by modern scholars in the Theravāda tradition to define the four stages. Based upon this, chapter four looks into the development of the concept "fetter" in the *Abhidhamma Piṭaka*.

Chapter three discusses the spiritual stages: stream-entry, once-returning, non-returning, and arahatship together with the methods of liberation with fetter and without fetters. In exploring the spiritual stages without fetters, we have shown that there are different ways for attaining the four stages of enlightenment. The methods without fetters were shown with (1) understanding and penetration into the Four Noble Truths including the Noble Eightfold Path, (2) insight into the five aggregates, (3) insight into the impermanent, suffering and non-self nature, (4) development and cultivation of mindfulness, (5) having abandoned the five things of selfishness (*macchariya*), (6) accomplishment of the five spiritual faculties, etc. These enumerations signify the value of understanding of the *dhamma*; indeed, all the methods demand an intellectual understanding of spiritual nature. In a similar approach, scholars Davids and Stede (1993, 143–44) claim that the stage of non-returning does not mean the abandonment of defilements, but the cultivation of certain good mental habits, such as *anatta* doctrines and the five *indriya*-s. These methods, however, can be explained mainly by emphasizing the realization of the spiritual stages in this very life, whereas the method with fetter emphasizes the existential binding from this world to another world.

When we look into the *Nikāya*-s for methods to attain the various stages of liberation, we find that the method with fetters provided by the first four *Nikāya*-s is different from the *Abhidhamma*. In the *Nikāya*-s, we have referred to the *Purisagati Sutta* (AN IV 70) which says non-returners are reborn in the Pure Abodes due to not having cut off the three latent tendencies: latent tendency of desire for becoming (*bhava-rāga-anusaya*), latent tendency of conceit (*māna-anusaya*), and latent tendency of ignorance (*avijjā-anusaya*).

In this regard, this study notes that no *Sutta*-s define a non-returner as one who is born in the Pure Abode due to not having given up the five higher fetters: desire for form, desire for formlessness, conceit, restlessness, and ignorance. To support this argument, reference was made to Somaratne (1999) who shows the weakness of the scheme of higher fetters in the *Sutta*-s. By showing this contrast, this study proposes that it is only the *Abhidhamma* which interprets the four stages of enlightenment entirely with giving up of the traditional ten fetters. The way the *Nikāya*-s emphasizes the four stages with the method of fetter links to existential binding. This method of fetter mainly denotes the rebirth into the three realms depending on the degree of the remaining fetters. On the other hand, the methods without fetters are emphasising the realization of the four stages in this very life. In this way, the third chapter reveals the four stages with fetters and without fetters.

Chapter two has only shown different variations of the concept "fetter" without referring to the four stages of enlightenment. It discusses different individual fetters such as the fetters of *taṇhā, nandi*, *bhava, gihi*, *lokāmisa*, *āneñja*, *ākiñcaññāyatana*, and *nevasaññānāsaññāyatana*. These fetters do not appear in the list of ten fetters. By consulting the *Sutta*-s, this study has presented that they are initial usages of the concept of fetter in the Buddhist teachings from which the other fetters grew. This chapter has argued that the concept "fetter" has three main variations in the Pāli Canon: (1) intra-psychic, (2) existential, and (3) householder bindings. The intra-psychic binding is defined with the fetter *chanda-rāga* which is examined as an earlier appearance of the concept of fetter in the Pāli Canon. The existential binding was examined with the three fetters: *nandi*, *taṇhā*, and *bhava-saṃyojana*. Here we have shown two interpretations of these fetters referring to intra-psychic and existential bindings. Each of these fetters appears in the earlier phase of Buddha's teachings and liberation was defined through abandoning each of these fetters.

Another variation of fetter was shown with the fetter of householder (*gihi-saṃyojana*) which refers to properties grain, wealth, and clothes, etc. of a householder. In this category the chapter has shown the list of eight kinds of fetter which is a different interpretation from any other lists of fetters. Including this variation of fetter another demarcation was shown in association with several *jhāna* states which is completely different from other cited categories. In addition, this study explores that the term *saṃyojana* initially was applied to denote the "intra-psychic binding" which is dependent on the sense bases and sense objects. Later this intra-psychic binding was superseded by the "existential binding" to show the rebirth in Buddhist teachings. And, this existential binding is prevalent in the Theravāda tradition.

Showing the different variations of the function of fetter, this study aims to prove that the concept "fetter" has different interpretations from context to context in the *Sutta*-s. But whenever it is associated with existential binding, the concept was developed from the *Sutta*-s to the *Abhidhamma*. The final development occurs to describe the four stages through giving up the fetters within the *Abhidhamma*. We hope that this study has charted the development of the concept "fetter" in the Pāli Canon. This study has shed some important light on the soteriological and historical concerns of the Buddhist teachings. We also hope that this work makes a contribution in respect of doctrinal development in the Pāli Canon. It is further hoped that our humble efforts in this study could inspire other scholars in the Pāli tradition to do research in the area of doctrinal development in the Pāli Canon.

Bibliography

PRIMARY SOURCES

The Pāli Text Society (PTS) Editions

The Dīgha Nikāya, Vols.I–III. Edited by T.W. Rhys Davids, and J.E. Carpenter. Oxford: PTS, 1889–2007.

The Majjhima Nikāya, Vols.I–III. Edited by V. Trenckner, T.W. Rhys Davids, J. Estlin Carpenter, Robert Chalmers. Oxford: PTS, 1888–2001.

The Samyutta Nikāya, Vols.I–IV. Edited by Mrs. C.A.F. Rhys Davids, Leon Feer, and G.A. Somaratne. Oxford: PTS, 1884–2000.

The Aṅguttara Nikāya, Vols.I-V. Edited by A.K. Warder, Rev. Richard Morris, E. Hardy. Oxford: PTS, 1855–1999.

The Dhammapada. Edited by O. von Hinüber, and K.R. Norman. Oxford: PTS, 1994–95.

The Sutta Nipāta. Edited by Dines Andersen, and Helmer Smith. Oxford: PTS, 1997.

The Theragāthā, and *The Therīgāthā*. Edited by H. Oldenberg, R. Pischel, K.R. Norman, and L. Alsdrof. Oxford: PTS, 1883–1990.

The Itivuttaka. Edited by Ernst Windisch. Oxford: PTS, 1975.

The Vipassana Research Institute (VRI) Editions

The *Dīgha Nikāya-aṭṭhakathā* (*Manorathapūraṇī*), Parts I–III. The Chaṭṭha Saṅgāyana (Sixth Council) resources. Igatpuri: VRI. http://www.tipitaka.org/pdf/romn/

The *Majjhima Nikāya-aṭṭhakathā* (*Papañcasūdanī*), Parts I–III. The Chaṭṭha Saṅgāyana (Sixth Council) resources. Igatpuri: VRI. http://www.tipitaka.org/pdf/romn/

The *Saṃyutta Nikāya-aṭṭhakathā* (*Sāratthappakāsinī*), Parts I–V. The Chaṭṭha Saṅgāyana (Sixth Council) resources. Igatpuri: VRI. http://www.tipitaka.org/pdf/romn/

The *Aṅguttara Nikāya-aṭṭhakathā* (*Manorathapūraṇī*), Parts I–III. The Chaṭṭha Saṅgāyana (Sixth Council) resources. Igatpuri: VRI. http://www.tipitaka.org/pdf/romn/

The *Majjhima Nikāya-aṭṭhakathā-ṭīkā*. The Chaṭṭha Saṅgāyana (Sixth Council) resources. Igatpuri: VRI. http://www.tipitaka.org/pdf/romn/

The *Cūḷaniddesa*, and The *Cūḷaniddesa-aṭṭhakathā*, Parts I–II.—The Chaṭṭha Saṅgāyana (Sixth Council) resources. Igatpuri: VRI. http://www.tipitaka.org/pdf/romn/

The *Mahāniddesa,* and the *Māhaniddesa-aṭṭhakathā*. The Chaṭṭha Saṅgāyana (Sixth Council) resources. Igatpuri: VRI. http://www.tipitaka.org/pdf/romn/

The *Paṭisambhidāmagga*, and The *Paṭisambhidāmagga-aṭṭhakathā*. The Chaṭṭha Saṅgāyana (Sixth Council) resources. Igatpuri: VRI. http://www.tipitaka.org/pdf/romn/

The *Dhammasaṅgaṇi,* and The *Dhammasaṅgaṇi-aṭṭhakathā* (*Atthasālinī*). The Chaṭṭha Saṅgāyana (Sixth Council) resources. Igatpuri: VRI. http://www.tipitaka.org/pdf/romn/

The *Vibhaṅga,* and The *Vibhaṅga-aṭṭhakathā* (*Sammoha-vinodanī*). The Chaṭṭha Saṅgāyana (Sixth Council) resources. Igatpuri: VRI. http://www.tipitaka.org/pdf/romn/

The *Puggalapaññatti,* and The *Puggalapaññatti-aṭṭhakathā* (*Pañcapakaraṇa aṭṭhakathā*). The Chaṭṭha Saṅgāyana (Sixth Council) resources. Igatpuri: VRI. http://www.tipitaka.org/pdf/romn/

The *Kathāvatthu*, and The *Kathāvatthu-aṭṭhakathā* (*Pañcapakaraṇa-aṭṭhakathā*). The Chaṭṭha Saṅgāyana (Sixth Council) resources. Igatpuri: VRI. http://www.tipitaka.org/pdf/romn/

The *Visuddhimagga*. The Chaṭṭha Saṅgāyana (Sixth Council) resources. Igatpuri: VRI. http://www.tipitaka.org/pdf/romn/

The Pāli *Tipiṭaka,* and The *Aṭṭhakathā*. The Chaṭṭha Saṅgāyana (Sixth Council) resources. Igatpuri: VRI. http://www.tipitaka.org

The Pāli *Tipiṭaka*, and The *Aṭṭhakathā*. The Chaṭṭha Saṅgāyana (Sixth Council) resources, CD ROM Version 4. Igatpuri: VRI, 1995.

Primary Sources Translated into English

A Buddhist Manual of Psychological Ethics (*Dhammasaṅgaṇi*). Translated by Rhys Davids. Oxford: PTS, 1997.

Points of Controversy (*Kathā-Vatthu*). Translated by Shwe Zan Aung, and Mrs. Rhys Davids. Oxford: PTS, 1915.

The Connected Discourses of the Buddha (*Saṃyutta Nikāya*), Vols.I&II. Translated by Bhikkhu Bodhi. Boston: Wisdom Publications, 2000.

The Numerical Discourses of the Buddha (*Aṅguttara Nikāya*). Translated by Bhikkhu Bodhi. Boston: Wisdom Publications, 2012.

The Path of Purification (*Visuddhimagga*). Translated by Bhikkhu Ñāṇamoli. Sri Lanka: Buddhist Publication Society, 1991.

The Path of Discrimination (*Paṭisambhidāmagga*). Translated by Bhikkhu Ñāṇamoli. Oxford. PTS, 2002.

The Middle Length Discourses of the Buddha (*Majjhima Nikāya*). Translated by Bhikkhu Ñāṇamoli, and Bhikkhu Bodhi. Wisdom Publications, 2009.

The Long Discourses of the Buddha (*Dīgha Nikāya*). Translated by Maurice Walshe. Boston: Wisdom Publications, 1995.

The Book of the Kindred Sayings (*Saṃyutta-Nikāya*) Vol.I. Translated by Mrs C.A.F. Rhys Davids. Oxford: PTS, 1917.

The Group of Discourses (*Sutta-Nipāta*). Translated by K.R. Norman. Oxford: PTS, 2001.

The Itivuttaka. Translated by Peter Masefield. Oxford: PTS, 2001.

SECONDARY SOURCES

Abeynayake, Oliver. *A Textual and Historical Analysis of the Khuddaka Nikāya*. Colombo: Tisara Press, 1984.

Akira, Hirakawa. *A History of Indian Buddhism From Sakyamuni to Early Mahayana*. Translated by Paul Groner. University of Hawaii: Asian Studies at Hawaii, 1990.

Anālayo, Bhikkhu. *Satipaṭṭhāna: The Direct Path to Realization*. Brimingham: Windhorse Publications, 2006.

———. "On the Five Aggregates (1)—A Translation of Saṃyukta-āgama Discourses 1 to 32." *Dharma Drum Journal of Buddhist Studies* 11(2012): 1–61.

———. *A Comparative Study of the Majjhima-nikāya* Vols.I &II. Taiwan: Dharma Drum Publishing Corporation, 2011.

———. *From Craving to Liberation—Excursions into the Thought-world of the Pali Discourses* (1). New York: The Buddhist Association of the United States, 2009.

———. *From Grasping to Emptiness—Excursions into the Thought-world of the Pali Discourses* (2). New York: The Buddhist Association of the United States, 2010.

———. "On the Five Aggregates (2)—A Translation of *Saṃyukta-āgama* Discourses 256 to 272." *Dharma Drum Journal of Buddhist Studies* 12 (2013): 1–69.

———. "On the Five Aggregates (3)—A Translation of *Saṃyukta-āgama* Discourses 59 to 87." *Dharma Drum Journal of Buddhist Studies* 13 (2013):1–66.

———. *The Dawn of Abhidharma*. Germany: Publishing house of the Hamburg State and University Library Carl von Ossierzky, 2014.

Beer, Robert. *The Handbook of Tibetan Buddhist Symbols*. Chicago: Serindia Publications, 2003.

Bodhi, Bhikkhu. Introduction to *The Numerical Discourses of the Buddha* (*Aṅguttara Nikāya*), translated by Bhikkhu Bodhi, 17–74. Boston: Wisdom Publications, 2012.

———. General Introduction to *The Connected Discourses of the Buddha* (*Saṃyutta Nikāya*) Vols.I &II, translated by Bhikkhu Bodhi, 21–55. Boston: Wisdom Publication, 2000.

———. Introduction to *A Comprehensive Manual of Abhidhamma* (*Abhidhammattha Saṅgaha*), translated by Bhikkhu Bodhi, 1–20. Sri Lanka: Buddhist Publication Society, 1999.

———. *Transcendental Dependent Arising—A Translation and Exposition of the Upanisa Sutta*. Sri Lanka: Buddhist Publication Society, 1980.

Bhikkhu, Thanissaro. *The Paradox of Becoming*. California: Metta Forest Monastery, 2008.

Buswell, Robert E. Jr., and Donald S. Lopez Jr. *The Princeton Dictionary of Buddhism.* New Jersey: Princeton University Press, 2014.

Buswell, Robert E. Jr., and Padmanabh S. Jaini. "The Development of Abhidharma Philosophy." In *Encyclopedia of Indian Philosophies*: *Abhidharma Buddhism to 150 AD*, Vol.VII, edited by Karl H. Potter, Robert E. Buswell Jr, Padmanabh S. Jaini, and Noble Rossreat, 73–119. Delhi: Motilal Banarsidass Publishers Private Ltd., 1996.

Bucknell, Rod. "The Buddhist Path to Liberation: An Analysis of the Listing of Stages." *The Journal of the International Association of Buddhist Studies* 7, No.7 (1984): 7–39.

Burford, Brace G. "Mahāniddesa." In *Encyclopedia of Indian Philosophies: Abhidharma Buddhism to 150 AD*, Vol.VII, edited by Karl H. Potter, Robert E. Buswell Jr, Padmanabh S. Jaini, and Noble Ross Reat, 305–12. Delhi: Motilal Banarsidass Publishers Private Ltd., 1996.

———. "Cūlaniddesa." In *Encyclopedia of Indian Philosophies: Abhidharma Buddhism to 150 AD*, Vol.VII, edited by Karl H. Potter, Robert E. Buswell Jr, Padmanabh S. Jaini, and Noble Ross Reat, 313–16. Delhi: Motilal Banarsidass Publishers Private Ltd., 1996.

Chandra Pande, Govinda. *Studies in the Origins of Buddhism*. Delhi: Motilal Banarsidass Publishers Private Ltd., 1999.

Collins, Steven. "On the Very Idea of the Pali Canon." *Journal of the Pali Text Society* 15 (1990): 89–126.

Committee, The Editorial. *Introduction to Dhammasaṅgaṇi*. Yangoon: Translation Section Department for the Promotion and Propagation of the Sasana Ministry of Religious Affairs, 1995. Accessed October 10, 2016. http://www.abhidhamma.com Introduction%20to%20 Dhammasangani.pdf

Dasgupta, Surendranath. *A History of Indian Philosophy* Vol.V. Delhi: Motilal Banarshidass Publishers Private Ltd., 1991.

Davids, T.W. Rhys & William Stede. *Pāli-English Dictionary*. Delhi: Motilal Banarsidass Publishers Private Ltd., 1993.

Davids, T.W. Rhys. *Buddhist India*. London: T. Fisher Unwin, and New York: G.P. Putnam's Sons, 1911.

———. *Buddhism: Being a Sketch of the Life and Teachings of Gautama, the Buddha*. London: Society for Promoting Christian Knowledge, 1912.

———. *Buddhism: Its History and Literature*. New York: G.P. Putnam's Sons, 1907.

Dawes, J. Charles. "The Path of Spiritual Progress in Theravāda Buddhism." PhD diss., California Institutes of Asian Studies, 1977.

Dhammajoti, Bhikkhu KL. *Sarvāstivāda Abhidharma*. Hong Kong: The Buddha-Dharma Centre of Hong Kong, 2015.

Frauwallner, Erich. *Studies in Abhidharma Literature and the Origins of Buddhist Philosophical Systems*. Translated by Sophic Francis Kidd. Albany: State University of New York Press, 1995.

Fuller, Paul. *The Notion of Diṭṭhi in Theravāda Buddhism: The Point of View*. London and New York: Routledge, 2005.

Garg, Ganga Ram, ed. *Encyclopaedia of the Hindu World* Vol.I. New Delhi: Concept Publishing Company, 1992.

Geiger, Wilhelm. *Pāli Literature and Language*. Translated by Batakrishna Ghosh. Calcutta: University of Calcutta, 1956.

Gethin, R.M.L. *The Buddhist Path to Awakening*. Oxford: Oneworld Publications, 2001.

———. "The Mātikās: Memorization, Mindfulness, and the List." In *The Mirror of Memory: Reflections on Mindfulness and Remembrance in Indian and Tibetan Buddhism*, edited by J. Gyatso, 149–72. New York: State University of New York, 1992.

Griffiths, Paul J. "Buddhist Jhāna: A Form-Critical Study." *Religion* 13 (1983): 55–68.

———. *On Being Mindless: Buddhist Meditation and the Mind-Body Problem*. New Delhi: Sri Satguru Publications, 1986.

Glasenapp, Helmuth Von. *Jainism: An Indian Religion of Salvation*. Delhi: Motilal Banarshidass Publishers Private Ltd., 1999.

Gombrich, Richard F. *How Buddhism Began: The Conditioned Genesis of the Early Teachings*. London and New York: Routledge, 2006.

———. *What the Buddha Thought*. London: Equinoxe, 2009.

Gowans, Christopher W. *Philosophy of the Buddha: An Introduction*. London and New York: Routledge, 2003.

Gunaratana, Henepola. *A Critical Analysis of the Jhānas in Theravāda Buddhist Meditation*. Washington: The American University, 1980.

Hinüber, Osker von. "A Handbook of Pāli Literature." In *Indian Philology and South Asian Studies* Vol.II, edited by Albrecht Wezler, and Michael Witzel. New York: Walter de Gruyter, 1996.

Hwang, Soonil. *Metaphor and Literalism in Buddhism: The Doctrinal History of Nirvana*. London and New York: Routledge, 2006.

Iggleden, R.E. Preface to *A Buddhist Manual of Psychological Ethics* (*Dhammasaṅgaṇi*), by Rhys Davids, viii-xii. Oxford: The Pali Text Society, 1997.

———. Introduction to *The Book of Analysis* (*Vibhaṅga*). Translated Sayadaw U Thittila, xv–lxxxi. London and Beccles: William Clowes and Sons, 1969.

Jayawickrama, N.A. *Sutta Nipāta: Text and Translation*. University of Kelaniya: Post-graduate Institute of Pali & Buddhist Studies, 2001.

Keown, Damien V. "Ethical Perfection in Buddhist Soteriology." PhD diss., University of Oxford, 1985.

Kuan, Tse-fu. *Mindfulness in Early Buddhism*: *New Approaches Through Psychology and Textual Analysis of Pali, Chinese and Sanskrit Sources*. London and New York: Routledge, 2008.

Lamotte, E. *History of Indian Buddhism: From the Origins to the Śaka Era*. Translated by Sara Wemm-Boin. Louvain-La-Neuve: Universite catholique de Louvain, 1988.

Lee, You-Mee. *Beyond Āsava & Kilesa: Understanding the Roots of Suffering According to the Pāli Canon*. Sri Lanka: Buddhist Cultural Centre, 2009.

Mahathera, Ven. Nyanatiloka. *The Ten Fetters of Existence* (*Dasa Saṃyojana*). Sri Lanka: Sarvodaya Shramadana Sangamaya, 1980.

Malalasekera, G.P. *Dictionary of Pāli Proper Names* Vol.II. New Delhi: Munshiram Manoharlal Publishers Pvt Ltd, 1998.

Matthews, Bruce Victor. "The Concept of Craving in Early Buddhism." PhD diss., McMaster University, 1975.

Matthews, Bruce. *Craving and Salvation: A Study in Buddhist Soteriology*. Canada: Wilfrid Laurier University Press, 1983.

Macdonell, A.A., and A.B. Keith. *Vedic Index of Names and Subjects* Vol.I. New Delhi: Motilal Banarsidass Publishers Private Ltd., 1995.

McClelland, Norman C. "Buddhist Stages of Liberation." In *Encyclopedia of Reincarnation and Karma*. North Carolina: McFarland & Company, Inc., Publishers, 2010.

McDermott, James P. "Paṭisambhidāmagga." In *Encyclopedia of Indian Philosophies: Abhidharma Buddhism to 150 AD*, Vol.VII, edited by Karl H. Potter, Robert E. Buswell Jr, Padmanabh S. Jaini, and Noble Rossreat, 219–64. Delhi: Motilal Banarsidass Publishers Private Ltd., 1996.

———. "Kathāvattu." In *Encyclopedia of Indian Philosophies: Abhidharma Buddhism to 150 AD*, Vol.VII, edited by Karl H. Potter, Robert E. Buswell Jr, Padmanabh S. Jaini, and Noble Rossreat, 265–304. Delhi: Motilal Banarsidass Publishers Private Ltd., 1996.

Min, U. Kyaw. *Buddhist Abhidhamma Meditation and Concentration*. Singapore: Times Books International, 1980.

Morris, Rev. Richard. Introduction to *The Puggala-paññatti* Part I, edited by Rev. Richard Morris, vii–xv. Oxford: PTS,1883.

Muller-Ortega, Paul E. *The Triadic Heart of Śiva*. Albany: State University of New York Press, 1989.

Mun-keat (Wei-keat), Choong. *The Fundamental Teachings of Early Buddhism: A Comparative Study based on the Sūtrāṅga Portion of the Pāli Saṃyutta-Nikāya and the Chinese Saṃyuktāgama*. Wiesbaden: Harrassowitz Verlag, 2000.

Nakamura, Hajime. *Indian Buddhism: A Survey with Bibliographical Notes*. New Delhi: Motilal Banarsidass Publishers Private Ltd., 1999.

Norman, K.R. "Pāli Literature." In *A History of Indian Literature* Vol.II, Fasc.2, edited by Jan Gonda. Wiesbaden: Otto Harrassowitz, 1983.

Nyanatiloka, Ven. *Buddhist Dictionary: Manual of Buddhist Terms & Doctrines*. Sri Lanka: Buddhist Publication Society, 1952.

Ñāṇamoli, Bhikkhu, and Bhikkhu Bodhi. Introduction to *The Middle Length Discourses of the Buddha* (*Majjhima Nikāya*), translated by Bhikkhu Ñāṇamoli, and Bhikkhu Bodhi. Wisdom Publications, 2009.

Ow, Gary. "Ananda's Path to Becoming an Arahat: How He Overcame the Ten Fetters to Attain the Four Stages of Enlightenment." PhD diss., California Institute of Integral Studies, 2000.

Payne, Richard K. "Ritual." In *Encyclopedia of Buddhism* Vol.I, edited by Robert E. Buswell, Jr. Gale: Thomson, 2004.

Potter, Karl H. *Encyclopedia of Indian Philosophies: Abhidharma Buddhism to 150 AD*, Vol.VII, edited by Karl H. Potter, Robert E. Buswell, jr., Padmanabhi S. Jain, and Noble Rossreat. Delhi: Motilal Banarsidass Publishers Private Ltd., 1996.

———. "Dhammasaṅgaṇī." In *Encyclopedia of Indian Philosophies: Abhidharma Buddhism to 150 AD*, Vol.VII, edited by Karl H. Potter, Robert E. Buswell Jr, Padmanabh S. Jaini, and Noble Rossreat, 137–64. Delhi: Motilal Banarsidass Publishers Private Ltd., 1996.

———. "Vibhaṅga." In *Encyclopedia of Indian Philosophies: Abhidharma Buddhism to 150 AD*, Vol.VII, edited by Karl H. Potter, Robert E. Buswell Jr, Padmanabh S. Jaini, and Noble Rossreat, 165–78. Delhi: Motilal Banarsidass Publishers Private Ltd., 1996.

———. "Puggalapaññati" In *Encyclopedia of Indian Philosophies: Abhidharma Buddhism to 150 AD*, Vol.VII, edited by Karl H. Potter, Robert E. Buswell Jr, Padmanabh S. Jaini, and Noble Rossreat, 189–202. Delhi: Motilal Banarsidass Publishers Private Ltd., 1996.

Schmithausen, L. "On Some Aspects of Descriptions or Theories of 'Liberating Insight' and 'Enlightenment' in Early Buddhism." *Stuien zum Jainismus und Buddhismus* (1981): 199–250.

———. "An Attempt to Estimate the Distance in Time between Aśoka and the Buddha in Terms of Doctrinal History." *Abhandlungen der Akademie der Wissenschaften in Göttingen* (1992): 110–47.

Sivaraman, K. *Śaivism in Philosophical Perspective: A Study of Formative Concepts, Problems and Methods of Śaiva Siddhānta*. Delhi: Motilal Banarsidass Private Ltd., 2001.

Somarante, G.A. "Intermediate Existence and the Higher Fetters." *Journal of the Pali Text Society* XXV (1999): 121–54.

Sujato, Bhikkhu, and Bhikkhu Brahmali. *The Authenticity of the Early Buddhist Texts*. Kandy: Buddhist Publication Society, 2014.

Sujato, Bhikkhu. *A History of Mindfulness: How Insight Worsted Tranquillity in the Satipaṭṭhāna Sutta*. Australia: Santipada, 2012.

Tan, Piya. "Saññojana Sutta," S41.1/4:281–83.143–46. Dharmafarer.org. Accessed date July 25, 2015.

Thittila, Sayadaw U. Preface to *The Book of Analysis* (*Vibhaṅga*), translated by Sayadaw U Thittila, xi–xiv. London and Beccles: William Clowes and Sons, 1969.

Walshe, Maurice. Introduction to *The Long Discourses of the Buddha* (*Dīgha Nikāya*), translated by Maurice Walshe, 19–53. Boston: Wisdom Publication, 1995.

Warder, A.K. *Indian Buddhissm*. Delhi: Motilal Banarsidass Publishers Private Ltd., 2000.

Watanabe, K. "A Chinese Collection of Itivuttakas." *Journal of the Pali Text Society* (1906–07): 44–49.

Weeraratne, W.G. "Saṃyojana." In *Encyclopaedia of Buddhism* Vol.VII, edited by G.P. Malalsekera, and W.G. Weeraratne, 683–84. Sri Lanka: Ministry of Religious Affairs, 2006.

Wen, Tzungkuen. "A Study of Sukkhavipassaka in Pāli Buddhism." PhD diss., The University of Queensland, 2009.

Williams, Paul, and Anthony Tribe. *Buddhist Thought: A Complete Introduction to the Indian Tradition*. London and New York: Routledge, 2000.

Winternitz, Maurice. *A History of Indian Literature* Vol.II. New Delhi: Oriental Books Reprint Corporation, 1977.

Williams, Monier. *Sanskrit-English Dictionary*. New Delhi and Madras: Asian Educational Services, 2003.

Wynne, Alexander. *The Origin of Buddhist Meditation*. London and New York: Routledge, 2007.

Zeyst, H.G.A. van. "Fetters." In *Encyclopaedia of Buddhism* Vol.V, edited by G.P. Malalsekera, and W.G. Weeraratne. Sri Lanka: The Government of Sri Lanka, 1990.

Secondary Sources Translated into English

Anuruddha, Ācariya. *A Manual of Abhidhamma* (*Abhidhammattha Saṅgaha*), translated by Narada Maha Thera. Kuala Lumpur: Buddhist Missionary Society, 1956.

———. *A Comprehensive Manual of Abhidhamma* (*Abhidhammattha Saṅgaha*), translated by Bhikkhu Bodhi. Sri Lanka: Buddhist Publication Society, 1999.

———. *Compendium of Philosophy* (*Abhidhammattha-saṅgaha*), translated by Mrs. Rhys Davids with Introductory Essay and Notes by Shwe Zan Aung. Oxford: PTS, 1910.

Svetasavatara Upanisad. Translated by T.N. Sethumadhavan. Nagpur: Shri Ganesh Chaturthi, 2011.

Index

This study explores the notion of fetter (*saṃyojana*) in the *Sutta* and the *Abhidhamma Piṭaka*-s of the Pāli Canon, by showing its three main functions as householder binding, as intra-psychic binding, and as existential binding. The study deliberates that the Theravāda tradition links the existential binding with the ten fetters which define the four stages of liberation; namely, stream-entry, once-returning, non-returning, and arahatship. It demonstrates this notion is a doctrinal development in the Pāli Canon. It examines different descriptions of the attainment of the four stages of liberation, the lexicons of which do not uniformly employ fetter as the standardized description of soteriological hierarchy in the *Sutta*-s, but the concept became widespread in the *Abhidhamma*. The Theravāda tradition simply inherits the *Abhidhammic* explanation of the Four Noble Persons with reference to giving up of the traditional ten fetters, and disregards other descriptions available in the *Sutta*-s. It is hypothesized that the earlier connotations of fetter in its mundane and psychological sense was almost superseded by its existential usage.

Born in Bangladesh, **Dipen Barua**, also known as BD Dipananda, is a PhD candidate at the Centre of Buddhist Studies at The University of Hong Kong (HKU). He has been granted a Hong Kong PhD Fellowship by the Hong Kong Research Grants Council for his PhD research. He obtained his Bachelor's degree from Calcutta University and his first Master's degree in Pali from University of Pune (now Savitribai Phule Pune University), India. He received a second Master's and an MPhil degree in Buddhist Studies from HKU. In addition to his research, he has published many articles in both Bengali and English about Buddhist studies, women's issues, and South Asian Buddhist art and cultural heritage.

After successfully completing his MPhil studies on the Buddhist concept of fetter (*saṃyojana*) at the Centre of Buddhist Studies (CBS) at The University of Hong Kong (HKU), Dipen Barua has revised his MPhil dissertation into a book. This important area of research that he conducted based on the Pāli Canon and its Commentaries makes an important contribution to Buddhist studies. In this study, he offers a comprehensive analysis of the concept of fetter from two perspectives: soteriological and doctrinal development in the Pāli Canon. I believe this work will be of considerable value to those who are interested in Theravāda Buddhism, particularly in the areas of historical and doctrinal studies.

– Venerable Sik Hin Hung, Director of CBS, HKU